Discovering Quacks, Utopias, and Cemeteries

Discovering Quacks, Utopias, and Cemeteries

Modern Lessons from Historical Themes

Cynthia Williams Resor

ROWMAN & LITTLEFIELD
Lanham • Boulder • New York • London

Published by Rowman & Littlefield
An imprint of The Rowman & Littlefield Publishing Group, Inc.
4501 Forbes Boulevard, Suite 200, Lanham, Maryland 20706
www.rowman.com

6 Tinworth Street, London, SE11 5AL, United Kingdom

Cover image credits: Photograph, Shakers at Pleasant Hill, Kentucky, late 1800s. (Courtesy of Archives of Shaker Village at Pleasant Hill, Kentucky); Trade Card, Ham's Oil of Gladness, c. 1870–1906. Courtesy of History & Special Collections for Medicine and the Sciences, UCLA Library Special Collections; Hand-colored Lithograph/Print by D. W. Kellogg & Company, c. 1840–1842. Courtesy of Library of Congress.

British Library Cataloguing in Publication Information Available

Library of Congress Cataloging-in-Publication Data

Names: Resor, Cynthia Williams, 1966– author.
Title: Discovering quacks, utopias, and cemeteries : modern lessons from historical themes / Cynthia Williams Resor.
Description: Lanham, Maryland : Rowman & Littlefield, 2019. | Includes bibliographical references and index.
Identifiers: LCCN 2019007893 (print) | LCCN 2019021864 (ebook) | ISBN 9781475832068 (electronic) | ISBN 9781475832044 (cloth) | ISBN 9781475832051 (pbk.)
Subjects: LCSH: Quacks and quackery—Social aspects. | Social history—Methodology.
Classification: LCC R730 (ebook) | LCC R730 .R47 2019 (print) | DDC 615.8/56—dc23
LC record available at https://lccn.loc.gov/2019007893

To David Wilson

Thanks for the gifts of antique hair jewelry to inspire my work.

Contents

Author's Note

Visit the companion website https://teachingwiththemes.com/ for the following:

- More primary sources, texts, and images related to quacks, utopias, and cemeteries.
- Additional classroom activities for learners of all ages.
- Primary Source Bazaar, my blog about the history of daily life.
- A feedback form. Please share your experiences and suggestions using the information, historical texts and images, and recommendations in this book.

If you like this book, please consider the first two books in this series:

- *Investigating Family, Food, and Housing Themes in Social Studies*
- *Exploring Vacation and Etiquette Themes in Social Studies*

Introduction

We all dream of better lives. We wish for health or wealth or happiness. We hope for long lives and for friends and family to remember us after we die. Hopes and dreams open worlds of limitless possibilities. They inspire efforts to improve ourselves and the world around us. Some are just daydreams, others become real. *Human hopes and dreams are the first underlying theme of this book.*

However, hopes and dreams make us vulnerable. Optimism can blind us. In our pursuit, we are influenced, misinformed, tricked, fooled, or manipulated. Quacks see this weakness and profit by selling fake cures to the sick or dying. Utopian dreams can be a fool's paradise, heaven on earth for some but dystopia for others. Efforts to remember friends and family can be transformed into unreasonable profits.

Someone always claims to have the solution, the answer, or the path to a better life. How do we know if the things being endorsed, promoted, advocated, or sold are legitimate? Choosing can be challenging; answers are rarely certain, simple, or easy. How do we decide? *Developing critical thinking skills to assess the claims of others (i.e., media literacy) is the second underlying theme of this book.*

Media literacy, the ability to analyze the content and understand the purpose of media,[1] is the modern label for age-old skills of critical analysis. Other names include historical primary source analysis and close reading. Seeking answers to key questions before making conclusions or decisions is at the core of all of these. Who created the message? What are the views and goals of the creator? Why is the message convincing? What does the creator gain? What do I gain or lose if I believe it? Where can I find more information?

Hopes and dreams and how to distinguish between what is beneficial or valuable and what is not are the issues connecting the three diverse topics of this book: quacks, utopias, and cemeteries. Since ancient times, people have been promoting solutions to life's challenges. These claims multiplied in the nineteenth century as technological, economic, and social changes caused by the Industrial Revolution dramatically changed daily life. Life shifted from the small communities of a pre-industrial world to new urban settings where neighbors became strangers. Answers and practices that seemed to work for centuries were suddenly called into question.

Nineteenth-century media promised the answers. People turned to these new, inexpensive sources of information—newspapers, magazines, advice books, and novels—for answers. New ideas, products, and services appeared, each promising to make life healthier, happier, or easier. Advertising expanded; age-old strategies were adapted and transformed to reach more people. Promoters of patent medicines and new medical treatments promised better health. Utopia communities offered answers in an uncertain world. Even the pain at the death of loved ones might be transformed or alleviated with the purchase of mourning stationary, jewelry, clothing, or the all-inclusive services of new funeral parlors.

Today, a new media revolution is transforming our daily lives. Old print and broadcast media fade in the face of modern forms of electronic communication: emails, smartphones, social media, and the internet. New technological, economic, social, and political uncertainties have appeared. We still search for the right answers to life's problems. Those claiming to have answers flood the old and new forms of media with a bewildering array of solutions. The media have changed, but the messages remain the same. Buy this, believe that, and your life will be better! We still struggle to decide.

In the following chapters, the histories of quacks, utopias, and cemeteries are examined with this theme in mind: developing critical analysis skills to make the best decisions in our search for better lives.

How to Use This Book

This book is a resource for teachers and learners who wish to explore the history of daily life. The study of everyday lives of ordinary people, or social history, is often overlooked. However, learning about the challenges faced by average people in the past gives us a new perspective on our own daily lives and choices. As we consider the everyday situations faced by historical working people, we consider what influences our choices in the modern world. Some things are age-old and have been recycled and reused for millennia; others are uniquely modern. Social history explores this continuity and change.

Quacks, utopias, and cemeteries are enormous fields of academic study and popular topics of discussion in every form of modern media. Books and articles on each topic by historians and other experts number in the thousands. Therefore, the focus of the following chapters is narrowed to highlight key themes related to media literacy and the essential questions at the opening of each chapter.

Essential questions are overarching questions that go beyond the basic facts like who, what, where, and when. Essential questions get at the *whys* and the *hows* of an issue. They explore how historical issues are significant in the present. Essential questions make history relevant.[2]

In each chapter, the essential questions are followed by historical overviews of quacks, utopias, and cemeteries with a focus on Western Europe and the United States. This emphasis is *not* a statement of the importance of Western culture over that of the rest of the world. Every culture is important. The Western focus represents my limitations as a historian. I hope this introduction to quacks, utopias, and cemeteries inspires you to learn more about these topics in your local community, the cultures of your students, and modern and historical cultures throughout the world.

At the end of each themed chapter are suggestions for learning activities. Historical images are featured throughout and several chapters include excerpted texts from historical print media. I have edited some of the excerpts for easier reading, but the meaning and language are as close to the original as possible. Please consult the endnotes for references to the full texts; many are available online. All of the images can also be found on the book's companion website.

Classroom teachers may ask, "Are the ideas in this book aligned with current education trends?" The answer is yes. The information and approaches align with media literacy education, thematic instruction, inquiry learning, and place-based education.

Media literacy, introduced above and highlighted in the following chapters, is the hottest new trend in education. Critical analysis skills are at its core. These skills can be developed through inquiry activities. Summarized briefly, inquiry learning activities begin with essential questions or problems. Students are asked to consider what they already know and are prompted to search for answers. However, the historical information in each chapter provides busy teachers with the background needed to guide student inquiry.

Thematic teaching is the selection and highlighting of a theme through a unit, a course, a series of social studies courses, or across disciplines. Themes can be topics, such as quacks or utopias, or overarching essential questions. Thematic teaching is most effective when the chosen theme and its essential questions are relevant to students' lives.

In place-based education, learners explore local history, cultures, landscapes, and experiences.[3] Explore the cemeteries in your community. Discover the historical and contemporary utopian communities in your state or region. Read old newspapers from your town to discover what quackery was promoted and advertised. Investigate the primary source collections in your local library, historical site or society, or university archives.

The book's companion website, https://teachingwiththemes.com/, offers more ideas and resources for teaching and learning about the history of daily life. If this book inspires you, learn more about the discipline of social history and how to research daily life themes in the first book in this series, *Exploring Vacation and Etiquette Themes in Social Studies*. The second book in the series, *Investigating Family, Food, and Housing Themes in Social Studies* uses daily life themes to contrast real and ideal, subjective and objective, in historical and modern media.

If you are a teacher, I hope you will be inspired to include daily life themes and essential questions in your lessons and instructional units. At the least, you may discover interesting anecdotes, activities, or historical documents and images to inspire you and your students to look at everyday life with new eyes.

Teachers are always searching for education utopia. We seek the miracle cure to magically transform our lessons, teaching, classrooms, or schools. I can't guarantee this book will revolutionize your classroom. I'm not selling education snake oil. I've encountered too many education quacks in my career to promise a panacea.

However, you and your students might see new relationships between current events and the past; gain insights into confusing and misleading media tactics; and recognize hazards and pitfalls in our age-old pursuit of hopes and dreams.

Notes

1. "What is Media Literacy? A Definition . . . and More," Center for Media Literacy, accessed December 2018, http://www.medialit.org/reading-room/what-media-literacy-definitionand-more.
2. Jay McTighe and Grant Wiggins, *Essential Questions: Opening Doors to Student Understanding* (Alexandria, VA: Association for Supervision & Curriculum Development, 2013).
3. "What Is Place-Based Education?" Center for Place-Based Learning and Community Engagement, accessed December 2018, https://promiseofplace.org/what-is-pbe/what-is-place-based-education.

CHAPTER ONE

Quackery

Every Age has its Hobby and Humbug—its seven-days Wonder—its week of Witchcraft—its Popular Delusion—its reign of Quackery. The Charlatan and Empiric—the False Prophet—the Miracle Worker, in what age of the world has not history recorded their false and arrogant pretensions; aye, full as wonderful and fully as much believed by a credulous public, as at the present day.

Impostors have ever practiced their deceits; Witches have rode the air on broomsticks; Prophets have ever been bawling the end of the world; Religious Enthusiasts building up fanatical sects; the sick have been miraculously cured, and the self-puffing Quack has promised an eternity of youth and vigor to mankind.

—Augustus Mason, *The Quackery of the Age: A Satire on the Times*, 1845.[1]

Essential question:

- Why do we fall for quackery?

As long as humans have had aches and pains, sickness or disease, quacks have offered false hopes for recovery. A quack is a person who dishonestly claims to have medical knowledge, skills, medicines, or cures. A quack is a fake. Quacks know the knowledge, treatments, or products they advertise and sell are false, fake, ineffective, worthless, dangerous, or even deadly.

Quacks have successfully adapted and flourished through time even though medicine and the media they use to promote their cures have changed dramatically, especially in the last two centuries. Despite media revolutions from word-of-mouth to print to electronic, quacks have successfully updated their techniques at deceiving and misleading customers. Quacks are experts at manipulating the public and many of their deceptive strategies have been used for centuries. If students can recognize and avoid these traps, they have mastered critical analysis, one of life's most valuable skills.

To successfully analyze the methods of quacks, one must understand two conceptual systems of medical practice: traditional and scientific medicine. In this chapter, the history of these types of medicinal practice and how quacks manipulate our understanding of both will be examined.

First, the meanings of quackery and other related terms are investigated. Second, the history of medical practice from ancient Europe to early twentieth-century America is outlined. The medical revolution beginning in the seventeenth century introduced scientific practice, but ancient theories continued to influence both legitimate practitioners and quacks. Third, pre-scientific methods of knowing are contrasted with the scientific method and its impact on human understanding of disease, health, and medical treatment. Fourth, the methods employed by quacks that manipulate understanding of both traditional and scientific medicine will be scrutinized. In the conclusion, the co-existence of traditional and scientific medicine in the twenty-first century is considered.

Quacks and Their Deceptive Allies

The word *quack* has many synonyms, historical and modern. *Quack*, a shorted version of a Dutch word, *quacksalver*, appeared in the English language in the sixteenth and seventeenth centuries. Many synonyms for *quack* are no longer used. For example, *medicaster*, a word with Latin roots, described a quack until the nineteenth century. *Water-caster* was a derogatory term for those who claimed to diagnose disease from looking at urine. In some eras, the names of famous quacks become a reference to all quacks. Dr. Sangrado or Dr. Bleeding was a nineteenth-century reference to a real French quack who promoted excessive bloodletting and drinking only water.[2] The words *charlatan*, *mountebank*, and *snake-oil salesman*, discussed later, also describe peddlers of fake cures.

Quackery is a euphemism for what the US Food and Drug Administration describes as health fraud. The twenty-first-century definition of health fraud is "the deceptive promotion, advertisement, distribution or sale of articles, intended for human or animal use, that are represented as being effective to diagnose, prevent, cure, treat, or mitigate disease or other conditions, or provide a beneficial effect on health, but which have not been scientifically proven safe and effective for such purposes. Such practices may be deliberate, or done without adequate knowledge or understanding."[3]

Figure 1.1. Quacks, charlatans, and mountebanks appear often in European paintings and prints between the fifteenth and seventeenth centuries. This Dutch genre painting depicts a quack cutting a stone from the head of a patient. This operation to remove the "stone of folly" symbolized a cure for foolishness and gullibility.
Painting, The Quack, *by Jan Steen, c. 1650–1660. (Courtesy of Wikimedia Commons)*

Quackery and its many synonyms often describe deceptions beyond the realm of medicine. These words can describe dishonest claims in any area of life. Quacks are also imposters, frauds, impersonators, counterfeiters, tricksters, scammers, swindlers, and most recently, purveyors of fake news.

While quackery is age-old, the medical marketplace where their cures are sold has changed over time. One must understand the wider history of medicine to effectively unmask the quack.

Hippocrates and Humors: The Long Life of Ancient Medical Theories

Ancient medicine in Egypt, Mesopotamia, and Babylonia combined theology with healing. Priests and physicians were usually one and the same, and they believed disease was a result of their gods' displeasure, disobedience to the gods, or magic. Diagnosis of disease often depended upon prayers, astrological readings, or divination methods such as interpreting animal entrails to discover how the patient offended the gods.

The ancient Greeks also practiced religious medicine. For example, Asclepeions were healing temples of Asclepius, the Greek god of medicine and could be found in both Greece and ancient Rome. Dream interpretation was one of the methods used to diagnose medical problems and sacred snakes were prominent in the healing process. The modern symbol of medicine, the winged caduceus or staff with two snakes, was originally associated with ancient Greek gods.

The ancient Greek physician Hippocrates is often referred to as the Father of Medicine. The name of this ancient Athenian teacher and physician is associated with a body of surviving Greek medical writings written between 410 and 360 BCE on medicine, surgery, diagnosis and treatment of disease, and disease prevention through diet and healthy living. Scholars believe these texts were likely written by several different authors over time.[4]

Rejection of magical and religious medical traditions made Hippocratic medical practitioners unique in the ancient world. Causes and cures of disease were not explained as the whims of gods but instead were assumed to have natural, observable causes.[5] The author of one of the Hippocratic treatises disapprovingly mentioned "conjurors, purificators, mountebanks, and charlatans" who, pretending to be religious healers, ineffectively used incantations to treat epilepsy, claiming it was caused by the gods.[6]

At the center of Hippocratic practice was the theory of humors. This doctrine proposed four body fluids, or humors, were the basis for health and disease: blood, phlegm, yellow bile, and black bile. In this holistic system, the body—mentally and physically—could maintain health if a proper balance of the humors was maintained. Disease was caused by an imbalance of the humors; therefore, treatments were meant to restore an equilibrium of the humors. Humoral theory was expanded upon by the Greek medical theorist Galen (c. 130 CE–c. 210 CE) and subsequently spread throughout the Roman Empire. Ancient Greek medical theories continued to influence Western medicine until the nineteenth century.

Three themes from ancient Greek humoral medicine—balance of the humors, moderation, and the use of plants as medicines—dominated Western medicine for centuries.[7] These same theories were restated, reinterpreted, and reused in both quack and legitimate medical practice for centuries and still reappear in the modern world.

On one hand, the ancient Greek medical theories of Hippocrates and Galen were a form of early science. Supernatural explanations for disease were rejected, and physicians relied upon careful observations of the patient and the progression of disease. The word *humor* is the Greek word for a fluid or juice. Some of their theories based on observations of the role of bodily fluids were insightful. For example, Greek physicians observed and noted that sap in plants and blood in animals and humans were key ingredients to life. Likewise, they saw that other bodily fluids appeared only when humans were sick, such as the mucus of a runny nose.[8]

On the other hand, from the perspective of modern science, ancient Greek humoral medicine was very flawed. The ancient Greeks disliked dissection of human bodies and performed no autopsies. Their knowledge of human anatomy was confined to the body's surface. Most of their theories of bodily fluids were just plain wrong. For example, bodily fluids do not correspond with psychological temperaments or the four seasons. The balance of the four humors is not holistically connected to one's social class, age, sex, or personality. Restoring the balance of the body's humors through bloodletting or inducing sweating, vomiting, or evacuation of the bowels were popular treatments through the nineteenth century. Today, these treatments are generally seen as ineffective in most circumstances and in some cases, even deadly.

Assumptions based on ancient Greek humoral theory persist even in the twenty-first century. For example, the common advice to "feed a cold, starve a fever" originated from the association of the four humors with cold, hot, wet, and dry weather and environmental conditions. Going outside with wet hair, getting feet wet, being caught in the rain, and failing to wear a hat on a cold day will not cause bacterial or viral infections. But these age-old ways of understanding illness persist. Modern physicians may even use these "common sense" explanations to help patients understand scientific treatments.[9]

Associations between the four humors and one's psychological state also endure in modern culture. Participants in a modern study agreed with the following statements: an improper diet can cause depression; a proper diet can protect from depression; regular bowel movements prevent depression; climate and weather conditions affect a person's likelihood of depression. Despite numerous scientific studies concluding depression is usually related to biochemical factors in the body, rather than the seasons or humors, traditional beliefs still persist. The study concluded people tend to agree with statements verified by personal experience over the views discovered through scientific research by medical experts.[10]

For two thousand years, ancient Greek medical theories dominated the field of medicine. Many still persist in how we perceive health and illness. Quacks exploit these enduring conscious or unconscious perceptions to sell their cures.

Revolutions in Science and Medicine

The discoveries of the Scientific Revolution laid the foundation for modern medicine, but ancient medical theories persisted alongside the new discoveries. Early medical scientists made revolutionary discoveries but continued to interpret their findings using the old paradigm of balancing the bodily fluids. For example, William Harvey discovered the circulation of blood (1628) but physicians did not completely reject humoral theories. Instead, the properties and functions of the other three humors, black bile, yellow bile, and phlegm, were shifted to blood.[11]

New tools such as the microscope and increased human dissection allowed for new observations and conclusions unknown by the ancient Greeks. Scientists began to recognize the contagious nature of some diseases and developed preventative measures. Edward Jenner (1749–1823) introduced the smallpox vaccine in 1796. Louis Pasteur (1822–1895) researched the connection between germs and disease and introduced the concept of pasteurization. John Snow (1813–1858) traced the source of cholera to public water supplies in London in 1854, which motivated improvements of the water and sewage sanitation systems of the city.[12]

The public health movement aimed at preventing disease grew throughout the nineteenth century. European and American cities improved sanitation systems. New York City completed the Croton Aqueduct to supply fresh water in 1842; public garbage disposal began in the 1880s and 1890s. Reformers took up the scientific causes in popular secular and religion newspapers, magazines, and pamphlets. Cleanliness was emphasized as a requirement for physical health as well as mental health and religious piety. Deaths due to infectious diseases such as cholera and typhoid declined.

A medical revolution in the treatment of disease began with developments in French hospitals in the early nineteenth century. In the 1840s, French doctors adopted new ways to study and diagnose disease using information from thorough physical examinations of patients. A French doctor, R. T. H. Laennec (1781–1826), invented the stethoscope, the instrument used to detect internal sounds of the body, which is still used in modern physical examinations. French doctors systematically connected data from autopsies and postmortem exams to observations about a patient's illness to better understand the progression of disease. The French physician Pierre Louis (1787–1872) was a pioneer in studying disease in large numbers of patients, a forerunner of modern clinical trials.[13]

Nineteenth-century doctors improved surgery techniques and began to effectively use anesthetics. In the late 1860s, Joseph Lister (1827–1912) discovered the bacterial origin of wound infections and used antiseptics to prevent infection from surgery. By the 1880s, the germ theory of disease became prevalent, based on the work of Louis Pasteur and Robert Koch (1843–1910).[14] Viruses were discovered in the 1890s. New synthetic drugs to reduce fever and treat pain were developed. The scientific discoveries of European scientists and medical experts laid the foundation for modern science-based medicine.

Attitudes toward medical care transformed in the twentieth century. Prior to World War I, people generally accepted that medical practitioners could do little to treat or actually stop the effects of serious disease, injuries, and disabilities.[15] Most care for the sick and dying took place in homes and was provided by the family. Today's minor ailments and accidents were serious problems before the twentieth century and frequently led to death. Death was usually slow and painful and always near.

The choices for medical advice and treatments were numerous, varied, and unregulated. As the money-based economy grew and industrialization and advertising increased during the eighteenth, nineteenth, and early twentieth centuries, the medical field became an expanding field of entrepreneurialism. One could purchase remedies based on ancient, religious, or traditional folk traditions. New scientific and pseudoscientific theories and cures were also promoted. Many medical practitioners blended both the old and the new. Anyone who could find a willing patient could practice medicine, since a system of medical licensing and scientific medical research did not exist.

By the 1920s, antibiotics, vaccines, transfusions, powerful diagnostic techniques, hygienic hospitals, scientific discoveries, and technology were transforming medicine. The age-old focus on care for the sick in the home was transformed into modern, scientific medical practice by licensed experts. Today, we expect more. For millennia, many merely hoped for a "Good Death," a painless death at home, surrounded by family. Today, we do not expect death. Rather we expect to be treated and cured with effective, reliable, and government-regulated treatments.

The Medical Marketplace: A Bewildering Array of Choices

Throughout history, patients could choose from a wide continuum of medical advice and treatment. Many sought medical advice and care from numerous sources at once. At-home treatment and family remedies, untrained folk healers, trained practitioners, and university-educated physicians offered treatments in all price ranges. These practitioners coexisted, usually peacefully, until the nineteenth century. Quacks also provided treatments, knowingly scamming customers at every level of society (see chapter 2, sources 3, 4, and 5).

The family was the first source of medical care and advice, and women usually fulfilled these roles. At first, family medical practice was shared through oral tradition and family recipes, letters, and diaries. As the costs of books declined and literacy grew in the eighteenth century, published medical guides promoting diverse theories gave readers advice and recipes for home health care. If traditional family care and cures provided no relief, additional medical advice was chosen based upon cost. Those who could afford to pay might choose university-trained physicians charging high fees, while simultaneously consulting other types of practitioners.[16]

University medical schools were established in the Middle Ages. From the eleventh century until the early nineteenth century, the authoritative texts of these universities were the works of Hippocrates, Galen, and other ancient theorists. Graduates were experts in theoretical medical knowledge but had little practical, hands-on training. Some sought additional training through apprenticeships; many did not. Their practice was usually confined to the wealthy, who could afford their services. University-trained physicians were from the upper class; the manual labor of medicine, requiring that patients be touched, was beneath them.

Many people, including the wealthy and educated who could afford their services, questioned the skills of the university-trained physicians and praised folk remedies and practitioners. King James I (1566–1635) noted academic medicine was useless because it was only conjecture and theoretical. Francis Bacon (1561–1626) said "empirics and old women are more happy many times in their cures than learned physicians."[17] Thomas Hobbes (1588–1679) said he would "rather have the advice or take physic from an old experienced woman that had been at many sick people's bedsides, than from the learnedst but unexperienced physician."[18]

The manual work of medicine was done by apothecaries and surgeons. Apothecaries prepared and sold drugs; surgeons bled patients to balance humors, dressed wounds, and performed surgery or other medical procedures. These medical practitioners lacked university training in ancient classical theories. Instead, they learned their trade through apprenticeships or on the job. Both apothecaries and surgeons were associated with medieval guilds. Guilds created rules and regulations for the trades and served as a sort of licensing agency by setting standards of knowledge and requiring apprenticeships to enter the trade.[19]

Next in the continuum of medical care were local specialists such as midwives, bone-setters, folk healers, wise women, and herb doctors. Traveling healers, referred to as mountebanks, charlatans, quacks, or snake-oil salesmen, also provided services such as tooth extraction, medicines, and entertainment. Priests, preachers, religious healers, and practitioners of magic and astrology might also be consulted.

Karen Cushman's historical novels for young adult readers, *Matilda Bone* and *The Midwife's Apprentice*, portray this medical hierarchy. Both stories are set in the Middle Ages and illustrate the differences between the local midwife, apothecary, surgeon, and the university-trained physician and the underlying importance of religion in medical treatment.

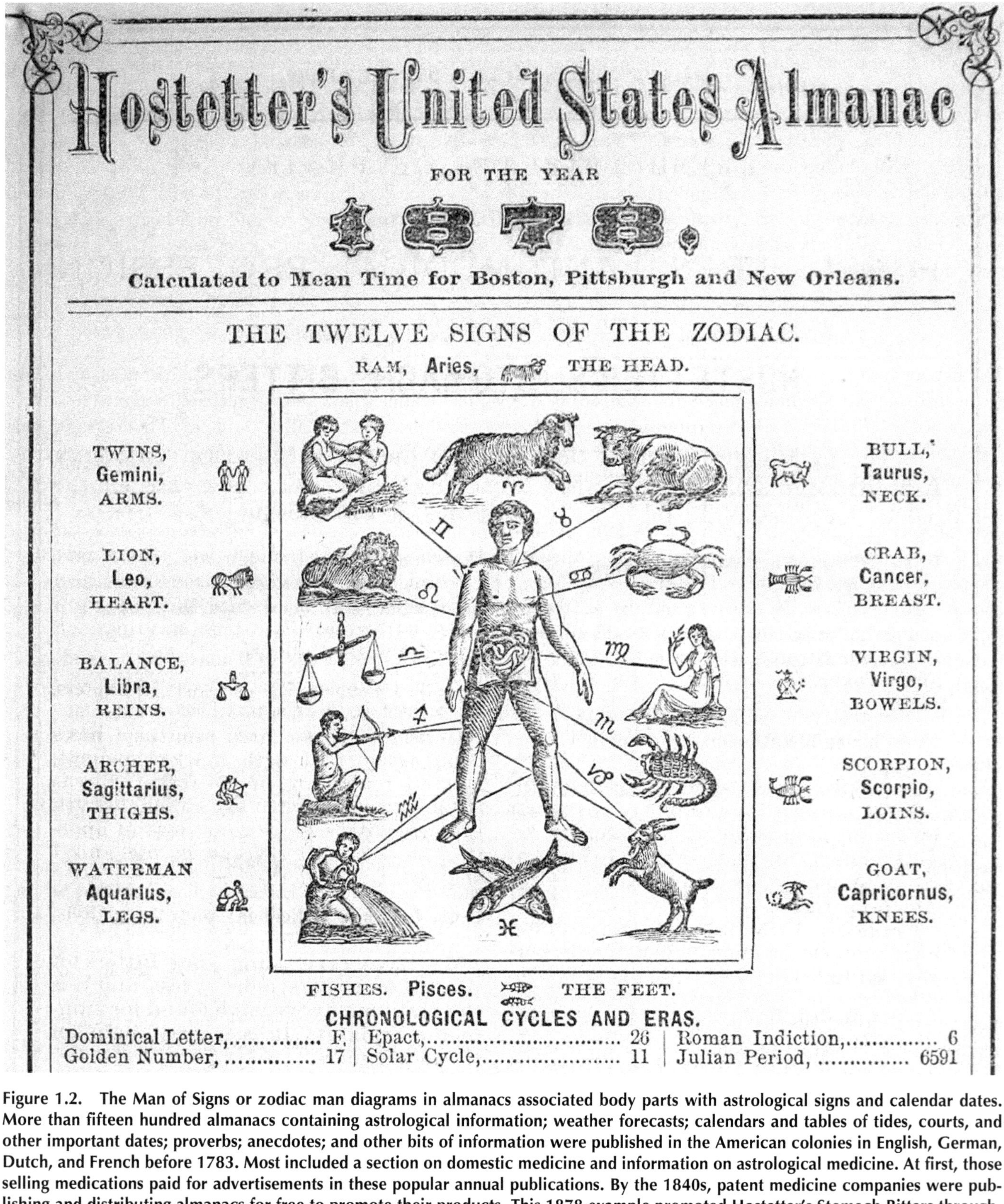

Figure 1.2. The Man of Signs or zodiac man diagrams in almanacs associated body parts with astrological signs and calendar dates. More than fifteen hundred almanacs containing astrological information; weather forecasts; calendars and tables of tides, courts, and other important dates; proverbs; anecdotes; and other bits of information were published in the American colonies in English, German, Dutch, and French before 1783. Most included a section on domestic medicine and information on astrological medicine. At first, those selling medications paid for advertisements in these popular annual publications. By the 1840s, patent medicine companies were publishing and distributing almanacs for free to promote their products. This 1878 example promoted Hostetter's Stomach Bitters throughout its forty-pages. Multiple articles promoted their product for unsettled nerves, insomnia, constipation, fever prevention, indigestion, biliousness, liver complaints, and rheumatism, as well as a safeguard against illness while traveling. Bitters usually contained water, alcohol, and bad-tasting herbs.

Bingham, The Snake-Oil Syndrome, 125; Guerra, "Medical Almanacs of the American Colonial Period," 254; Hostetter's Illustrated United States Almanac, *Hostetter & Smith, 1878. (Courtesy of Archive.org)*

Medicine in America: Merging the Old and the New

European medical traditions arrived in the New World with the colonists, who also adopted and adapted Native American and African healing traditions. From the sixteenth through the nineteenth century, diverse practitioners offered a wide range of health and medical services. While European universities began teaching scientific approaches to medicine, colonial America lacked medical schools and university-trained physicians were in short supply.

For most colonial Americans, medical care was primarily a family responsibility, especially in the sixteenth and seventeenth centuries. Therefore, American colonists depended more on their own resources, consulting apothecaries, surgeons, and local or itinerant healers such as midwives, "Indian doctors," or "root and herb doctors." Americans living on the frontier were even more likely to be medical pluralists, choosing from the limited options available and creating their own do-it-yourself approach.[20]

Home remedies were the most common form of medical treatment. The well-off might purchase imported medicines for home use, but most relied upon traditional remedies prepared at home from family recipes, almanacs, newspapers, or published advice books.

The ingredients used for home remedies were little different from the medical ingredients available to physicians and other medical practitioners. Most ingredients were botanical, originating from herbs or other plants. Many American botanical remedies were a mix of European, Native American, and African traditions. For example, taking a spring tonic made from sassafras was common among Southerners of all different backgrounds, but was originally a Native American practice. Natural remedies were also believed to have religious value because the plants from which they were derived were considered God-given gifts.[21]

An existing inventory of drugs from the seventeenth century listed spirits, oils, ointments, pills, and powders with little reference to the actual ingredients. Instead, the drugs are described by the desired effect and influence on the body's humors. For example, cordials stimulated the heart, juleps were sweet potions with cooling effects, diaphoretics caused sweating, pectoral syrups cleared chest congestion, restringents worked like modern anti-diarrheal medications, and purges loosened the bowels. Special diets of fruit, sugar, spices, prunes, or beer were recommended for those with deficient humors.[22]

American remedies were also associated with the astrological information communicated through almanacs. Diagrams of the Man of Signs or zodiac man in almanacs associated body parts with astrological signs and calendar dates (see figure 1.2). The phases of the moon played an important role in decisions about planting and harvesting, as well as the health of animals and humans. The success of treatments, such as bloodletting, were believed to be influenced by the sun, phases of the moon, or positions of the planets or constellations.[23]

Commercially published manuals and recipes books for do-it-yourself domestic medicine were available in the colonies beginning in the seventeenth century. Households treated their apprentices, domestic workers, and slaves with recommended medicines, ointments, and treatments to balance humors such as bleeding, sweating, or inducing vomiting or bowel movements. John Tennent's *Every Man His Own Doctor; or, The Poor Planter's Physician* (1735) was one of the first of these popular medical manuals.[24] John Wesley, founder of the Methodist Church, published *Primitive Physick* (1747). This work emphasized practical remedies and recipes with an underlying religious focus on the health of the soul.

In the last half of the eighteenth century, books of medical advice written by university-trained physicians for home use by lay people became increasingly popular. The best known was William Buchan's *Domestic Medicine; or, The Family Physician*, first published in Edinburgh in 1769 and republished in dozens of American editions over a century.[25] According to Buchan, his goal was to educate readers so they would not fall prey to "quacks and conjurers, and the folly of their own superstitious notions" (see chapter 2, source 1).[26]

Buchan's work was unique for the time. Previous medical advice books for home use addressed preserving good health, usually in a religious context, but with little information on treating disease or illness. Others were books of recipes and home treatments for various illnesses. Buchan's work combined both formats with the most up-to-date medical knowledge of his era in a secular, scientific manner.

Domestic Medicine was organized by specific illnesses with a description of the disease and its symptoms, the causes, and recommended treatments including recipes. He discounted superstitious or magical medical thinking. However, his work also illustrates how the humoral model of the ancient Greeks was incorporated into early medical science. His work stressed how moderation and balance of diet, temperature, weather, exercise, stress, and clothing maintained health, while expelling various bodily fluids and feces rid the body of illness.[27]

"Licensed" Physicians in an Unregulated Marketplace

Anyone could claim to be a physician or healer and provide medical advice and treatment in seventeenth- and eighteenth-century America. Formal training programs or licensing systems did not exist. An inventory of seventeenth-century medical practitioners and medicines from government records reveals the bewildering diversity. The medical specialties of men and a few women were described with the following terms: *doctor, licentiate in physic, chirurgeon* (surgeon), *barber, a practitioner of physic and Divinity*, and *apothecary*.[28] The word *physic* in the seventeenth century could refer to a healthy practice or habit, a medicine, or more specifically a cathartic or purgative to cause vomiting, or a laxative.[29]

Those claiming to be physicians rarely had university training. Only one in nine of seventeenth-century Virginia's physicians attended medical school; only one of Boston's ten physicians had a university degree in 1720. The few university-trained physicians in America were educated at European universities. Prominent colonial families sent sons to Europe, especially Edinburgh, Scotland, for training. Throughout the eighteenth century, most of these trained physicians lived in prosperous towns and cities along the coast. Few ventured into the rural frontier.[30]

The first American medical universities were founded in Philadelphia in 1765 and New York in 1767. After the American Revolution, the College of William and Mary and Harvard offered medical training. Those holding medical degrees created exclusive medical societies, first in Pennsylvania and New Jersey. A focus of these early medical societies was to provide rudimentary regulation or oversight of medical practice. Some state legislatures enacted laws to license doctors in the late eighteenth and early nineteenth centuries. But these early efforts at government regulation of medical practice were overturned by 1844 in the egalitarian spirit of the Jacksonian era.[31]

In the absence of a comprehensive licensing system, the American Medical Association formed in 1847 and began campaigns denouncing other medical practitioners. The professional class of university trained physicians, also referred to as regular, orthodox, or allopathic doctors, sought to gain a higher status in a crowded market. Any not conforming to the standards of the American Medical Association were indiscriminately labeled as quacks.

However, many American physicians were slow to adopt European scientific advances in medicine, so their practice was often little different than their competitors. Not until the early twentieth century did the American Medical Association gain a science-based reputation by raising the standards of medical schools, testing prescription drugs, and licensing doctors who used scientific procedures.[32]

The nineteenth century was a period of conflict and transformation in health care and treatment. A bewildering array of medical practitioners and treatments were categorized under various titles such as alternative, irregular, botanical, eclectic, empiric,[33] pseudoscience, or quack. An 1866 New Jersey survey reported 596 "regular" practitioners and 151 "irregular" health practitioners in twelve different categories.[34]

In the eighteenth and nineteenth centuries, an increasing number of medical practitioners, the growth of a cash economy, and a lack of government regulation of the medical field provided quacks with unlimited opportunities. At one end of the continuum were university-trained doctors who were attempting to create a new professional status and discount the reputation of competitors; at the other end, home care and do-it-yourself medicine. In the middle were traditional apothecaries, surgeons, midwives, and herb doctors; a growing number of commercial or patent medications; and new pseudoscientific approaches to health care. Tradition, science, and pseudoscience competed in a confusing and unregulated array of medical approaches and treatments (see chapter 2, sources 3, 4, and 5).

Quackery before and after Scientific Medicine

From a twenty-first-century viewpoint, the effectiveness of *all* historical medical practice is questionable. Modern scientific studies demonstrate that some historical treatments were effective, some were dangerous and even deadly, and others made no difference. George Washington's death was hastened by too much bloodletting. Patrick Henry was probably poisoned with doses of mercury. But both were confident in their physicians, and both practices were a part of the mainstream medical practice of their day.[35] Many intelligent people in the past believed in the value of medicine that has, in retrospect, been proven ineffective.

A quack is a fraud, both now and in the past. However, a key distinction must be made when applying the term to medical treatments before and after the development of scientific medicine in the late nineteenth and early twentieth centuries. Indiscriminately labeling all historical medical practices currently known to be ineffective would be anachronistic, judging past decisions using a modern mind-set.

The twenty-first-century definition of health fraud asserts that deceptions can be committed with or *without* adequate knowledge or understanding.[36] Yet, throughout history, *honest* medical practitioners and their patients were unknowingly ignorant about the scientific prevention, causes, or treatments of disease. For millennia, quacks and true believers often promoted the exact same treatments. Therefore, the modern standard for quackery cannot be applied to prescientific medicine.

Many cures used throughout history by well-meaning medical practitioners have turned out to be dead wrong when scientifically investigated. Since ancient times, mercury, referred to as cinnabar, quicksilver, or calomel, was administered as an ointment or pill or inhaled as a vapor to treat skin diseases, typhoid, yellow fever, parasites, constipation, syphilis, mental illness, and other complaints. It was an especially popular cure in the nineteenth century, administered by physicians and used as a key ingredient in medicines.

Mercury was often taken internally to induce vomiting and sweating so the humors could be balanced. Over the centuries, ancient Greek theories of the humors had become common knowledge. Sweating and vomiting were considered tried-and-true treatments. Few realized that vomiting was a symptom of mercury poisoning. Instead, the symptoms of mercury poisoning were attributed to the disease being treated.

The long-term brain damage and neurological effects of mercury—headaches, memory loss, and emotional problems—were associated with other illnesses. If a patient died, common sense said the disease had already progressed too far to treat effectively.[37] For thousands of years, using mercury to treat disease was acceptable. Today, it would be a clear case of quackery (see figure 1.3).

Figure 1.3. Medicine companies distributed free or low-cost pamphlets and books promoting their products. Most included testimonials and descriptions of dramatic cures. Some were probably authentic; others were false. Nancy Linton's cure from scrofula, or the King's Evil, was featured in publications promoting Swaim's Panacea. The image featured Nancy after she had been cured! Scrofula was a skin disease, probably a form of tuberculosis affecting the lymph nodes of the neck that caused chronic abscess. From the thirteenth century to the eighteenth century, the monarchs of England and France were believed to have the supernatural power to cure the disease by touching patients, thus the name "King's Evil." Swaim's Panacea was promoted as a cure for many afflictions including syphilis. Skin diseases and syphilis were often treated with mercury; Swaim's Panacea contained this dangerous ingredient. See chapter 2, sources 7 and 9 for more about testimonials and scrofula.
Engraving, Nancy Linton, Swaim's Panacea. (Courtesy of US National Library of Medicine)

On the other hand, some traditional remedies have been shown to be effective with modern research methods. Botanical ingredients historically used in medicine have been scientifically examined and show a range from ineffective or harmless to dangerous or deadly. Over the last thirty years, up to 50 percent of approved drugs are derived either directly or indirectly from plants.[38] For example, the plant foxglove, while extremely poisonous, was recommended in small amounts as a medication in the ancient and medieval worlds. For centuries, this botanical remedy was used for various illnesses, but the science behind its effectiveness was unknown. In the 1930s, the drug digoxin was derived from the plant, and scientific studies proved it safe to treat heart conditions. Conversely, unscientific use of the plant, also known as digitalis, is extremely dangerous.

Before the twentieth century the difference between quackery and medicine was that the former was *knowingly* practiced as deception. The absence of scientific knowledge meant there were few tools to determine the safety and effectiveness of medical treatments. Today, we are held to a higher standard. Innovations in science, medicine, technology, education, and communication have improved both medical practice and our ability to determine the effectiveness of health care. We have access to more quality medical information than ever before. Ignorance is no longer an excuse for committing malpractice. Yet despite the knowledge and tools at our fingertips, quackery continues to flourish. We still fall for health scams. Why?

While the transition from traditional to scientific medical practice began several centuries ago, human methods of understanding still often fall back on thousands of years of cumulative experience. Old traditions are slow to disappear. Furthermore, scientific knowledge evolves over time. Uncertainty created by coexisting ancient and modern ways of knowing is compounded in a world of rapidly changing communication and technology. Quacks exploit the confusion.

Traditional Ways of Knowing: Common Sense

The term *common sense* describes knowledge of the world that appears sensible and confirmed by experience, derived from the five senses, the social milieu, and the wider culture. Common sense is thought to be true because it has been repeated and recirculated over decades, centuries, or millennia and because society believes it to be true. However, common sense can be false; it can be common ignorance.

Quack cures are often presented as common sense handed down through the ages and "tested" by time over hundreds or thousands of years. Positive cultural associations with long-held religious beliefs, traditional cultural practices, or historical institutions or theories make these remedies seem safe, wholesome, reliable, and natural.

Quacks work to portray their products as "natural" because it suggests that they are in harmony with nature, assisting the body to heal itself or aligning with or conforming to natural forces. When we say it is natural to act in a certain way, we imply it is reasonable and instinctual.[39] However, *natural* is a vague enough term that quacks can use it to influence our perceptions of their products.

In the prescientific era, common sense was the best method humans had for explaining the world. Knowledge was based upon what humans saw, heard, touched, tasted, and smelled. Conclusions about how the world worked could only be based upon that sensory information. Because knowledge of one's environment and the behavior of others was required for survival, humans developed systems of simple, quick, and practical decision-making strategies for learning and problem solving. These strategies and their associated body of knowledge, or common sense, accumulated over time. It was adequate. Common sense worked for enough humans, over time, to allow humanity to survive.

However, decisions based on instinct may not be found to be the *best* solution when additional time is taken to analyze all available information. Scientific tools and better technology allow access to much more information. Yet we still often turn to these quick commonsense solutions, which frequently lead to bad results.

Commonsense thinking regularly incorporates cognitive biases. A cognitive bias is a widespread, persistent, psychological error in judgment that causes mistakes in remembering or evaluating information and impacting decision-making.[40] Researchers have identified dozens of cognitive biases and their effects on daily decision-making. Marketing and advertising efforts routinely manipulate reliance on cognitive shortcuts.

When a quack presents a cure confirming our existing opinions, hopes, or fears, we are likely to fall for it, even with additional research. When contradictory scientific evidence is discovered, we are likely to discount its value because of confirmation bias and availability bias:

- Confirmation bias leads to selectively searching for or interpreting information confirming existing hopes, beliefs, or preconceptions while ignoring or neglecting evidence proving otherwise.

- Availability bias is the tendency to value firsthand experience, information from acquaintances, or easily obtained information over statistics and scientific data that can be difficult to read or understand.

Even when we discover scientific evidence discrediting a quack cure or when people we know warn us against it, we often continue to believe in quackery because of these cognitive biases:

- The belief perseverance effect causes humans to continue to have faith in a cure even when faced with contrary evidence.
- The optimism bias and the above-average effect causes people to be overly optimistic about their own future and believe their results will be better than most.

After using a quack cure for a period of time, we may even convince ourselves it is effective because of these cognitive biases:

- Illusionary correlation is the tendency to believe or create a cause-and-effect relationship where it does not exist. For example, if symptoms disappear after taking a quack cure, improvement is incorrectly attributed to the quack cure. In fact, recovery for most problems is likely to occur anyway, with or without a cure. Or, when quack cures are used along with scientific medical approaches, improvements are credited to the quackery instead of the legitimate approach.
- Mere exposure effect is the tendency to develop a preference for something because it is familiar. People may prefer a traditional remedy, even though research has proven it has absolutely no effect.
- Rationalization causes one to use false excuses to justify previous actions. For example, after investing money or time in a quack cure, we hate to admit its ineffectiveness to ourselves and others. We might even continue to take or recommend the cure, believing we need to take more or take it longer for the effect to be evident.[41]

Age-old habits, beliefs, and ways of knowing and understanding the world still exist in the twenty-first century even though knowledge based on scientific experimentation and reasoning dominates our modern, technology-laden lives. Human traditions formed over thousands of years are difficult to discard in the face of just a few centuries of scientific thought.

Science or Pseudoscience?

Beginning with the Scientific Revolution (c. 1550–1700), humans began devising improved methods of thinking and learning. New tools and technologies enabled humans to learn about phenomena that could not be perceived with the five senses and were unexplainable using traditional common sense. Unseen realities such as the circulation of blood, viruses, germs, DNA, oxygen, electricity, and radioactivity were discovered and scientific medical practice developed. Humans learned old or traditional or popular perceptions of the world might not be true.

While scientific thinking has led to astounding progress in recent centuries, its uses are often misunderstood. It is not a method to instantly know with timeless certainty what is true or false, right or wrong. The scientific method is a *process* for inquiry based upon evidence and reasoning. Scientists ask questions, hypothesize, observe, predict, measure, experiment, test, analyze the data, and rehypothesize. As new technology is developed such as the telescope, microscope, or computer, scientists observe and analyze new data and arrive at new, better informed conclusions.

The science of medicine rarely produces one right answer that remains true for all time. Science is a collective effort; many scientists observe, experiment, and interpret data. Scientists may form different or conflicting medical conclusions. The road to new discovery is twisted, with dead ends and false leads. Most famous medical discoveries took years or decades, with many contributors, false leads, and incorrect conclusions. Over time, the community of scientists abandons flawed theories and conclusions. If one scientist clings to an inaccurate conclusion or a faulty theory, over time the wider scientific community will call attention to the mistakes.

Ideally, scientists do not have financial, ideological, or religious commitments to a particular answer. But because scientists are human, mistakes are made or outside interests may sway the outcome. Intentionally misleading or unintentionally mistaken conclusions can lead to medical disasters. But these do not negate the entire process. Over time and over all, medical care based on scientific method is better than most historical alternatives. Good science continues to improve medical knowledge and practice.

On the other hand, pseudoscience is fake science. Pseudoscientists claim to follow the steps of real scientific method. But usually, the intent is to deceive others with misleading or false information presented as scientific. The word *pseudoscience* was first used in the late eighteenth and early nineteenth centuries to distinguish older ways of knowing, such as magic, astrology, and alchemy from the new scientific disciplines such as astronomy and chemistry.[42]

Pseudoscience depends upon a culture's acceptance of the scientific method. Eighteenth-century quacks quickly took advantage of the public's interest in scientific discovery, deceiving customers with pseudoscientific evidence and arguments. Quacks, then and now, depended upon vague understandings or misunderstandings of the scientific terms and methods to create false perceptions of their products.

Today, broad scientific-sounding claims are made using vague words such as proven, tested, or clinical. Words such as *detoxify*, *cleanse*, *enhance*, *boost*, *revitalize*, *energize*, *deficiencies*, and *imbalances* are popular. Potential customers are informed of problems with their metabolism and hormones.[43] Metabolism is a scientifically proven process through which the body converts food into energy. Hormones are chemical substances created in the endocrine glands to stimulate cells and tissues. But the wider public lacks a detailed scientific understanding of the metabolic process. Quacks take advantage of that gap in understanding, inventing commonsense explanations to sell their cures for low metabolism or vague hormone problems.

Quack cures lack scientific evidence to prove their effectiveness. These pseudoscientists pretend biased anecdotes and personal experiences are valid substitutes for objectively collected data and multiple scientific studies. Quacks assert that because their methods or cures have not been proven false, they must be true. They avoid careful peer review of their methods by other scientists or medical experts, claiming someone will steal their ideas if the secret is revealed. Quacks allude to scientific certainty but fail to produce valid evidence to back their claims.

Quacks rely upon the public's belief in scientific progress while simultaneously arguing the scientific process is unreliable. They criticize any scientific study or information discrediting their cures. They provide real, bogus, and distorted examples of studies where scientists and medical experts were wrong. Sadly, some scientifically proven methods have subsequently been found to be ineffective or dangerous. These unfortunate failures are highlighted by quacks to create uncertainty and fear.

Pseudoscientists claim to be groundbreaking scientists ahead of their time who are persecuted by those jealous of their discovery or ignorant of the truth. Quacks deflect the attention from the lack of scientific data to irrelevant historical examples. Quacks note Galileo was persecuted for his groundbreaking discoveries, even though he accurately concluded that planets revolve around the sun. This argument is misleading because contemporary scientists did not persecute Galileo; it was the seventeenth-century Catholic Church that placed Galileo under house arrest.

Quacks effectively manipulate and employ old and new methods for understanding the world. They distort modern science, exploit misconceptions of science, and employ pseudoscientific arguments to promote products. At the same time, they beguile customers by drawing on thousands of years of traditional ways of knowing. They contrast natural and commonsense remedies with unnatural or artificial scientific medicine. Quacks adopt ancient theories of health such as a balance of humors or vital fluids; a harmony of the body, mind, and spirit; a vital force, energy, or essence. Quacks promote astrological, supernatural, or magical forces and allude to good health or illness as a divine reward or punishment to fatten their profits, not to improve the health or well-being of others.[44]

Fear, Uncertainty, and Promises of a Better Life: The Universal Tools of Quacks

Humans have always looked for certainty and the truth, seeking solutions to the most basic challenges in life—health, youth and beauty, love, success, and happiness. A quick or easy solution to these age-old challenges rarely exists, but someone is always selling something to make us healthier, wealthier, happier, or more attractive. Quacks are especially adept at manipulating hopeful dreams for the future.

Quacks also manipulate feelings of uncertainty; confusion; and fear of pain, disease, and death to sell their cures. They promote their impossible cures for the most common or frightening diseases of their time—the plague, scrofula, tuberculosis, influenza, polio, HIV/AIDS, cancer, Ebola, or MRSA. They invent fearful syndromes and illnesses for which only they have the cure. Quacks overemphasize the importance of generic symptoms and exaggerate the impact of benign conditions or the normal aging process. Many employ "disease mongering"—convincing healthy people they are sick or people with minor conditions they are seriously ill.[45] Quacks overemphasize the expense or side effects of surgery and other legitimate treatments, promising inexpensive or painless cures with no side effects.

Figure 1.4. Many have sought to expose quacks and warn the public of their dangers. This cartoon referenced the fraud of Dr. John St. John Long, a successful London quack in the 1820s and 1830s. He began his career as a painter but proclaimed himself a physician to make more money. Long claimed all conditions were caused by "acrid humours." He gave medication to make the patient sicker, then substituted a placebo. Patients recovered and attributed their miraculous cure to Long. Note that Long is dressed as an undertaker. He was tried for murder when a patient died, but the case was dismissed when former patients defended his practice.

George Humphrey, "Dr Long, the Oracle of Harley Street, 1830," July 14, 2015, https://bit.ly/2Vjw4ko; Image, "A Long Way through a Short Life: The Oracle of Harley Street," 1830. (Courtesy of US National Library of Medicine)

Quacks promise hope in desperate situations, preying upon the most vulnerable. Terminally ill patients or the family members resort to desperate measures to avoid death or relieve pain and the suffering of loved ones. When scientific medicine has no answer and legitimate treatments offer no relief, quacks know patients will spend unreasonable amounts of money on untested, risky, and questionable treatments.

If their treatments or methods are questioned, quacks claim competitors or evil conspiracies threaten their miracle cures, further exploiting fear and uncertainty. All rivals are accused of dishonesty, regardless of the effectiveness of the rivals' treatments. Quacks convince consumers their products are not well-known, widely used, or accepted because evil or corrupt groups do not want the average person to know.

Conspiracy theories are explanations or justifications involving secret plots by powerful and malevolent groups. Who are these supposed evil conspirators, according to quacks? The answer varies based on the audience or purpose of the quack. Modern quacks may accuse the government, the US Food and Drug Administration, American Medical Association, the entire scientific medical community, pharmaceutical companies, or even rival quacks.

Why do these conspirators want to withhold information? According to the quack, their miraculous cures will cause the conspirator's profits or power to decline. In reality, all of these organizations have played a role in the improvement of medical care and treatment over the past century. But, sadly, political controversies, unethical decisions, and tragic mistakes have created enough doubt in the minds of consumers to make conspiracy claims seem plausible.

Fear and uncertainty are compounded by conflicting information about health, disease, and treatments appearing daily in the media. Much of this information overload is advertising, pure and simple. Print, broadcast, and internet "news" stories are often sponsored information paid for by quacks. Talk show hosts on radio, television, and the internet invite those selling questionable or popular cures to tell their story.

News reporters contribute to the confusion by reporting on the latest study or new popular cure without assessing the quality of the study, actual value of the cure, or history of its development. Through this type of reporting, medical products or cures are widely publicized, regardless of their quality. By omitting critical analysis, the reporter or talk show host lends a legitimacy to what may be outrageous or ridiculous quackery.[46]

Legitimate medical professionals may refuse to comment on the latest popular craze, hoping to avoid controversy. Furthermore, as scientists conduct research on health and disease, new studies may change or sometimes even reverse widely accepted evidence from the past. Quacks use this bewildering confusion of information and lack of information to their advantage.

People also turn to quack cures because they do not have the money to pay for more expensive, legitimate medical treatment. Quacks highlight the high costs of health insurance and legitimate medical care; costs out of reach of many. The reality of the high cost of quality medical care is used to justify cheaper quack cures. Quacks often portray themselves as champions of average people struggling to pay for medical care.[47] But quacks are not heroes. Instead quacks waste the time and money of unfortunate victims and may contribute to additional medical problems or even premature death.

Three infamous quacks, John Brinkley, Norman Baker, and Harry Hoxsey, effectively used these tactics to swindle thousands of patients in the 1930s, 1940s, and 1950s. All three championed common Americans and promoted traditional rural values while denouncing scientific practice and the medical establishment. They tapped into the fears of many Americans of their era by attacking elitism, the power of the American Medical Association, government interference, and urban growth. All three used pseudoscience, common sense, religion, and populism in print media and the radio to sell useless medicines, revitalizing goat gland cures, and fake cancer cures.[48]

Finally, quack cures, if not inherently harmful, may result in relief for a patient because of the placebo effect, thus bolstering sales. The placebo effect is a seeming improvement in the patient's condition that occurs simply because the patient *believes* in the cure. A placebo is a substance with no impact or effect on the patient's health in itself, although a positive psychological or possibly even physical effect may result. Patients given a placebo may report positive effects if they believe it is a real cure that works.

Why does this occur? Some argue patients are mentally resolving worries about an expensive treatment by convincing themselves their money has purchased an effective treatment. Others argue most medical conditions naturally get better or worse. After patients take a placebo, they may be entering a phase where the condition improves anyway. Patients also make faulty cause-and-effect assumptions, crediting the placebo for feeling better. Another possibility is that if the person recommending the placebo has a positive demeanor and tells the patient it will work, the patient believes it and reports improvements.

The placebo response is somewhat different. This phenomenon occurs when the patient both believes there are fewer symptoms, and physically there really are fewer symptoms. In other words, the improvement is not "all in the patient's head." Research is still being conducted, but some treatments may cause the release of endorphins occurring naturally in the body and make a person literally feel better.[49]

Quackery and Medicine in the Twenty-First Century

Traditional and *scientific* medicine are convenient labels for describing the historical development of medical practice. In the twenty-first century, scientific medicine is referred to as conventional, allopathic, or biomedicine. All other approaches to health care are commonly referred to as alternative or complementary medicine. Alternative medicine implies treatments that are used *in place of* scientific medicine. Complementary means nonconventional treatments are used *along with* scientific treatments.

Scientific and alternative treatments continue to be viewed in opposition to each other. One is commonly considered true or effective; the other labeled as false or quackery. A new term, *integrative medicine*, describes a fusion of scientific and alternative approaches. This new term suggests the old dichotomy between regular, orthodox, university-educated physicians and "irregular," "unorthodox," or traditional practitioners is being re-evaluated.

Modern alternative medicine encompasses a huge, unlimited range of practices. Historical, prescientific, traditional approaches reappear alongside a multiplicity of new health lifestyles and treatments. Many have ancient origins in cultures from around the world. Some were revived or reinvented in the New Age movement of the 1960s and 1970s. Practices falling under this wide umbrella include systems integrating the body, mind, and spirit with cosmic, religious, or natural forces. Other alternative practices may be completely new discoveries or inventions.[50]

Because the range of alternative medicine is so all-encompassing, it is impossible to characterize all alternative medicine as good or bad, science or pseudoscience, effective or quack. For example, some alternative treatments have been scientifically proven to be effective; others have failed that test or studies are inconclusive. Nonconventional therapies lacking scientific evidence of effectiveness now may be the subject of future studies confirming or denying their worth.

The wide historical continuum of medical care described in this chapter is similar in scope to the range of medical options available in the modern world. As in the past, decisions are based on the cost and availability of treatment, the seriousness of the illness, and belief in the efficacy of the treatment. The wealthiest continue to seek medical advice and care from a top tier of medical specialists and treatment facilities. Those with limited means consult less expensive medical practitioners.

People from all socioeconomic levels still choose alternative practitioners and do-it-yourself approaches using over-the-counter, herbal, or other legal and illegal medications and treatments. Quacks still exist across the continuum and take advantage of both rich and poor.

Today, as in the past, people consider information from many sources when choosing health care providers or approaches. People continue to mix and match treatments based upon their own past experience, advice from people they know and medical practitioners, religious beliefs, cultural traditions, and information published in print media and on the internet. Multiple studies from around the world confirm a growing reliance on the internet for medical information and the need for media literacy skills among those seeking health information online.[51] A 2012 survey found nearly 60 percent of American adults looked online for health information and 35 percent sought to diagnose their own condition.[52]

A critical analysis of the history and techniques of medical quackery equips students with media literacy skills applicable to every area of their lives. The purpose of this work is not to label modern conventional or alternative medicine as effective or ineffective, but rather to encourage students to consider health care and quackery in a historical context and apply those lessons in their own lives. Quacks take advantage of how humans understand and misunderstand medical information; distorting what is true and adding what is false. Even the most careful and observant can be duped.

Why Do We Fall for Quackery?

Quackery has existed over the millennia of human history, even though medical knowledge and practice have changed dramatically. Modern medical diagnoses and treatments of disease, health care technology, and knowledge of how to maintain health have significantly increased the health and lifespan of humans. Beginning with the Scientific Revolution of the sixteenth and seventeenth centuries, new discoveries have contributed to the twenty-first-century scientific practice of medicine.

McClure's—The Marketplace of the World

MEDICAL OPINIONS OF BUFFALO LITHIA SPRINGS WATER

A. F. A. King, A. M., M. D., *Prof. of Obstetrics and Diseases of Women and children in the Medical Department of Columbia University, Washington, D. C., and in the University of Vermont, Ex-President Washington Obstetrical and Gynecological Society; Fellow of the British Gynecological and of the American Gynecological Societies, etc., etc.,* in the eighth edition of his Manual of Obstetrics recommends **BUFFALO LITHIA WATER** as a diuretic in diseases of the Kidney and Bladder.

T. Griswold Comstock, A. M., M. D., *St. Louis, Mo.,* says: "I have made use of it in gynecological practice, in women suffering from acute Uræmic conditions, with results, to say the least, very favorable."

Dr. Jos. Holt, *of New Orleans, Ex-President of the State Board of Health of Louisiana,* says: "I have prescribed **BUFFALO LITHIA WATER** in affections of the kidneys and urinary passages, particularly in Gouty subjects in Albuminuria, and in irritable condition of the Bladder and Urethra in females. The results satisfy me of its extraordinary value in a large class of cases usually most difficult to treat."

Voluminous medical testimony on request. For sale by the general drug and mineral water trade.

BUFFALO LITHIA SPRINGS WATER CO BUFFALO LITHIA SPRINGS, VIRGINIA

Remember.

Whether naturally perfect or not, your teeth require daily care, and will well repay the regular use of

Calvert's

Carbolic Tooth Powder.

Price from 15cts. Sample and Booklet from Park & Tilford, 927 Broadway, New York.
Makers: F. C. Calvert & Co., Manchester, England.
Canadian Depot: 349 Dorchester Street West Montreal.

LABLACHE

FACE POWDER

THE WOMAN WHO KNOWS

that her good looks—her success in society—depend chiefly on her complexion, uses always that greatest of beautifiers, **Lablache.** It keeps the skin smooth and velvety. Prevents redness, roughness and chaps caused by winter winds, and imparts to its users the appearance of perennial youth. *Refuse substitutes.* They may be dangerous. Flesh, White, Pink, or Cream, 50c. a box, of druggists or by mail.

Send 10c. for sample box.

BEN. LEVY CO., French Perfumers
Dept. 19 125 Kingston St., Boston, Mass.

The Berkshire Hills Sanatorium

Established Thirty-one Years.

For the exclusive treatment of cancer and all other forms of malignant and benign new growths (except those in the stomach, other abdominal organs, and the thoracic cavity).

With the Escharotic Method

(without resorting to surgical procedure).

Ask your family physician to make a personal investigation. This institution is conducted upon a strictly ethical basis. Complete information given upon request. Address,

WALLACE E. BROWN, M. D.
NORTH ADAMS, MASS.

Figure 1.5. The curative powers of water have been promoted since ancient times. In this advertisement, lithia water is promoted as a cure for kidney and bladder problems. Lithia water contains lithium salts and natural springs of this type are rare. Buffalo Springs was a popular water spa; the waters were bottled and sold nationally from the 1880s through the early twentieth century. Calvert's Tooth Powder, an early form of toothpaste, contained carbolic acid or phenol with antiseptic qualities. It can be poisonous in large quantities. The Berkshire Hills Sanatorium was a private hospital offering cancer treatment. The Escharotic Method involved chemically burning cancerous tumors. The method was not scientifically tested and the cancer often returned after the treatment. It is still promoted by quacks.
Advertisements, McClure's Magazine *(December 1909): 77. (Courtesy of the author)*

Despite this shift toward scientific ways of knowing and medicine, the success of quacks has not diminished. Quacks continue to profit selling unrealistic promises. Modern quacks effectively merge and twist age-old conceptions of health and disease with modern scientific understanding and pseudoscience to sell their products. They adapt sales strategies to the newest forms of media and technology and tailor appeals to every socioeconomic class of men and women. Medical quacks, now and in the past, skillfully create unrealistic hopes and manipulate fears of illness and death. Although life is uncertain and one right answer rarely exists, we keep looking and quacks keep promising.

In the Classroom

Quackery is an ideal theme for examining daily life on three levels—individual, societal, and historical. Students can figurately wear three pairs of glasses to examine issues in their own lives, the wider modern culture, and the past. This process encourages analysis of one's beliefs and decision-making processes.

First, prompt students to examine their own experiences. Assemble examples of current popular but questionable approaches to health from various media to prompt discussion. Ask students to share their individual opinions and experiences with these products or trends.

Second, ask students to explore the reasons for their approval or disapproval of these dubious health care options. Invite students to explore how each individual's experience is shaped by family, culture, and community. For example, cultural or religious traditions influence opinions of products using appeals to religion, tradition, or nature in advertising. Socioeconomic levels also influence health care choices.

Students, individually or in groups, can create a continuum of modern health care options from quackery to best or most acceptable. Require students to explain their rationale for the placement of each option. Student rationales will differ based on their own experiences and impressions from the media and the wider culture.

Finally, investigate how historical quackery and responses to it reflected past realities and cultural expectations for men, women, and children; just as modern responses are reflective of unique circumstances and cultures. This provides opportunities to examine continuity and change over time in the medical marketplace.

Some issues have remained constant over time—a confusing and often conflicting array of health care choices, the impact of wealth or poverty on health care choices, advertising and marketing tactics, the presence of quackery, and the debate about who is a quack and how to combat the problem.

Other factors have changed dramatically—the development of scientific medical practice, evolving forms of media used to promote health care options, and increasing government regulation of the medical marketplace. The development of the health insurance industry in the twentieth century is an element in the medical marketplace that should be discussed, but unfortunately is not within the scope of this work.

Individual lessons or instructional units focused on modern and historic medical care and quackery provide the perfect context for teaching how to distinguish between traditional, scientific, and pseudoscientific ways of knowing; identify common cognitive biases; and recognize the persuasive strategies employed in marketing and advertising. In the following chapter, additional essential questions, the history of patent medicines and several nineteenth-century medical approaches, and primary source text excerpts are provided.

Notes

1. Augustus Mason, *The Quackery of the Age: A Satire on the Times* (Boston: White, Lewis & Potter, Printers, 1845), 5, https://collections.nlm.nih.gov/bookviewer?PID=nlm:nlmuid-101198816-bk#page/1/mode/2up.
2. *Oxford English Dictionary Online*, s.v. "quack, n.2"; "quacksalver, n."; "medicaster, n."; "water-caster, n."; "Sangrado, n.," http://www.oed.com/.
3. United States Food and Drug Administration, "CPG Sec. 120.500 Health Fraud—Factors in Considering Regulatory Action," accessed July 2018, https://www.fda.gov/ICECI/ComplianceManuals/CompliancePolicyGuidanceManual/ucm073838.htm.
4. Vivian Nutton, "Humoralism," in *Companion Encyclopedia of the History of Medicine*, vol. 1, ed. William Bynum and Roy Porter (New York: Routledge, 1997), 282.
5. A contemporary of Hippocrates, the historian Thucydides (c. 460–400 BCE) also rejected the role of deities when recounting historical cause and effect in histories.
6. Toby Gelfand, "The History of the Medical Profession," in *Companion Encyclopedia of the History of Medicine*, vol. 2, ed. William Bynum and Roy Porter (New York: Routledge, 1997), 1120.

7. William Bynum, *History of Medicine: A Very Short Introduction* (Oxford: Oxford University Press, 2008), 5–18.
8. Nutton, "Humoralism," 282.
9. Cecil. G. Helman, "'Feed a Cold, Starve a Fever': Folk Models of Infection in an English Suburban Community, and Their Relation to Medical Treatment," *Culture, Medicine and Psychiatry* 2 (1978): 107–37.
10. Vicky Rippere, "The Survival of Traditional Medicine in Lay Medical Views: An Empirical Approach to the History of Medicine," *Medical History* 25, no. 4 (1981): 411–14.
11. Nutton, "Humoralism," 282.
12. Bynum, *History of Medicine*, 68–90.
13. Ibid., 43–67.
14. Ibid., 91–117.
15. Arthur L. Caplan, "The Concepts of Health, Illness, and Disease," in *Companion Encyclopedia of the History of Medicine*, vol. 1, ed. William Bynum and Roy Porter (New York: Routledge, 1997), 235.
16. William G. Rothstein, "The Medical Profession," in *Encyclopedia of American Social History*, vol. 3, ed. Mary Kupiec Cayton, Elliott J. Gorn, and Peter W. Williams, (New York: Charles Scribner's Sons, 1993), 2363–78.
17. Francis Bacon, *The Advancement of Learning* (1605), 2nd book, X 5, http://www.philosophy-index.com/bacon/advancement-learning/ii-x.php.
18. Lamar Riley Murphy, *Enter the Physician: The Transformation of Domestic Medicine 1760–1860* (Tuscaloosa: University of Alabama Press, 1991), 3.
19. Bynum, *History of Medicine*, 19–42.
20. Robert C. Fuller, "Alternative Medicine" in Cayton, Gorn, and Williams, *Encyclopedia of Social History*, vol. 3, 2379.
21. Erika Brady, "Folk Medicine" in *The New Encyclopedia of Southern Culture*, vol. 22, ed. Charles Reagan Wilson and James G. Thomas (Chapel Hill: University of North Carolina Press, 2012), 77–78.
22. George B. Scriven, "Doctors, Drugs, and Apothecaries of Seventeenth Century Maryland," *Bulletin of the History of Medicine* 37, no. 6 (November/December 1963): 516–22, http://www.jstor.org/stable/44446987.
23. Francisco Guerra, "Medical Almanacs of the American Colonial Period," *Journal of the History of Medicine and Allied Sciences* 16, no. 3 (July 1961): 234, http://www.jstor.org/stable/24620679.
24. John Tennent, *Every Man His Own Doctor; or, The Poor Planter's Physician* (ca. 1727), National Humanities Center Resource Toolbox, accessed July 2018, http://nationalhumanitiescenter.org/pds/becomingamer/ideas/text7/homemedicalguides.pdf; Whitfield J. Bell Jr., "Medical Practice in Colonial America," *Bulletin of the History of Medicine* 31, no. 5 (September/October 1957): 442–53, http://www.jstor.org/stable/44449174.
25. William Buchan, *Domestic Medicine* (Philadelphia: Joseph Crukshank, 1774), https://archive.org/details/2544042R.nlm.nih.gov.
26. Quoted in Murphy, *Enter the Physician*, 7, from William Buchan, *Domestic Medicine*, ix–xiv, 1769 edition.
27. Murphy, *Enter the Physician*, 7–8.
28. Scriven, "Doctors, Drugs, and Apothecaries of Seventeenth Century Maryland," 516–22.
29. *Oxford English Dictionary Online*, s.v. "chirurgeon, n.2."; s.v. "physic, n."
30. Kay Moss, *Southern Folk Medicine, 1750–1820* (Columbia: University of South Carolina Press, 1999), 226, eBook Collection, EBSCOhost; Bell, "Medical Practice in Colonial America," 444.
31. Bell, "Medical Practice in Colonial America," 449–53.
32. Jane B. Donegan, *Hydropathic Highway to Health, Women and Water-Cure in Antebellum America* (New York: Greenwood Press, 1986), 10; Rothstein, "The Medical Profession," 2363–78.
33. Empirics relied on experience over theory.
34. David Cowen, *Medicine and Health in New Jersey: A History* (Princeton, NJ: D. Van Nostrand, 1964), 71, cited in William H. Helfand, *Quack, Quack, Quack: The Sellers of Nostrums in Prints, Posters, Ephemera and Books* (New York: Grolier Club, 2002), 40.
35. Moss, *Southern Folk Medicine, 1750–1820*, 2.
36. United States Food and Drug Administration, "CPG Sec. 120.500 Health Fraud—Factors in Considering Regulatory Action."
37. Patricia A. D'Itri and Frank M. D'Itri, *Mercury Contamination: A Human Tragedy* (New York: John Wiley & Sons, 1977), 177–97.
38. Ciddi Veeresham, "Natural Products Derived from Plants as a Source of Drugs," *Journal of Advanced Pharmaceutical Technology & Research* 3, no. 4 (October–December 2012): 200–201, doi:10.4103/2231-4040.104709; US National Library of Medicine, National Institutes of Health, https://www.ncbi.nlm.nih.gov/pmc/articles/PMC3560124/.
39. Paul A. Offit, *Do You Believe in Magic? The Sense and Nonsense of Alternative Medicine* (New York: HarperCollins, 2013), 41; Maarten Boudry, Stefaan Blancke, and Massimo Pigliucci, "What Makes Weird Beliefs Thrive? The Epidemiology of Pseudoscience," *Philosophical Psychology* 28, no. 8 (2015): 1189, http://dx.doi.org/10.1080/09515089.2014.971946.

40. The term *cognitive bias* was first introduced in the early 1970s by psychologists Amos Tversky and Daniel Kahneman in their research on how people make decisions.

41. Joe Y. F. Lau, *An Introduction to Critical Thinking and Creativity: Think More, Think Better* (Hoboken, NJ: John Wiley & Sons, 2011), 185–94; A. Wilkie and R. Mata, "Cognitive Bias," in *Encyclopedia of Human Behavior*, vol. 1, ed. V. S. Ramachandran, 2nd ed. (Cambridge, MA: Academic Press, 2012), 531–35.

42. *Oxford English Dictionary Online*, s.v. "pseudoscience."

43. Timothy Caulfield, *The Cure for Everything* (Boston: Beacon Press, 2012), 186.

44. Bonnie B. O'Connor and David J. Hufford, "Understanding Folk Medicine," in *Healing Logics: Culture and Medicine in Modern Health Belief Systems*, ed. Erika Brady (Logan: Utah State University Press, 2001), 18–25, doi: 10.2307/j.ctt46nwrq.

45. Howard Wolinsky, "Disease Mongering and Drug Marketing," *EMBO Reports* 6, no. 7 (2005): 612–14, doi 10.1038/sj.embor.7400476, US National Library of Medicine, National Institutes of Health, https://www.ncbi.nlm.nih.gov/pmc/articles/PMC1369125/.

46. Caulfield, *The Cure for Everything*, 154–58

47. Ibid., 132; Eric S. Juhnke, *Quacks and Crusaders: The Fabulous Careers of John Brinkley, Norman Baker, and Harry Hoxsey* (Lawrence: University Press of Kansas, 2002).

48. Juhnke, *Quacks and Crusaders*.

49. Offit, *Do You Believe in Magic?*, 223–31.

50. Erika Brady, "Introduction," in *Healing Logics: Culture and Medicine in Modern Health Belief Systems*, 4, 10.

51. J. T. Chu, M. P Wang, C. Shen, K. Viswanath, T. H. Lam, and S. S. C. Chan, "How, When and Why People Seek Health Information Online: Qualitative Study in Hong Kong," *Interactive Journal of Medical Research* 6, no. 2 (2017), doi: 10.2196/ijmr.7000, https://www.i-jmr.org/2017/2/e24/; J. Moreland, T. L. French, and G. P. Cumming, "The Prevalence of Online Health Information Seeking among Patients in Scotland: A Cross-Sectional Exploratory Study," *JMIR Research Protocols* 4, no. 3 (July 2015), doi: 10.2196/resprot.4010, https://www.researchprotocols.org/2015/3/e85/; J. Car, B. Lang, A. Colledge, C. Ung, and A. Majeed, "Interventions for Enhancing Consumers' Online Health Literacy," *Cochrane Database of Systematic Reviews* 15, no. 6 (June 2015), doi: 10.1002/14651858.CD007092.pub2, US National Library of Medicine National Institutes of Health, https://www.ncbi.nlm.nih.gov/pubmed/21678364.

52. "The Internet and Health," Pew Research Center, Internet & Technology, February 12, 2013, accessed December 2018, http://www.pewinternet.org/2013/02/12/the-internet-and-health/.

CHAPTER TWO

Caveat Emptor

Let the Buyer Beware

Never meddle with medicines, unless some disorder of the system renders them really necessary. Remember the friendly warning in the epitaph on an old gravestone: "I am well; would be better; took physic: and here I am.

—Lydia Maria Child, *The Family Nurse*, 1837[1]

Essential questions:

- What is the best way to stop quackery?
- To what extent should *Caveat emptor*—"let the buyer beware"—be applied to the medical marketplace?
    - Who is to blame for quackery? People buying it? The quack? The media? The government?
- What is the function of government regulation in the medical marketplace?
    - To educate the public?
    - To research, test, and approve medications and medical treatments?
    - To protect consumers? To protect the health care industry?
        - What regulations are appropriate? What regulations are too restrictive?
    - To regulate marketing and advertising in the medical marketplace?

The tales of historical quacks are interesting and entertaining. As the details unfold of their ridiculous cures, astonishingly deceptive sales techniques, and gullible customers, we are amused by the credulity and naivety of people in the past. We congratulate ourselves on our hindsight. We are certain we know better in the modern world and are confident we would never have fallen for it.

However, quackery is alive and well in the modern world. Quacks continue selling dubious cures using the same tactics and schemes. The names and contents of the panaceas may have changed, the buzzwords updated, and the message carried through new forms of media, but people continue to be conned, tricked, and deceived. Honest introspection usually leads to the realization that we too have been fooled by a quack.

After realizing we've been duped, whom do we blame? The quack, the media, ourselves? Do we say, "Someone should have warned me"? Perhaps we console ourselves because "everybody was buying it." Or we may blame the government for not banning it. Do we scrutinize our own decision-making process? Do we make a better choice the next time?

The problem of quackery and reliable methods of recognizing and avoiding it are topics that have been debated for centuries. The tactics of quacks, our age-old complicity, and how to overcome it are the themes of this chapter. The histories of several popular or fashionable nineteenth-century cures are outlined to illustrate four key concepts relevant to quackery in the modern health care marketplace.

First, popularity does not guarantee effectiveness. These products or cures were widely promoted by honest believers, celebrities, and quacks. Then, as today, customers mistakenly equated popularity with effectiveness.

Second, the contrast between conventional and alternative treatments is highlighted, a dichotomy that continues today. Nineteenth-century "irregular" practitioners provided alternatives to the treatments of "regular" physicians. By modern standards, the treatments of both sides prior to the twentieth century were questionable, but ignorance and lack of information created a marketplace of confusion and uncertainly, the perfect opportunity for quacks.

Third, the debate over the role and extent of government regulation of the marketplace is explored. Government regulation was nonexistent or minimal prior to the twentieth century. Individuals had the primary responsibility for their choices and the consequences. A shift in attitude began in the Progressive Era when consumers began to demand government oversight. However, the role of government in the medical marketplace is still debated in the twenty-first century.

Fourth, media may have transformed from print to electronic, but nineteenth-century advertising and marketing strategies were the forerunners of those used today. Testimonials, direct marketing, pyramid or multilevel marketing schemes, promotional campaigns, and infotainment are not new concepts. Quacks of any era are adept at using the newest strategies to dupe their customers.

Natural Cures: Samuel Thomson and Botanic Physicians

Nineteenth-century botanical or eclectic medicine was the most popular alternative to the regular physicians of the era. Plant-based and "natural" approaches were used for the prevention and treatment of illness. This movement organized medical societies, journals, and their own medical schools in the first half of the nineteenth century. At its height in the 1830s, botanical medicine was a system of patients, general supporters, family subscribers, dedicated practitioners, professional salespeople, and quacks selling instructional literature and medicines.[2]

Samuel Thomson (1769–1843) was the most prominent of the botanic medical practitioners. He developed, promoted, and sold a household system of botanical medicine that enabled people to become their own doctor. Samuel Thomson began his career as a New Hampshire farmer and in 1805 became an itinerant, self-trained botanical healer. In 1822 he published *New Guide to Health.* He employed people to sell his book and botanical drugs and organized Friendly Botanical Societies to promote his products. He was labeled a quack by regular physicians (see source 2).

Thomson's treatments centered on the same three themes prominent in ancient Greek medicine: balance of the humors, botanical medications, and moderation. His cures were especially popular for several reasons.

First, the treatments recommended by Thomson and other botanical healers were viewed as more moderate and easier on the body than other contemporary approaches. Both Thomson and regular doctors were seeking to correct imbalances of the humors. However, many university-trained physicians practiced heroic medicine. Heroic medicine used bloodletting; powerful chemicals such as calomel, a form of mercury and antimony/tartar emetic to induce sweating, vomiting, and bowel evacuation; and addictive opiates such as laudanum. Thomson's treatments also induced emptying fluids from various orifices but were considered gentler and more natural. Instead of potent chemical agents, Thomson recommended botanicals such as lobelia, cayenne pepper, or steam baths to heat the body and remove obstructions of the humors (see figure 2.1).[3]

Second, botanical medicine corresponded with traditional beliefs in the healing power of God-given natural cures. The moral and religious climate in America before the Civil War encouraged individuals to take responsibility for their own moral and physical shortcomings. The belief in human perfectibility was evident in evangelical religious movements and efforts to reform society through temperance. Individuals were expected to reform themselves physically as well as morally and spiritually. Disregarding the laws of healthful living was equated with sin.[4]

Finally, Thomson's be-your-own-doctor approach coincided with the political philosophies of the Jacksonian democracy and the era of the common man. Americans sought to determine their own destiny without government interference. Botanical medicine also appealed to average people and frontier families with limited money to pay or access to regular physicians. Every man, woman, or family could be their own physician (see source 7).[5]

Thomson controlled the rights and profits of his self-treatment system through what is known in the twenty-first century as multilevel marketing. Thomson sold the instructions, called "family rights," to use his system for $20. Users of Thomson's system were encouraged to create local Friendly Botanic Societies. These local networks, in turn, further publicized the system. Members could become designated agents authorized to sell additional "family rights," creating a

Figure 2.1. Samuel Thomson's multilevel marketing system made his botanical cures especially popular and profitable in the first half of the nineteenth century. Subscribers to his system could purchase the medicines for their own use as well as become agents to sell his books and products.
Engraving, Advertisement for Thomsonian Botanic Medicine Store, 1834. (Courtesy of US National Library of Medicine)

pyramid of distributors and new customers.[6] Today, both questionable and legitimate businesses employ the multilevel marketing system or network marketing. Many modern pyramid schemes are illegal.

By the 1840s, Thomsonian medicine was beginning to decline, but other approaches to health and medical care captured the attention and dollars of Americans.

Hydropathy: Reforming Body and Spirit

Hydropathy, or the water cure, was another health reform movement and treatment popular in the United States in the decades before the Civil War. Patients soaked in cold baths, took showers, or were wrapped in cold wet compresses, sheets, belts, or special wet dresses; they also drank copious amounts of water.

The curative power of water was recognized by the ancient Greeks and Romans and mineral springs were frequented in both Europe and America for centuries before the hydropathy craze. In eighteenth-century Bath, England, upper-class visitors to the Pump Room drank mineral water from the nearby hot spring. This "watering place" was located on the ruins of ancient Roman baths. In America, the wealthy vacationed at mineral spring resorts such as White Sulphur Springs, Virginia (now The Greenbriar in West Virginia) and Saratoga Springs, New York, as well as dozens of smaller, local springs for both their health and entertainment.

The nineteenth century hydropathy fad began when a European peasant, Vincenz Priessnitz (1799–1851), treated animals and himself through cold water applications and sweating and reported his methods could cure gout and rheumatism. In just a few years, Priessnitz had hundreds of patients. Physicians and other medical practitioners and patients across Europe and the United States adopted and adapted the water cure. Proponents of hydropathy and the botanical movement were united in their criticism of the methods of regular physicians of the era.

Nineteenth-century hydropathy focused on more than just curing existing ailments. The movement also tapped into contemporary trends focusing on a healthy lifestyle. Healthful living was viewed as a moral imperative; unhealthful living was viewed as sinful in the evangelical reform climate of the era. Hydropathy regimes include prescriptions for fresh air, exercise, special diets, and the elimination of various habits negatively associated with a fast-paced, urban lifestyle. The recommendations were similar to those promoted by contemporary health reformer Sylvester Graham (1794–1851)—a vegetarian diet, no rich food or "stimulating" beverages containing alcohol or caffeine, and restrictions on sexual activity.

Between 1843 when the first American establishments were opened in New York City and 1860, at least twenty-seven hydropathic treatment centers opened, two medical schools of hydropathy were established, several water cure journals were published, and over one hundred male and female practitioners provided therapy in the United States. The water cure regime could be followed at home with the help of water cure practitioners and advice publications. Those who could afford the expense visited water cure spas offering treatments in scenic settings, educational classes and lectures, amusements, and interaction with other patients.[7]

The water cure movement was especially promoted by and for women. These women advocated new approaches to pregnancy and childbirth and challenged contemporary beliefs that women should avoid strenuous exercise and wear tight corsets and voluminous skirts. Between 1850 and 1852, the *Water Cure Journal* called for less restrictive clothing for women and even asked readers to submit ideas. Most were similar to outfits worn by the women of the utopian Oneida Community and popularized by women's rights activist Amelia Bloomer.[8]

Testimonials from well-known authors and reformers increased the popularity of the treatments. Lucy Stone, Amelia Bloomer, Susan B. Anthony, Horace Greeley, and William Alcott praised hydropathy. Harriet Beecher Stowe spent almost a year at one of the most expensive and exclusive water cure spas located in Brattleboro, Vermont (see source 8).[9]

Alfred Tennyson promoted the hydropathic cure in 1844 when he described his treatment at a hydropathy center in England in a letter (February 2, 1844). "Much poison has come out of me, which no physic ever would have brought to light. . . . I have been here already upwards of two months. Of all the uncomfortable ways of living . . . hydropathical is the worst; no reading by candlelight, no going near fire, no tea, no coffee, perpetual wet sheet in cold baths and alternation from hot to cold: however have much faith in it."[10]

Despite its popularity, hydropathy was not praised by everyone. Critics reported deaths due to improper treatment, questioned its effectiveness, and accused hydropaths of being quacks. The hydropathy craze reached its zenith in the mid-1850s, but it did not disappear. Its concepts of cleanliness, exercise, and diet were prominent in other pseudosci-

Figure 2.2. Electric cures appealed to customers in the late nineteenth and early twentieth centuries because they represented the newest technology. Dr. Scott heavily marketed his electric tooth brushes, hair brushes, corsets, insoles, and other products in newspapers, magazines, and by direct mail. His products actually contained magnets, not electric current. He claimed his devices could cure nearly every ailment of both men and women. Note the message in the bottom left corner of this image. The belt was promoted as safer than medications taken internally: "Away with physics and quack nostrums." Physics were "cleansing" medications causing patients to vomit or empty the bowels.
Dr. Scott's Genuine Electric Belt Postcard, c. late 19th century. (Courtesy of US National Library of Medicine)

entific approaches and legitimate efforts at hygienic reform. The enthusiasm of its promoters brings to mind modern trends focusing on bottled mineral or vitamin water or health and beauty spas.

Electrical Devices: New Technology for the New Urban Lifestyle

In 1869, physician George Miller Beard (1839–1883) invented a word for a new disease affecting America's urban white-collar middle-class: neurasthenia. According to Beard, this frightening new affliction was the underlying cause of an epidemic of physical and mental problems rampant in Europe and America. Consumption, fatigue, nervousness, impotence, heart palpitations were all caused by the demands of modern life in a new industrial and urban world. Beard claimed the body had a finite or fixed amount of energy. In the slower-paced rural life of the past, the body's energy was sufficient to deal with the demands of daily life. But fast-paced city life, the demands of higher education, and the "brainwork" required for white-collar occupations caused a premature depletion of the bodies "nerve force."

The symptoms of neurasthenia were numerous and varied from case to case: sleeplessness, anxiety, weariness, fatigue, depression, indigestion, or weak muscles. All parts of the body could suffer. Those affected complained of headaches, back pain, groin discomfort, or overall physical fatigue. Today, these would be characterized as non-specific symptoms, complaints reported by a patient that do not clearly point to a specific disease or involve a specific organ or body system. While non-specific symptoms can indicate larger medical issues, they are also routinely referenced by quacks to convince consumers they suffer from a disease that only the quack can cure.

Prescribed treatments for neurasthenia were different for men and women, reflecting contemporary views on the inherent difference in male and female biology and mental capacity. By 1900, physical and mental depletion of middle-class white men appeared to be an epidemic. Fresh air and strenuous exercise were the preferred treatments for men. Theodore Roosevelt and Frederic Remington regained their health in the wilderness of the American West. Women, who were expected to conserve their energy for reproduction, were supposed to have complete bed rest, no intellectual stimulation, and a bland diet. Charlotte Perkins Gilman, social reformer and writer, wrote about her treatment in the short story "The Yellow Wallpaper" (1892).[11]

Modern and "scientific" appliances and tonics were invented and prescribed for neurasthenia by regular physicians, unlicensed practitioners, and quacks. Between 1870 and 1930, electrical devices were popular. Electrical belts, collars, vibrators for various body parts, and even suppositories were supposed to contribute electrical energy to make up for the depletion caused by modern life.

Promoters of electrical devices popular in the late nineteenth century repeated many of the claims of mesmerists from the previous generation. Mesmerism, or magnetism, was introduced in 1778 by Franz Mesmer in Europe; it was introduced in the United States in the 1830s. Proponents claimed disease was caused by obstructions of an electrical or magnetic "universal fluid." Mesmer and his followers cured disease by moving their hands, magnets, or other devices over or touching patients' bodies to move this internal force. This popular treatment was dismissed by some as quackery but embraced and promoted by many, including Mary Baker Eddy (1821–1910).

By the 1870s, various electric devices were used by medical practitioners of all sorts to create muscle contractions, stimulate digestion and evacuation, or to remove moles, ulcers, and tumors. More powerful currents were used as a nerve tonic or general energy stimulant. By the 1880s, practitioners claimed electrotherapy could cure everything from poor eyesight to sexual dysfunction, as well as relieve pain or stop blood flow. Various devices were sold for home use such as the Magnetic Machine and electric belts to wear on the body. These devices were heavily promoted and offered for sale in popular magazines, mail-order catalogs such as Sears, Roebuck and Company, direct mail campaigns, and door-to-door sales.

The I-ON-A-CO electric device was especially popular in the 1920s through the 1940s. Promoters claimed this plug-in belt cured disease by electrically magnetizing the body's iron to increase absorption of oxygen. The product was heavily promoted by Henry Gaylord Wilshire, a wealthy California real estate developer, through free clinics, newspaper advertising, and radio health shows. Millions of Americans purchased, used, and praised the I-ON-A-CO device.

The I-ON-A-CO device represents the difficult-to-discern line between quackery and true believers, between science and pseudoscience, and between popularity and genuine effectiveness. In the decades the device was sold, many doubted its effectiveness and publicly labeled the device as quackery. Did it really work, or was it the placebo effect? While the I-ON-A-CO belt could not cure major diseases as claimed, the light electric massage may have remedied minor ailments such as fatigue or stiff necks. Even today, licensed physicians and physical therapists apply electrodes to muscles and tendons to alleviate pain.[12]

I-ON-A-CO devices were endorsed by a well-known personality who made a fortune from its sale. Wilshire's marketing blended science and pseudoscience. The public's interest in the new science of electricity merged with their unfamiliarity with the untested applications of electricity in medicine. These electric devices were purchased by average people who attested to their usefulness. Popularity came to equal effectiveness.

Radium: The Popular Poison

By the early twentieth century, scientific medicine had a firm hold. Physician training and licensing programs were well-established and new discoveries and scientific practices were improving health care. But many still hoped to fulfill the age-old dream of a fountain of youth. Science and pseudoscience merged again in the first forty years of the twentieth century to produce the radioactive elixir craze. This especially dangerous panacea was supposed to alter the cellular composition of the body so it could continuously produce its own renewable energy. The reality of its effect was much different.

In 1902, Marie and Pierre Curie announced their discovery of a new element, radium. This scientific discovery fascinated the American public, largely because of its seeming ability to grow in energy even as it diminished in quantity. Scientists and the public alike believed radium could kill damaged cells and renew depleted energy levels.

Radium enthusiasm inspired thousands of articles, songs, fictional stories, games, entertainments, and health cures between 1900 and 1940. Scientists, physicians, quacks, and consumers wanted to believe radium was a miracle cure for aging. With little evidence and even less scientific proof, the American press made dramatic claims for the future potential of radium. Science and pseudoscience merged. Radium-enhanced consumer products were sold including toothpaste, hair tonic, and even chocolate bars. The products were touted as brightening, glowing, invigorating, and healthful. The popularity of natural hot spring spas was declining in the 1910s, but new claims that spring waters contained radium to reinvigorate the body and stop aging created a new flood of customers.

Radium experts, such as William Hammer, an electrical engineer on Thomas Edison's team who studied with the Curies in Paris, promoted radium therapy across the country between 1902 and 1907. At the time, even the most respected radium scientists believed radium was physically beneficial in every case. Despite her declining health, Marie Curie believed in the positive effects of radium until her death. Her demise in 1934 was caused by years of radioactive exposure.

Throughout the 1920s, radium water dispensers were marketed for home use. Consumers were told this "liquid sunshine" could revive their energy through a natural healing process. Radium water jars were sold by many manufacturers through the mail, door-to-door, and in stores with names such as Radium Ore Revigator, the Vitalizer, the Radiumator, and VigoRadium. Some of these jars provided minuscule radium doses; others provided none at all. Consumers were advised to drink multiple glasses of water every day from the radium water for sixty to ninety days to get the full effect.

Larger doses of radium were offered by licensed physicians and other types of practitioners during office treatments. Bottled radium treatments with higher amounts of radium, such as Radithor, could also be purchased for home consumption. In 1925, William Bailey, a self-proclaimed doctor without a license or medical degree began to sell Radithor, half-ounce bottles of radium water. He claimed if one took the prescribed dose of one to three bottles a day, the body would be flooded with energy and the glands of the endocrine system (hormones) would be invigorated. Between 1925 and 1930, more than four hundred thousand bottles of Radithor were sold worldwide.

Even though radium poisoning had been discovered as early as 1920, the popular enthusiasm around its curative properties caused many to ignore its dangers. When the well-known industrialist and millionaire sportsman Eben Byers died in 1932 from radium poisoning, caused by consuming Radithor, the popular press finally noticed.[13] By 1933 William Bailey's business was shut down. The high-profile legal battle of radium-poisoned women using the element to paint watch dials was settled in 1928, about the time that Eben Byers began to consume Radithor, hoping to stop the natural aging process. Popular enthusiasm blinded scientists, physicians, the popular press, and regular Americans to the danger of radium consumption.[14]

Patent Medicine

Patent medicine, proprietary medicine, panacea, and nostrum—all these words described medicines or medical devices sold directly to consumers in the eighteenth, nineteenth, and early twentieth centuries. Today, all of these terms imply quackery. The evolution of our perception of these terms reflects the twentieth-century transformation in the availability of medicine to consumers and increased government regulation.

Before the twentieth century, *all* medications and medical devices could be purchased without a doctor's prescription. Individuals medicated themselves without government oversight. Anyone could purchase the ingredients used in medicines, create and sell various pills, powders, and liquid medications. Physicians might recommend a particular medicine, but doctors' formal approvals were not required for purchase. Drugs were sold through mail order, by traveling salesmen, and in pharmacies and other stores. Powerful drugs were not locked behind the counter of a licensed pharmacist as in the twenty-first century. The modern distinction between prescription drugs and over-the-counter medications did not exist.

Technically, patent proprietary medications are made from legally protected formulas that can only be made or sold by the patent owner. Patents grant the exclusive right to make, sell, or import a product and exclude others without the consent of the owner. Patenting has a long history in Europe; monarchs granted "letters patent," exclusive rights to produce goods or services. These traditions continued in the colonies and were reiterated in the US Constitution.

In seventeenth-century Britain, patent rights were extended to include the proprietors of popular medical remedies. A seventeenth-century list of British medical patents listed six: four for baths and devices, one for an improved method to prepare alum, and one for making Epsom salts. Compounded medicines, based on unique recipes of various natural

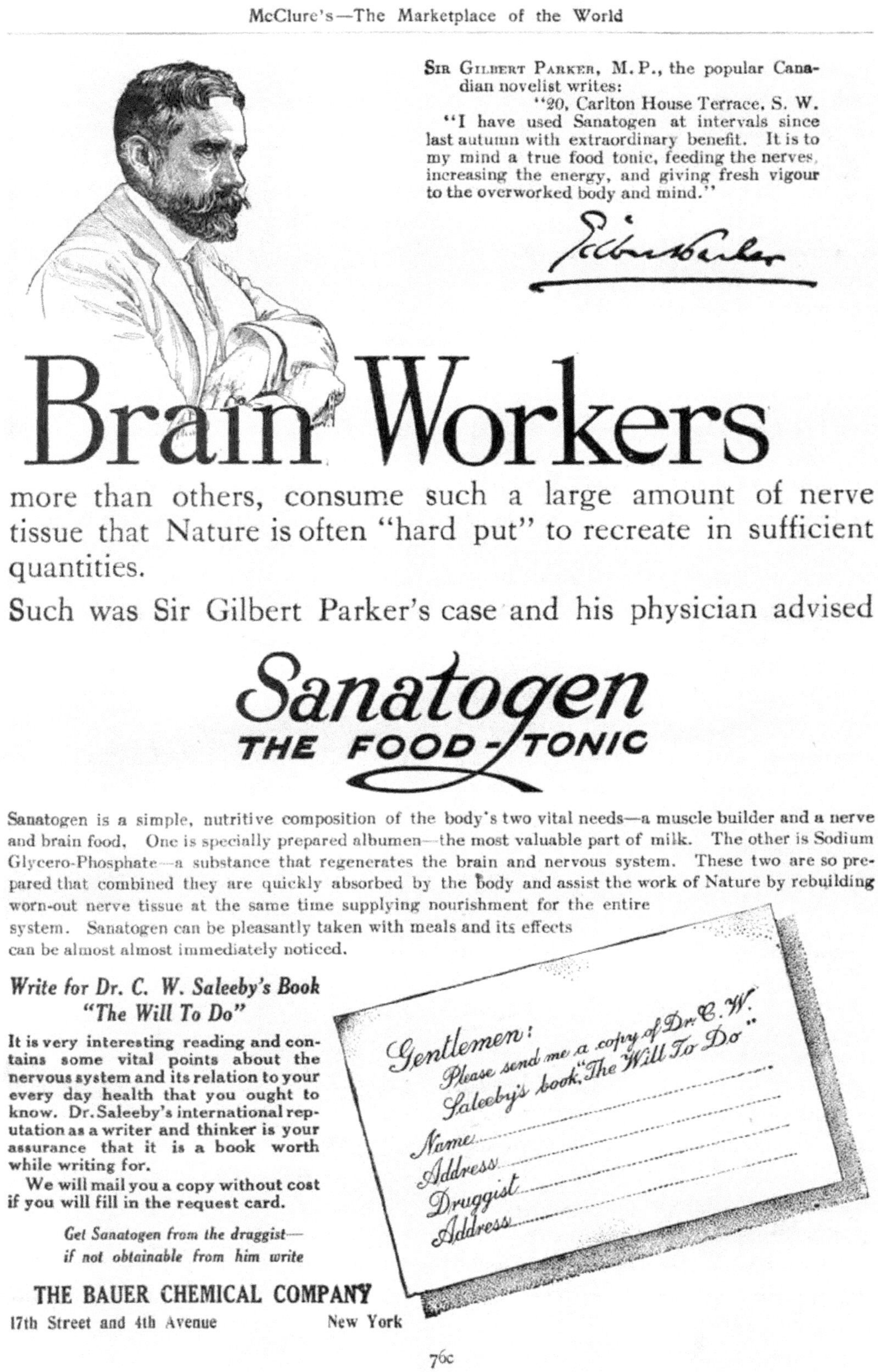

Figure 2.3. Americans were worried about a new disease caused by the new demands of fast-paced urban life in the late nineteenth century—neurasthenia. White-collar men, "brain workers," were especially susceptible. In this magazine ad, a testimonial from a politician and an offer for additional information was used to convince readers they needed to buy Sanatogen, a tonic to assist nature in revitalizing the body. Phosphate, an ingredient of this product, was thought to be linked to brain health by nineteenth-century scientists. However, recent studies suggest that phosphate supplements may be harmful.

Advertisement McClure's Magazine *(December 1909): 76c; Alan Dronsfield and Pete Ellis, "Phosphorus—Food for Thought," November 1, 2009,* Education in Chemistry, *Royal Society of Chemistry, https://rsc.li/2CgJpCl. (Courtesy of the author)* and chemical ingredients, were also patented, such as the twenty-two-ingredient Stoughton's Elixir in 1712 or Hooper's Female Pills in 1743. The first patent granted by the British government to a person living in the American colonies was for a device created by Sybilla Watson for grinding corn to be used for food and as an "Excellent Medicine for Consumptions & other Distempers."[15]

Popular British medications such as Dr. Bateman's Pectoral Drops, Hooper's Female Pills, and Daffy's Elixir were available in Britain and shipped to the colonies. However, blockades during the American Revolution reduced colonial access to British medications. Some formulas were legally protected against duplication; others were not. Enterprising Americans began reproducing British medications, with or without legal patentholder approval, to meet the demand in the colonies. For liquid medications, the distinctive bottles of British medications were recycled and refilled with American imitations. American glass factories manufactured new imitation bottles and enterprising business people filled them with similar formulas.[16]

In 1796, the first American patent for medicine under the new United States Constitution was granted to Samuel Lee Jr. for Bilious Pills. Until a new patent law in 1836, no proof of effectiveness, usefulness, or novelty was required. However, most American medications were not legally patented. Gaining a patent required that the ingredients be revealed, which allowed others to create a similar medicine. Patenting the design of the bottle or copyrighting the label and advertising literature were more lucrative ways to protect one's unique formula.[17]

Proprietary medicines were recommended and sold by practitioners and quacks across the continuum of medical care. Versions of the same medicines were marketed, some under the original proprietary label, others under competing labels. Some were created by apothecaries whose mixtures were endorsed by physicians. Similar medicines could also be made at home. Recipes for commercial medications were published in domestic medical advice and recipe books. For example, John Wesley's *Primitive Physic* included formulas for Daffy's Elixir and other popular patent medicines.

The ingredients in patent medicines included active substances that impacted the body. Some ingredients are known to be scientifically safe or useful today, others have been proven dangerous or deadly. Botanicals known in Europe for thousands of years; newer botanicals from Africa, Asia, and the Americas; various chemicals; alcohol; and highly addictive narcotics such as opium and morphine were common. Various flavorings and inactive fillers were also used. Since the precise scientific effect of various ingredients was unknown, there was a tendency to mix numerous ingredients in the same formula to treat every possible illness and complaint. Complex mixtures protected one's unique formula from rivals because only the original inventor knew the precise amounts of ingredients.

Drug makers were not required to inform customers about ingredients or list the ingredients of their products on the label. In 1822, the Philadelphia College of Pharmacy compared the ingredients of American imitations to the British drugs of the same name. They found two drugs with the same name often had very different ingredients or proportions of ingredients. A pamphlet printed by the college listing eight standardized formulas of British medications was so popular it was reprinted twice. As the formulas became publicly known, the proprietary names for the British medications fell out of use. New, distinctly American proprietary medications took their place such as Swaim's Panacea or Brandreth's Pills.[18]

Selling Snake Oil: Patent Medicine Advertising and Traveling Medicine Shows

Opportunities for quackery were abundant in this unregulated drug market. Anyone could create medication and sell it directly to customers. Patent medication promoters saw opportunity, employing legitimate and fraudulent advertising and marketing strategies to sell their products.

Patent medicine makers were leaders in the emerging field of advertising, distinctive packaging, and the psychology of consumers, using every media of the era. By the late nineteenth century, growing profits from print advertising fueled the growth of inexpensive magazines and newspapers, enabling cures to be sold to wider and wider audiences.

Patent medicine promoters knew patents and copyrights on unique packaging or advertising literature was more valuable than the contents of the container. Trademarks and distinctive symbols, such as Lydia Pinkham's maternal face, differentiated a product in a crowded market and became more important than the actual ingredients. Colorful and creative packages caught the attention of customers and inspired brand loyalty. Images and symbols were used to frighten, amuse, or inspire patriotism or love of family. Text and illustrations alluded to secret formulas and ingredients from new scientific discoveries, ancient or exotic lands, Indian secrets, natural sources, or biblical knowledge.

As transportation networks expanded across the nation, successful brands became nationally known, generating more sales. Store owners received perks for carrying or promoting certain brands. Consumers were instructed in marketing materials to buy only the name brand product and reject substitutes. Money-back guarantees and special prices were offered. Nostrum sellers developed early forms of customer loyalty programs with rewards, rebates, and free merchandise. Trial samples, toys, and other items were given away to promote products. Improved methods of selling medicines directly to consumers were developed using door-to-door salesmen, multilevel marketing systems, and mail-order schemes.

Free or low-cost pamphlets, almanacs, calendars, posters, and other literature promoting patent medications were distributed. Trade cards with colorful images and catchy advertising slogans on the front and additional text and testimonials on the back were especially popular. Most were three by five inches and were distributed for free by merchants and salespeople. Between the 1870s and the early 1900s, trade cards promoting all types of products were collected, traded, and pasted in scrapbooks.[19]

Critics of the nineteenth-century proprietary medicine industry claimed only quacks advertised; real physicians did not. Samuel Adams Hopkins advised readers to "Study the medicine advertising in your morning paper, and you will find yourself in a veritable goblin-realm of fakery, peopled with monstrous myths."[20] However, this distinction was not a reliable method of identifying a quack. Then and now, all types of medical practitioners advertise, using numerous methods. Even the American Medical Association journal, the official publication of licensed physicians, carried proprietary medication advertisements until 1901.[21]

The career of Clark Stanley exemplifies patent medicine quackery of the late nineteenth and early twentieth centuries. Stanley marketed his rattlesnake oil as a cure for aches and pains, claiming his secret formula came from the Hopi Indians. Stanley's snake oil was just one of the cures marketed to Americans through a creative blend of live entertainment, informational or entertaining pamphlets and books, and print advertising. In 1916, Stanley's snake oil cures were proven to contain no snake oil at all and he was fined $20.[22] Stanley's career made the term snake oil a synonym for quack.

Medicine shows, a blend of entertainment, advertising, and marketing, were known as far back as the Middle Ages. These early traveling showmen entertained with a variety show of songs, magic tricks, and skits and sold various goods and medical remedies or services such as tooth pulling. They offered entertainment, escape, laughter, novelty, and promises to ease daily suffering. Skits acted out miraculous cures. For example, charlatans pretended to drink poison or be bit by a snake so they could be "cured" by the antidotes they sold.[23]

Quacksalver, *charlatan*, and *mountebank*, from Dutch, French, and Italian, are archaic words describing an itinerant salesman of medicine and entertainment.[24] In the sixteenth and seventeenth centuries, these labels did not always imply dishonesty. For example, the word mountebank literally referred to someone selling goods from a stage or platform.

The remedies sold by European charlatans and mountebanks were virtually the same as those of regular physicians, apothecaries, or other healers. However, Italy, France, the Dutch Republic, and Spain passed laws or licensing rules for these itinerant medical providers. Licensing records from sixteenth-century Italy indicate charlatans usually sold plaster or oils to treat pain, ointments for scabies, and powder for teeth or for treating intestinal worms. Only a few sold self-proclaimed secret remedies; some made grandiose claims for cures for fatal diseases such as the plague.[25]

The long tradition of charlatans and mountebanks became known in America as the traveling medicine show. American medicine shows combined elements of many different forms of entertainment—dime museums such as P. T. Barnum's American Museum; circus routines; black-face and slapstick minstrel shows and vaudeville acts; religious tent revivals; and Wild West reenactments. The healing power of Native American herbs and cures had a special appeal to Americans. Many traveling shows and proprietary medicines, such as Clark Stanley's snake oil, claimed Native American names or origins.

The Kickapoo Indian Medicine Company produced one of the most prosperous turn-of-the-century medicine shows. The founders, cure-all salesmen John Healy and "Texas Charlie" Bigelow, selected the name Kickapoo because it was amusing. They claimed to be agents for the tribe and sold secret formula patent medications with unique names like Kickapoo Buffalo Salve, Kickapoo Indian Worm Killer, and Sagwa.

The Kickapoo Medicine Show included entertaining and often lurid interpretations of Indian customs such as powwows and dances, and bloody battles between white settlers and Indians. Singing, dancing, acrobatics, comedy sketches, and a five-thousand-foot moving painted panorama of the Wild West was also featured. They claimed to employ eight hundred Indians making medicine, performing in the traveling shows, or appearing in advertisements.

In the 1890s, up to one hundred different troupes of traveling Kickapoo shows were on the road in the United States and Canada. The Kickapoo Company also advertised in newspapers and magazines and distributed dozens of publications and pamphlets at little or no cost containing medical advice, stories, jokes, general information, and lots of ads for Kickapoo products.

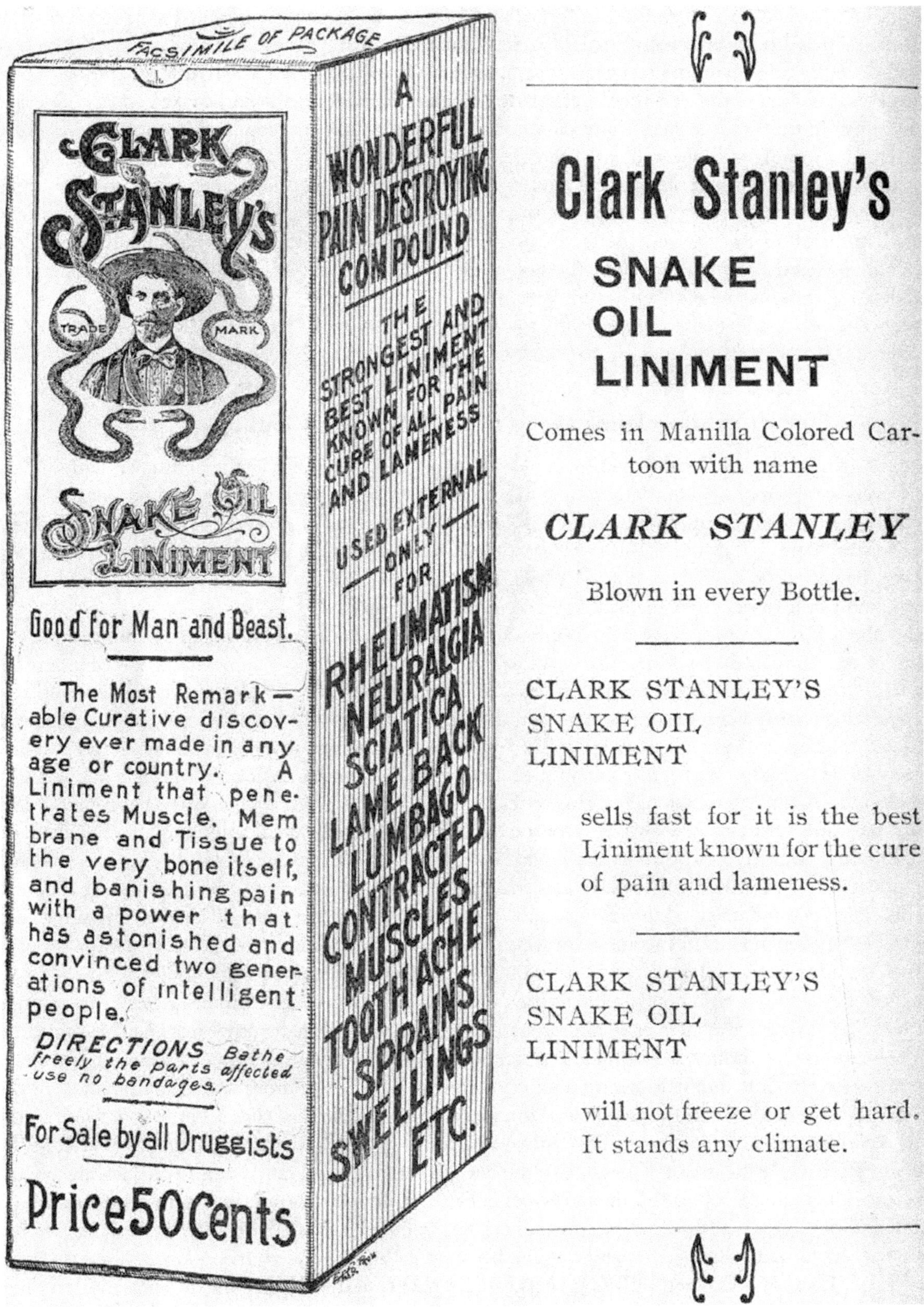

Figure 2.4. Snake oil became a synonym for quackery thanks to the career of Clark Stanley, the Rattlesnake King. He used his experience as a cowboy to promote his cures, which he claimed to learn from the Hopi Indians. This advertisement was featured in a promotional book, *The Life and Adventures of the American Cowboy*, featuring information about cowboys, snakes, and numerous advertisements for his snake oil liniment.

Advertisement, The Life and Adventures of the American Cowboy: Life in the Far West, *Clark Stanley, 1897, 70. (Courtesy of Archive.org)*

In the first two decades of the twentieth century traveling medical shows disappeared as new forms of media and entertainment such as movies and radio captured American audiences and advertising dollars. The Kickapoo Medicine Show closed in 1912.[26] However, old techniques were adapted to new technology by a new generation of quacks.

John Brinkley, inventor of the goat gland transplant, and Norman Baker, purveyor of fake cancer cures, opened their own radio stations in the 1920s in rural Kansas and Iowa. Brinkley and Baker dispensed medical advice and entertainment on the radio, earning millions selling quack cures.[27]

In the early twentieth century, the medical landscape was changing. Reformers called for government regulation of both drugs and the methods used to advertise medicine. Due to advances in medical science, reliable tests could determine if medicines and treatments were ineffective or dangerous. For example, Brinkley's fraudulent goat gland career ended in malpractice and tax fraud lawsuits, the loss of his medical credentials, and bankruptcy. Government action also succeeded in closing Baker's cancer-healing resorts and radio stations.

However, strategies blending entertainment with sales have been reinvented for new generations. Medicine shows have been transformed by new media technology into modern infomercials, shopping channels, and internet infotainment.

Regulating Drugs in the Twentieth Century

Until the twentieth century, drugs and medical devices were purchased directly by the consumer, without government oversight. Buyers were responsible for determining the quality of medical goods and services, not local, state, or federal governments. *Caveat emptor*, a Latin phrase meaning "let the buyer beware" described this legal understanding inherited from early Roman, Germanic, and English law.[28] In the eighteenth and nineteenth centuries, efforts were made to reduce quackery by educating the public. But in a marketplace with so many choices and no clear method of determining what was the most or least effective, medical fraud continued to flourish.

Attitudes about the need for government regulation in the industrial economy began to change in the late nineteenth century era of progressive reform. Many realized the growing scale and complexity of the economy limited the information any one individual could gather on drugs and medical services. Local and state governments passed the first laws restricting the sales of some drugs. However, the drug industry fought back. In 1881, the Proprietary Medicine Manufacturers and Dealers Association was formed to promote the interests of medicine manufacturers. The organization lobbied against legislation restricting patent medicine production and sales at both the state and federal levels.[29]

Samuel Hopkins Adams's series of muckraking articles about the patent medicine industry, published in 1905 in *Collier's Weekly* magazine, created a new awareness of the dangers of proprietary medications and unethical advertising. In his series of articles, collectively known as *The Great American Fraud*, Adams published shocking results of laboratory tests of proprietary medications. He revealed widespread use of fake testimonials (see source 6) and explained the "red clause." This clause was included in advertising contracts between patent medicine advertisers and print publications. Newspapers, heavily dependent on income from patent medicine advertising, were forced to accept stipulations preventing them from reporting on laws or other news unfavorable to the patent medicine industry.[30]

The impact of Adams's work is comparable to the new awareness created by Upton Sinclair's exposé on the meatpacking industry, *The Jungle*. Adams's publications, along with the work of many other reformers, led to the passage of a series of regulations governing the drug industry. In the first decades of the twentieth century, two types of federal legislation impacted the drug industry—restrictions on the use and quality of drugs and regulation of advertising.

The Pure Food Act of 1906 was the first federal attempt to regulate the ingredients of medications, but the law did not limit who could purchase medications. This early regulation focused on product labeling, not government oversight of the safety or effectiveness of drugs. According to the law, drug labels could not be false or misleading about ten dangerous substances including alcohol, heroin, and cocaine. False labeling claims about the effectiveness of the drug were not prohibited until 1912 when the Sherley Amendment to the Pure Food and Drug Act was enacted.

Restricted access to narcotics, opiates, and cocaine began in 1914 with the Harrison Anti-Narcotics Act. In 1938, the Federal Food, Drug, and Cosmetic (FDC) Act created a new category of non-narcotic prescription drugs and required more information on labeling for drugs sold directly to consumers. The clear distinction between prescription and over-the-counter drugs familiar today was not established until 1951 with the passage of the Durham Humphrey Amendment.[31]

Federal legislation of the medical marketplace continued throughout the twentieth and into the twenty-first century. Every phase of this complicated story impacts Americans' choices and access to medical care. Government regulation of industry, then and now, is a balancing act between the interests of consumers and those of the drug and health care industry. In some decades, such as the 1930s and 1960s, consumers' campaigns against and regulatory control of quackery has dominated this negotiation. But these crests of reform are often followed by periods in which regulatory control is loosened.

In the 1990s, two federal actions occurred affecting the broad category of modern medical care often referred to as alternative medicine. First, in 1991, the federal National Center for Complementary and Integrative Health was created to investigate alternative medicine and to oversee scientific research on practices and products not generally considered part of conventional medicine. This government agency has both supporters and critics. Critics question the political motivation behind its creation and funding and the quality of its research, yet the new focus on studies of dietary supplements and other alternative methods has been praised.[32]

Second, in 1994, the Dietary Supplement Health and Education Act defined how dietary supplements should be regulated by the US Food and Drug Administration. This law defines a dietary supplement as a product taken by mouth, other than food, intended to supplement the diet and includes vitamins, minerals, herbs or other botanicals, and other substances. Similarly to the Food and Drug Act of 1906, this law primarily regulates the labeling of supplements. The act does *not* require scientific testing to demonstrate the safety or effectiveness of the product. Contrary to what many believe, the US Food and Drug Administration does not test or approve dietary supplements.[33]

Regulatory laws always reflect competing priorities—personal, professional, political, and economic interests of individuals, businesses, and government. The unknown benefits and dangers of many twenty-first-century alternative therapies make legislative oversight even more complicated. Some of these untested treatments may prove to be scientifically viable. Others believed to be safe and effective today may be shown to be ineffective or dangerous in the future. Science and society have rejected many historical quackeries but new panaceas continually appear to replace them.

Regulating Medical Advertising in the Twentieth Century

Prior to 1938, the federal government did little to regulate misleading or false advertising to consumers. While the contents and safety of drugs was relegated to the Food and Drug Administration, drug advertising was the job of the Federal Trade Commission (FTC). In 1914, the original Federal Trade Commission Act created this regulatory agency and authorized it to prevent unfair methods of competition in commerce. In these early years, only practices unfair to market competitors were regulated. Unfair and deceptive advertising that was a threat to consumers was not the focus.

In 1929, Consumers' Research was formed. The organization called for the strengthening of consumer protection laws and stronger enforcement of the 1906 Federal Food and Drug Act. The organization published several books including *100,000,000 Guinea Pigs: Dangers in Everyday Foods, Drugs, and Cosmetics* (1933). Their work created more awareness of the dangers of drugs and deceptive advertising. Misleading advertising began to be seen as a health issue, not just an unfair form of business competition.

In 1938, the Wheeler-Lea Act amended the Federal Trade Commission Act so the FTC could also impose civil penalties for "unfair or deceptive acts or practices" in food, drugs, device, or cosmetic advertising. False advertising was clearly defined.

Between 1938 and 1951, federal legislation had a significant impact on how drugs were purchased and advertised. The wildly false, misleading, and entertaining elements of patent medicine advertising aimed at the consumer came to an end. As more and more drugs were available only with a doctor's prescription, advertising shifted from direct marketing to patients to promotions aimed directly at the health professionals prescribing medications. By the 1960s, more than 90 percent of pharmaceutical company spending on marketing was aimed at health care professionals; a complete reversal of nineteenth-century practices.[34]

In recent decades, due to changing federal regulations on the marketing and advertising of drugs, the trend has reversed. Since 1997, the FDA has loosened prescription drug advertising regulations and direct-to-consumer advertising has dramatically increased.[35]

Drug marketers across the continuum of conventional and alternative medicine have successfully adapted to new forms of media. Live medicine shows have transformed into infomercials, infotainment, and commercial sponsorship of sports, concerts, and other live events. Old tactics used in magazine, newspaper, and television advertising appear in internet and email advertising (see source 9). Eighty percent of internet users have searched for health information online.[36] As always, quacks are there, ready to capture the attention and money of new victims.

Figure 2.5. Trade cards were a popular form of advertising between the 1870s and early 1900s. They came in packages of various products or were distributed free to customers. Collecting trade cards became a popular hobby, and the cards often featured images that had little connection with the product advertised. Sets of trade cards featuring pictures of animals, birds, historical scenes, sites around the world, and other themes were issued to encourage collecting. Extensive collections of trade cards are available online. Horsford's Acid Phosphates contained phosphoric acids, which are still used as a food and beverage additive to create a tangy or sour taste.
Trade card for Horsford's Acid Phosphate, c. late 1800s. (Courtesy of US National Library of Medicine)

In the Classroom

Examples of promotion and advertising of questionable health care are especially useful for teaching historical primary source analysis and media literacy skills. In the following inquiry activity, students can practice these skills using either historical or modern examples.

First, ask students to choose a nineteenth-century patent medicine trade card they find especially appealing. Several collections of digitally reproduced trade cards are available online. Consult this book's companion website, https://teachingwiththemes.com/, for recommendations. Do not explain the wider context of trading cards and medical marketplace at the beginning of the activity. Allow students to deduce or discover as much information as possible before providing historical context.

Trade cards, advertisements with colorful images on the front and text on the back, were a popular form of advertising between the 1870s and early 1900s. They came in packages of various products including tea, coffee, soap, or patent medicines. Others were distributed to retailers who added the names and addresses of their stores and distributed them free to customers. Collecting trade cards became a popular hobby. To encourage collecting, sets with pictures of animals, birds, historical scenes, sites around the world, and other themes were created.

Second, ask students to analyze the image and text on both sides of their chosen trade card and identify the elements or advertising strategies used to make the product appealing to potential customers. Some tactics are discussed in this and the previous chapter. In the spirit of inquiry, students can be asked to identify sales tactics before the teacher introduces common examples. After students speculate on their own, the teacher should follow with explicit instruction about common advertising strategies.

Third, ask students what additional information about the historical context of their trade card would be helpful in understanding the appeal of the product. For example, what words need to be defined in the text? Have the meanings of some words changed over time? What needs to be known about the ingredients or effectiveness of the product? Do the medical problems described still exist? What additional information should be obtained about how people purchased medicine in the late 1800s? Is the image appealing to modern audiences? If not, what might have caused the change in tastes?

Fourth, direct students to practice their internet research skills to discover additional information about the product advertised, its ingredients, the medical problems it was claimed to cure, and the wider patent medicine industry. Research has shown that students often lack the ability to distinguish the quality of various websites.[37] Teach students how to choose the best sites. Many of the best choices are listed far down the list of search results instead of at the top where the most popular or commercially sponsored sites appear. This activity also provides an opportunity to teach students about Wikipedia, both its advantages and disadvantages.

Depending upon the trade card selected, students are likely to discover a wealth of additional information. For example, an internet search conducted to learn more about Horsford's Acid Phosphate (figure 2.5) turned up more advertising ephemera including an advertisement in the 1884 *American Medical Journal* and a promotional brochure with recipes using the product; information about dyspepsia; the fact that this product was falsely claimed to treat cholera; a history of the product's creator, Eben Horsford; more historical and modern uses of acid phosphate known today as phosphoric acid; and that this key ingredient continues to be used in modern products, some of which are promoted as healthful.

If time or the curriculum do not allow for research on historical patent medicines and quack cures, the same media literacy skills can be modeled and practiced using examples of modern cure-alls. Ask students to perform lateral reading, the practice of opening several websites with information on the same topic, and to compare and contrast the information provided.[38]

Searches for modern popular panaceas can be especially challenging. Often the first several pages of search results will be free or paid testimonials and other promotions. Reliable scientific information is often buried far into the search results. Lateral reading across the internet highlights how consumers are easily confused by conflicting information about health care.

Many quality instructional resources for assessing media literacy skills and teaching students to analyze the author, format, audience, content, and purpose of every form of modern and historical media are available. See this book's companion website, https://teachingwiththemes.com/, for recommendations.

The Primary Sources

The following primary source excerpts range over one hundred years and focus on three themes.

First, sources 1, 2, 3, 4, and 5 were selected to illustrate the array of health care choices available in the nineteenth century and the debate on how to best unmask and stop quackery. Most believed educating the public about the dangers of quackery was the best solution. However, in the late nineteenth and early twentieth century, public opinion began to favor government regulation of the medical marketplace as a remedy to quackery. Source 4, from a British medical journal, is the only one is which the author suggests members of Parliament should be elected who would be brave enough to tackle the complicated issue of government regulation.

Second, prior to the scientific medical advances of the early twentieth century, the medical practice of regular physicians and alternative medical practitioners was often indistinguishable. Traditional methods, emerging scientific practice, and pseudoscience competed. Both experts and consumers lacked reliable scientific tests and quality information to determine the actual safety and effectiveness of cures. The derogatory label *quack* was as likely to be applied to one's competition as to an actual scammer and deceiver.

Third, sources 6, 7, 8, and 9 were selected to demonstrate continuity and change in media, marketing, and advertising of both legitimate and fraudulent health care. Several tactics were invented or perfected in the nineteenth century, including direct marketing, multi-level marketing, testimonials, endorsements, and media monitoring. Forms of media may have changed, but most promotional and advertising strategies are old news.

Statements from average people, celebrities, politicians, writers, and other well-known people influence potential buyers by building trust. They make products appear credible and reliable. Some testimonials, endorsements, and reviews or ratings by customers are genuine; many are not.

Longer published accounts of popular treatments also served to promote cures, quack or legitimate. True believers offer their testimonials free of charge by word-of-mouth and in published articles, books, blogs, social media, or YouTube videos. Numerous versions of endorsements by celebrities or well-known "influencers" help to build what is now called buzz or viral marketing. The repetition of enthusiastic endorsements, free or paid, reinforces beliefs in the efficacy of the cure, a phenomenon referred to today as an echo chamber. The popularity of a cure is often mistaken for a sign of its effectiveness (source 8).

One fraudulent direct-marketing tactic exposed to the public in the early twentieth century was the sale and reuse of private letters seeking medical advice. Advertisements encouraged individuals to write letters describing their health problems to patent medicine companies. Letter writers were promised that doctors would review the descriptions of their illness and send free personal responses, recommending the proper treatment. These patent medicine advertisers promised the letters would be kept "sacredly confidential."

This tactic appealed to those unable to afford care from reliable physicians and to those with embarrassing medical conditions. Women were especially likely to write private letters seeking medical advice instead enduring the embarrassment of visiting male physicians.

In reality, the thousands of letters received were quickly read by clerks and categorized by the nature of the complaints. Each letter writer was mailed a form letter appearing to be a personal response from a physician. Every form letter recommended the purchase of one of the patent medicine company's products, usually by mail order. Then, the company profited a second time by selling or renting the letters to letter-brokers. These brokers sold the information to other medicine companies for use in their own direct-mail campaigns.

This practice was exposed in *Ladies' Home Journal* in 1906 (source 6). The title of this article, "Did Mr. Bok Tell the Truth?", referred to a previous incident related to the patent medicine industry. Edward Bok, publisher of *Ladies' Home Journal* and temperance supporter, often criticized patent medications for their high alcohol content in his magazine. In 1904, Bok published an editorial entitled "The Patent Medicine Curse" exposing the alcohol content of popular patent medicines.[39] He singled out Dr. Pierce's Favorite Prescription as containing alcohol, opium, and digitalis.

The maker of Dr. Pierce's Favorite Prescription sued Bok. Bok lost the suit and published a retraction stating he unknowingly used the results of a twenty-five-year-old report.[40] Source 6 is a portion of that retraction. Mark Sullivan, the author of the retraction, was also Bok's lawyer in the suit. Sullivan became an influential muckraker, publishing numerous articles criticizing the drug industry and its marketing tactics.[41]

Mark Sullivan also exposed the practices of "testimonial-brokers." He learned the testimonials of important politicians were obtained by paying women, reporters, or poverty-stricken veterans to get signatures of politicians on a product endorsement. Sullivan noted that often politicians were unaware of how their names would be used and most had not even tried the medication. In other cases, a few bottles of the medication were sent to the home of those providing the testimonial.

Sullivan learned the testimonials of average people were often complete fiction. In other situations, real people were paid to sign a written testimonial or appear in photographs with the medication. To convince readers that testimonials were real, readers were encouraged to write the author of the testimonial at an address provided in the advertisement. Sullivan followed up on this offer. He discovered the woman at one such address was being paid twenty-five cents for every letter she sent to those making inquiries. Sullivan also discovered a few testimonials were actually genuine.[42] Source 6 is an example of what was likely a genuine testimonial by a real person.

Testimonials and endorsements continue to be powerful marketing and advertising tools. Endorsements by people known to the customer are especially effective. In direct, multilevel, referral, or word-of-mouth marketing systems, salespeople convince friends, family, neighbors, and coworkers to purchase their products. "It worked for me, and it can also work for you!" is especially persuasive coming from someone known and trusted. The availability cognitive bias causes people to value firsthand experience, suggestions from acquaintances, or easily obtained information instead of difficult-to-understand scientific data and statistics.

The multilevel marketing system depends upon the availability bias as well as the human tendency to rationalize the effectiveness of cures after investing time and money in them. In this business model, individuals sell the product and recruit additional salespeople. Large investments in the product are usually required. However, the scheme sounds attractive because the original salesperson earns money from his or her own sales as well as a percentage of the sales of recruits. Thus, salespeople are even more motivated to endorse the cure and its effectiveness. Samuel Tomson's Friendly Botanic Societies, discussed in this chapter, utilized this approach.

Media monitoring and the collection of data about potential customers gained from their internet activity are standard practices in the marketing and advertising industry. These practices were invented in the nineteenth century. In the 1870s, new services known as clipping bureaus collected information of interest from newspapers and other print publications for their customers.[43] Stories and notices in newspapers about illnesses of community members were requested by those selling medical services and cures. The people identified in these collected articles become potential customers. They were mailed samples and information about cures they could purchase. Source 9 describes this practice.

The primary source texts and images provided in this and the previous chapter can be used independently or in sets in relevant lessons or instructional units. The essential questions at the opening of each chapter should be used to focus student attention on wider issues relevant to both the past and the present.

Source 1

Excerpt from the introduction of *Domestic Medicine* by William Buchan, 1784.[44]

> No two characters can be more different than that of the honest physician and the quack; yet they have generally been very much confounded. The line between them is not sufficiently apparent; at least to the general eye. . . . No laws will ever be able to prevent quackery, while people believe that the quack is as honest a man, and as well-qualified, as the physician. A very small degree of medical knowledge, however, would be sufficient to break the spell. . . . It is the ignorance and credulity of the multitude. With regard to medicine, which renders them such an easy prey. . . .
>
> Diffusing medical knowledge among the people would not only tend to improve the art, and to banish quackery, but likewise render Medicine more universally useful, by extending its benefits to society. . . . Indeed, men of every occupation and condition in life might avail themselves of a degree of medical knowledge; as it would teach them to avoid the dangers peculiar to their respective stations.

Source 2

Excerpt from *Guide to Health, or Botanic Family Physician* by Samuel Thomson, 1831.[45]

> The word quackery when used by the doctor against me, was a very important charm to prejudice the people against my practice. But I would ask . . . the following question. . . . Which is the greatest quack, the one who relieves them from their

sickness by the most simple and safe means, without any pretensions to infallibility or skill, more than what nature and experience has taught him? Or the one who, instead of curing the disease, increases it by administering poisonous medications, which only tend to prolong the distress of the patient, till either the strength of his natural constitution, or death relieves him?

Source 3
Excerpt from *Humbugs of New-York: Being a Remonstrance against Popular Delusion* by David Meredith Reese, M.D., 1838.[46]

While the reign of humbug continues, our citizens have neither eyes nor ears; and experience itself seems to have been lost upon them. . . . Every year, and indeed almost every month, brings to our city some imported mountebank; some foreign or domestic humbug; each of which in its turn is greedily swallowed while the rage of novelty lasts, until another more clamorous, or more showy, succeeds it. . . . Each of these acquires proselytes . . . the same individuals, in many instances, deliberately swallow them all. Indeed there are gentlemen and ladies in this city, who have been successively gulled by **Matthias, Fanny Wright**, the **moon story**, and the **Crawcours**. They have taken the pills of foreign and domestic quacks by the thousand, with **Lobelia, Cayenne pepper**, and **vapour baths**. They have swallowed **Maria Monk**, abolitionism, and **homeopathia**; and are now equally busy in bolting down **Phrenology** and **Animal Magnetism**. These several humbugs having been disposed of, the same persons, and thousands more, will be prepared for still farther experiments in gullibility, ad infinitum.

Matthias—a man claiming to be a prophet in the 1830s in New York who swindled wealthy businessmen and promised salvation.
Fanny Wright—controversial abolitionist, feminist, reformer, and founder of Nashoba, a utopian community.
moon story—also known as the Great Moon Hoax; a series of articles published in *The Sun*, a New York newspaper, in 1835. The articles claimed life had been discovered on the moon.
Crawcours—Brothers who introduced highly controversial but inexpensive dental fillings made from an amalgam of mercury and silver in 1833. Previous dental fillings had been made of gold.
Lobelia, Cayenne pepper—natural ingredients especially popular in Samuel Thomson's botanical medicine.
vapour baths—steam bath popular in hydropathy.
Maria Monk—reference to sensational popular book published in 1836 claiming nuns were sexually abused and their babies were murdered. The story was false but the book fueled anti-Catholic sentiment.
homeopathia—system of alternative medical treatments.
Phrenology—pseudoscience claiming the shape of the skull indicated quality of one's mental ability and character.
Animal Magnetism—also known as mesmerism, pseudoscience based on manipulating one's invisible natural forces or magnetism to improve health.

Source 4
Excerpt from "Four Strongholds of Quackery in the Fourth Estate," *Association Medical Journal*, a weekly newspaper for physicians, 1853.[47]

One of the most discouraging features of the times in connection with quackery is the ease with which portions of the press can be seduced to circulate the manifestoes of charlatans. Another cause of sorrow is the apathy with which our profession regards the dissemination of pseudo-medical journals, and tolerates those quasi-professional men. . . .

There are in the Fourth Estate Four strongholds of quackery, to which at present we particularly wish to direct attention.

I. NEWSPAPERS, especially those published in the Provinces and in the Colonies
II. RELIGIOUS (?) PERIODICALS
III. PSEUDO-MEDICAL PAPERS
IV. MEDICAL JOURNALS

A standing order from half a dozen quacks for the insertion of their long advertisements . . . are with 9 of every 10 provincial and colonial newspapers necessary elements of existence. A paper with a limited local circulation, and a small number of legitimate advertisements, requires assistance from the advertising quacks. . . . Piles of provincial and colonial newspapers are now before us, the majority of which are actually choked with . . . indecent advertisements of notorious medical swindlers. We have found upon careful and extensive inquiry, that these papers, containing the fraudulent declaration of pill-cheats, and the beastly blackguardism of **venerealists**, circulate freely both at home and abroad, and the family circles of the high and the low, of the rich and the poor. . . .

It is not upon mere professional grounds that the quacks ought to be driven from their great stronghold of provincial and colonial newspapers. Public morality demands this; and public opinion might, we are confident, be easily made to accomplish it. If there is no man in Parliament who will ceaselessly agitate this question till redress be obtained (*legislation is passed*), we must get someone to enter Parliament with this special mission. . . .

The Religious Periodicals constitute another stronghold of quackery. What is popularly designated as the "religious" press, is preeminent as the accomplice of the medical quack. All sects seem equally to participate in this iniquity (*sin*). . . . With very few honorable exceptions, the publishers of religious periodicals seem to be so blinded to all decency by their thirst for profit, that the piety and morality of the interior of their publication forms a violent contrast to the impiety, fraud, and filth in the advertisements on its covers. Probably the explanation of the degraded condition of the religious press lies in the fact, that these publications are mere business ventures of mean capitalists, who look upon religious readers, and quack advertisers, equally . . . for the sake of their cash. . . .

Pseudo-medical Papers are published in London by Homeopathists, **hygeists**, **chronothermalists**, **Mesmerists**, hydropaths, and **Coffinites**. Each of these sects has its own publication; and several individual quacks support and disseminate journals for their own trade. Speaking generally, there is a close alliance among all the quack journals, and most of the open charlatans, as well as the quasi-medical authors, use all of these papers . . . for keeping their names before the public. . . . The pseudo-medical press is a stronghold from which quackery may never be dislodged; but the profession can materially weaken it, by disowning those false brethren who clandestinely accept the meretricious blandishments of its commanders. . . .

And now the shortcomings of the medical press. Here, the faults are occasional and not systematic. . . . Yet they are of too serious a character to be passed over in silence. [*The author describes a quack's ad published in the* Association Medical Journal, *in which a well-known physician's name was used to advertise quack medications without the permission of the physician.*] . . .

Upon future occasions, it is our intention to throw strong lights upon the strongholds of quackery in the fourth estate; because we believe that by following such a course, we shall be able to drive some detachments of the enemy from their entrenchments, and to seize and punish various parties of renegades and pirates.

venerealists—quacks promoting cures for sexually transmitted diseases.
hygeists—followers of James Morison, creator of a cure-all named Hygeian Vegetable Universal Medicine.
chronothermalists—followers of the controversial Samuel Dickson's medical theories. Dickson claimed all illnesses were forms of fever and criticized blood-letting and other practices of regular physicians.
Mesmerists—followers of a pseudoscience and medical treatment based on manipulating one's invisible natural forces or magnetism to improve health.
Coffinites—British health practitioners who recommended the botanical system of Samuel Thomson.

Source 5

Excerpt from *Quackery Unmasked* by Dan King, 1858.[48]

In this comprehensive 331-page book, the author, a physician, defends "regular" medicine and seeks to educate the public and medical professionals about the many types of quackery and "irregular" medicine of his day. In the excerpt below, readers were warned about the dangers of female physicians. In the conclusion of the book, also excerpted below, he provided estimates of the numbers of irregular medical practitioners.

When a female resolves to become a doctor in medicine, she must also resolve to violate a law of her being, and vow perpetual celibacy. She may shut her eyes and stop her ears to all the pleasures of social intercourse, and look upon mankind and the world with stoical indifference. It cannot be otherwise. The mother cannot leave her nursing infant at the hour of midnight, and launch out amid the howling tempest to attend the sick. She must not expose herself to the thousand hardships and dangers that are incident to a life of medical practice. These are duties which do not belong to her, and should not be expected of her.

The female arm was never intended to wield the sledge or swing the scythe, nor her hand to grasp the dissecting knife, the **trephine** or the **gorget**. In her own sacred home, amid her domestic duties, or in her own parlor surrounded by groups of friends, or abroad as business or pleasure or inclination may dictate; whenever we behold her in her own province, she shines the ornament and glory of the race. But when she enters the fetid laboratory of the anatomist, and plunges her hands into the gore of dead men, she loses all her feminine loveliness, and appears like a fallen angel, an object of universal horror and disgust.

. . .

Irregulars, as follows:
Homoeopathists, about 1000
Hydropathists, about 400
Female Physicians, 300
Eclectics, 800
Botanies, 600
Chrono-Thermalists, 300
Besides the foregoing, there are—Indian doctors, Astrologic, Clairvoyants, Magnetic, Natural Bone-setters, **Uriscopic**, Mesmerists, **7th sons**, **Galvanic**, Blowpipe doctors, &c. &c. &c.
With a large number of itinerant **nostrum venders**; perhaps, in all, three or four thousand.

trephine/gorget—surgical instruments.
Eclectics—medical practitioners using herbal medicines and any approach believed beneficial; rejected the practices of regular physicians such as bloodletting.
Uriscopic—practitioners who examined patients' urine to diagnose disease.
7th sons—a folk healer believed to have religious or magical power to heal because he is the seventh son of a seventh son.
Galvanic—medical practitioners claiming electricity cured various medical problems.
nostrum venders—people selling medicine.

Source 6

Excerpt from "Did Mr. Bok Tell the Truth?" in *Ladies' Home Journal* by Mark Sullivan, January 1906.[49]

I found three of these letter-brokers: clearinghouses for patients' letters to patent-medicine makers. They buy letters from one patent-medicine company and sell them, or rent them and reread them to others. One of these brokers has over seven million letters. "There are five million chronic sick and incurables in the United States," said the broker, "and I've got letters from one million of them right here in that building"—pointing to his storage warehouse. "To be sure, they've all tried one remedy or more; but that's all right, they'll keep on trying new remedies till they die. Buy or rent a few thousand of those letters from me at a few dollars a thousand, tackle 'em with a new proposition—something new, with a new name—Jolly 'em along a little, and they'll all come up with money for a new treatment."

One of these letter-brokers assured me he could give me "choice lots" of "medical female letters"! Another sent me a list of hundreds of thousands of letters which he had—all from women. . . . Showing the absurdity and criminal falsehood of the declaration that "your letters are treated by us in sacred confidence." The business of letter brokerage is perfectly well-known and understood in patent medicine and quack doctor circles.

[*The author lists various categories of letters that can be purchased for a half cent each.*]
55,000 Female Complaint Letters
44,000 Bust Developer Letters
40,000 Women's Regulator Letters
7,000 Paralysis Letters
9,000 Narcotic Letters
52,000 Consumption Letters
3,000 Cancer Letters
65,000 Deaf Letters

Source 7

The excerpt below is one of several testimonial statements from a book describing the treatments of Richard Carter, a frontier herb doctor. Carter settled near Versailles, Kentucky, in the early nineteenth century. He developed a large practice despite his lack of university credentials. His book, Valuable Vegetable Medical Prescriptions, for the Cure of All Nervous and Putrid Disorders, *printed in 1813 and reprinted three times, described his methods and medicines.*[50] *Carter's book, like many publications promoting medical systems or cures, used testimonials of famous and average people. Some, such as the one below, appear to be genuine. Nathaniel McClure, James Finnel, and John Wray all appear on Garrard County, Kentucky, census records and tax lists in 1800 and 1810.*

Testimonial from *Valuable Vegetable Medical Prescriptions* by Richard Carter, 1815.[51]

January the 16th, 1815.—I, Nathaniel McClure, was taken with the **King's Evil**, about four years past; it grew very fast, about a year and a half before I applied to a doctor. I was under his care five months, he gave me ease; then it grew about a year, and was very bad. Then I applied to another doctor, he done me no good, still grew worse. Then I applied to doctor Richard Carter, and since it feels as well as ever; and I believe it is a sound cure. It has been about three months since he quit treating me—Given under my hand. NATHANIEL M'CLURE. Test. [*witnessed by*], John Wray, James Finnel.

King's Evil—The King's Evil, also called scrofula, was a skin disease, probably a form of tuberculosis that caused chronic masses and abscesses to appear on the body. From the thirteenth century to the eighteenth century, the monarchs of England and France were believed to have the supernatural power to cure the disease with "the royal touch."

Source 8

In this excerpt, William Gilmore Simms (1806–1870), a Southern novelist, helped to popularize hydropathy in a lengthy magazine article. Large sections of his article were quoted from the work of an English supporter of hydropathy, Richard T. Claridge.[52] *These glowing accounts were confirmed by other well-known personalities of the era such as Harriet Beecher Stowe and Horace Greeley, creating what is today called buzz or an echo chamber.*

Excerpt from "Hydropathy: or the Cold Water Cure," 1842.[53]

Hydropathy completely supersedes the dreadful necessity of cutting men's flesh or amputating their limbs. For chronic diseases . . . all persons suffering from the effects of mercury, in its many dangerous forms, will derive instant benefit, and, in the end, perfect health, from Preissnitz's water cure. I can affirm that half of Preissnitz's patients are under the influence of this pernicious drug [*mercury*]. The water cure treats obstinate complaints such as gout, rheumatism, hemorrhoids, obstructions of the bowels and their associated ills; also scrofula, syphilis; in fact, all disease known by the term chronic, or connected with the nerves. . . . Everyone who is not acquainted with the water cure, will naturally doubt its wonderful power. And every doctor, when he reflects upon the number of patients laboring under acute diseases, who have perished under his hands, will, no doubt laugh loudly at the new water system. Nevertheless, I'm ready by deeds, as well as with words, to prove all that I have stated as to the healing power of water.

Source 9

Excerpt from the *Journal of the American Medical Association*, 1911.[54]

Of the many charges . . . against the "patent medicine" makers, a lack of enterprise in obtaining prospective victims is not one of them. . . . More recently two cases have been brought to our attention in which patent medicine makers have resorted to the use of the press-clipping bureaus, for lists of possible purchasers. The following news item appeared in the Brockton (Mass.) Times.

"Mrs. Wm. Wilcox is at the Jordan Hospital, suffering from an attack of acute rheumatism."

This piece of news was garnered in by a clipping bureau and sent to one of its customers, the exploiters of the nostrum Angeline. If its manufacturers are to be believed, which they are not, Angeline will permanently cure acute and chronic rheumatism. So the Angeline booklet is sent to Mrs. Wilcox, evidently in the belief that advertising bead cast on the waters may come back after many days in the form of an order.

Raymond & Co., who sell Raymond's Pectoral Plasters also use press-clippings. A Sunday-school superintendent, of a small village in Virginia, recently received one of Raymond's "positive cures" for whooping-coughs, bronchitis, etc., with the following ingenious note:

Dear Sir: We noticed in the ____ Journal that Whooping Cough is interfering with the attendance of your school and are of the opinion that RAYMOND'S PECTORAL PLASTERS are not known in your vicinity, or this would not be the case. We wish you would hand the one enclosed to the mother of one of the little ones affected, that she may see for herself what they ACCOMPLISH. Then when you are both satisfied as to their MERIT will you kindly advise us, on the enclosed card the name of the merchant in ____ who sells medicines of any kind that we may take up with him the sale of these Pectoral Plasters in your community.

Notes

1. Lydia Maria Child, *The Family Nurse; or, Companion of the Frugal Housewife* (Boston: C. J. Hendee, 1837), 5, https://catalog.hathitrust.org/Record/006125465.
2. Toby A. Appel, "The Thomsonian Movement, the Regular Profession, and the State in Antebellum Connecticut: A Case Study of the Repeal of Early Medical Licensing Laws," *Journal of the History of Medicine and Allied Sciences* 65, no. 2 (April 2010), 156–57, http://www.jstor.org/stable/24632012; William G. Rothstein, "The Medical Profession," in *Encyclopedia of American Social History*, vol. 3, ed. Mary Kupiec Cayton, Elliott J. Gorn, and Peter W. Williams (New York: Charles Scribner's Sons, 1993), 2363–78.
3. Appel, "The Thomsonian Movement," 156–57.
4. Robert C. Fuller, "Alternative Medicine," in *Encyclopedia of Social History*, vol. 3, ed. Mary Kupiec Cayton, Elliott J. Gorn, and Peter W. Williams (New York: Charles Scribner's Sons, 1993), 2379.
5. Lamar Riley Murphy, *Enter the Physician: The Transformation of Domestic Medicine 1760–1860* (Tuscaloosa: University of Alabama Press, 1991), 70–71.
6. Michael A. Flannery, "The Early Botanical Medical Movement as a Reflection of Life, Liberty, and Literacy in Jacksonian America," *Journal of the Medical Library Association* 90, no. 4 (2002): 442–54, US National Library of Medicine, National Institutes of Health, https://www.ncbi.nlm.nih.gov/pmc/articles/PMC128961/.
7. Marshall Scott Legan, "Hydropathy in America: A Nineteenth Century Panacea," *Bulletin of the History of Medicine* 45, no. 3 (May–June 1971): 267–80, http://www.jstor.org/stable/44451210; Jane B. Donegan, *Hydropathic Highway to Health, Women and Water-Cure in Antebellum America* (New York: Greenwood Press, 1986), 7; Arthur Wrobel, *Pseudo-Science and Society in 19th-Century America* (Lexington: University Press of Kentucky, 2015), 74–99, eBook Collection, EBSCOhost.
8. Amy Kesselman, "The 'Freedom Suit': Feminism and Dress Reform in the United States, 1848–1875," *Gender and Society* 5, no. 4 (December 1991): 496–97, http://www.jstor.org/stable/190097; Donegan, *Hydropathic Highway to Health*,138.
9. Joan D. Hedrick, *Harriet Beecher Stowe, A Life* (New York: Oxford University Press, 1994), 173–85.
10. Christopher Ricks, *Tennyson* (Berkeley: University of California Press, 1989), 166.
11. Carolyn Thomas de la Piña, *The Body Electric: How Strange Machines Built the Modern American* (New York: New York University Press, 2003), 4–5.
12. Ibid., 89–136.
13. "Eben M. Byers Dies of Radium Poisoning," *New York Times*, April 1, 1932; "Death Stirs Action on Radium 'Cures,'" *New York Times*, April 2, 1932.
14. de la Piña, *The Body Electric*, 171–212.
15. George B. Griffenhagen and James Harvey Young, "Old English Patent Medicines in America," *Pharmacy in History*, 34, no. 4 (1992), 199–229, https://www.jstor.org/stable/41111487; James Harvey Young, *The Toadstool Millionaires: A Social History of Patent Medicines in America* (Princeton, NJ: Princeton University Press, 1961, 2015), 19.
16. Griffenhagen and Young, "Old English Patent Medicines in America," 199–229.
17. James Harvey Young, "Patent Medicines: An Early Example of Competitive Marketing," *Journal of Economic History*, 20, no. 4 (December 1960): 649, http://www.jstor.org/stable/2114405; James Harvey Young, "Patent Medicines: The Early Post-Frontier Phase," *Journal of the Illinois State Historical Society* 46, no. 3 (Autumn 1953): 256, http://www.jstor.org/stable/40189311.
18. Griffenhagen and Young, "Old English Patent Medicines in America," 199–229.
19. A. Walker Bingham, *The Snake-Oil Syndrome: Patent Medicine Advertising* (Hanover, MA: Christopher Publishing House, 1994), 113–29.

20. Samuel Hopkins Adams, *The Great American Fraud*, 1912, 57, reprinted from *Collier's Weekly*, February 17, 1906, https://www.gutenberg.org/files/44325/44325-h/44325-h.htm.

21. Griffenhagen and Young, "Old English Patent Medicines in America," 199–229; Young, "Patent Medicines: The Early Post-Frontier Phase," 260.

22. United States Department of Agriculture, Bureau of Chemistry, *Service and Regulatory Announcements*, Supplement 29, issued October 17, 1917. Notice 4944, 592, accessed July 2018, http://goo.gl/a2AXI.

23. David Gentilcore, "'Charlatans, Mountebanks and Other Similar People': The Regulation and Role of Itinerant Practitioners in Early Modern Italy," *Social History* 20, no. 3 (October 1995): 308, http://www.jstor.org/stable/4286294.

24. *Oxford English Dictionary Online*, s.v. "charlatan, n. and adj."; s.v. "quacksalver, n," http://www.oed.com/.

25. Peter Burke, *Popular Culture in Early Modern Europe* (New York: New York University Press, 1978), 94–95.

26. Ann Anderson, *Snake Oil, Hustlers and Hambones: The American Medicine Show* (Jefferson, NC: McFarland, 2002), 48–67; Brooks McNamara, "The Indian Medicine Show," *Educational Theatre Journal* 23, no. 4 (December 1971): 431–44, http://www.jstor.org/stable/3205750.

27. Eric S. Juhnke, *Quacks and Crusaders: The Fabulous Careers of John Brinkley, Norman Baker, and Harry Hoxsey* (Lawrence: University Press of Kansas, 2002).

28. John C. Reitz, "A History of Cutoff Rules as a Form of Caveat Emptor," *American Journal of Comparative Law* 36, no. 3 (Summer, 1988): 437, https://www.jstor.org/stable/840343.

29. James Harvey Young, *The Medical Messiahs: A Social History of Health Quackery in Twentieth Century America* (Princeton, NJ: Princeton University Press, 1967), 24.

30. Samuel Hopkins Adams, "The Magic Red Clause," in *The Great American Fraud* (New York: Collier and Son, 1912), 5, https://www.gutenberg.org/files/44325/44325-h/44325-h.htm#link2H_4_0004.

31. Peter Temin, "The Origin of Compulsory Drug Prescriptions," *Journal of Law & Economics* 22, no. 1 (April 1979): 91–105, http://www.jstor.org/stable/725214.

32. Paul A. Offit, *Do You Believe in Magic? The Sense and Nonsense of Alternative Medicine* (New York: HarperCollins, 2013), 96–97.

33. "Dietary Supplements," National Institutes of Health, Office of Dietary Supplements, updated June 24, 2011, accessed March 2018, https://ods.od.nih.gov/factsheets/DietarySupplements-HealthProfessional/.

34. Julie Donohue, "A History of Drug Advertising: The Evolving Roles of Consumers and Consumer Protection," *Milbank Quarterly* 84, no. 4 (2006): 668, http://www.jstor.org/stable/25098137.

35. C. Lee Ventola, "Direct-to-Consumer Pharmaceutical Advertising: Therapeutic or Toxic?" *Pharmacy and Therapeutics* 36, no. 10 (2011): 669–84, US National Library of Medicine, National Institutes of Health, https://www.ncbi.nlm.nih.gov/pmc/articles/PMC3278148/.

36. Susannah Fox and Maeve Duggan, "Health Online 2013," Pew Research Center, Internet & Technology, January 15, 2013, accessed March 2018, http://www.pewinternet.org/2013/01/15/health-online–2013/.

37. Sam Wineburg, Sarah McGrew, Joel Breakstone, and Teresa Ortega, "Evaluating Information: The Cornerstone of Civic Online Reasoning" (2016), Stanford Digital Repository, http://purl.stanford.edu/fv751yt5934.

38. Sarah McGrew, Teresa Ortega, Joel Breakstone, and Sam Wineburg, "The Challenge That's Bigger Than Fake News: Civic Reasoning in a Social Media Environment," *American Educator* 41, no. 3 (Fall 2017): 9.

39. Edward Bok, "The 'Patent-Medicine' Curse," *Ladies' Home Journal* 21 (May 1904): 18, https://babel.hathitrust.org/cgi/pt?id=mdp.39015020919042;view=1up;seq=343.

40. Edward Bok, "Dr. Pierce's Favorite Prescription: A Retraction," *Ladies' Home Journal* 21 (July 1904): 18, https://babel.hathitrust.org/cgi/pt?id=mdp.39015020919042;view=1up;seq=465.

41. Robert J. Valuck, Suzanne Poirier, and Robert G. Mrtek, "Patent Medicine Muckraking: Influences on American Pharmacy, Social Reform, and Foreign Authors," *Pharmacy in History* 34, no. 4 (1992): 183–92, http://www.jstor.org/stable/41111483.

42. Mark Sullivan, "The Inside Story of a Sham, by Which Thousands of People Are Daily Hoodwinked, and to Which the Most Prominent Men and Women in America Have Loaned Their Names," *Ladies' Home Journal* 23 (January 1906): 14, https://babel.hathitrust.org/cgi/pt?id=mdp.39015011447888;view=1up;seq=105.

43. Ellen Gruber Garvey, *Writing with Scissors: American Scrapbooks from the Civil War to the Harlem Renaissance* (Oxford: Oxford University Press, 2013), 236, 243–45.

44. William Buchan, *Domestic Medicine* (London: Joseph Crukshank, Robert Bell, and James Muir, 1784), xxv–xxvi, https://archive.org/details/domesticmedicin00buchgoog/page/n4.

45. Samuel Thomson, *Guide to Health, or Botanic Family Physician* (Brockville, ON: W. Willes by Wm. Buell Jr. & Company, 1831), 46–47, https://archive.org/details/cihm_01684/page/n5.

46. David Meredith Reese, *Humbugs of New-York: Being a Remonstrance against Popular Delusion* (New York: John S. Taylor, 1838), 21–22, https://archive.org/details/humbugsofnewyork01rees/page/n5.

47. "Four Strongholds of Quackery in the Fourth Estate," *Association Medical Journal* 1, no. 24 (June 17, 1853): 518–20, accessed July, 2017, http://www.jstor.org/stable/25494700.

48. Dan King, *Quackery Unmasked* (Boston, D. Clapp, 1858), 215–16, 333, https://archive.org/details/57310420R.nlm.nih.gov.

49. Mark Sullivan, "Did Mr. Bok Tell the Truth?" *Ladies' Home Journal* 23 (January 1906): 18, https://babel.hathitrust.org/cgi/pt?id=mdp.39015011447888;view=1up;seq=109.

50. Douglas C. McMurtrie, "Early Kentucky Medical Imprints with a Bibliography to 1830," *Register of Kentucky State Historical Society* 31, no. 96 (July 1933), 256–70.

51. Richard Carter, *Valuable Vegetable Medical Prescriptions, for the Cure of All Nervous and Putrid Disorders* (Frankfort, KY: Gerard & Berry, 1815), xi, https://collections.nlm.nih.gov/catalog/nlm:nlmuid–2545048R-bk.

52. R. T. Claridge, *Hydropathy; or, The Cold Water Cure* (London: J. Madden and Company, 1842), 74–75, https://archive.org/details/39002086176733.med.yale.edu/page/n7.

53. William Gilmore Simms, "Hydropathy: Or the Cold Water Cure," *Magnolia*, October 1842, 257–60, http://simms.library.sc.edu/view_item.php?item=152559.

54. "Press Clippings and the Nostrum Enterprise," in *Nostrums and Quackery: Articles on the Nostrum Evil and Quackery*, reprinted from the *Journal of the American Medical Association* (Chicago: American Medical Association, 1911), 499–500, https://archive.org/stream/nostrumsquackery00amerrich#page/498/mode/2up.

CHAPTER THREE

Imagining Utopia

A map of the world that does not include Utopia is not worth even glancing at, for it leaves out the one country at which Humanity is always landing. And when Humanity lands there, it looks out, and, seeing a better country, sets sail. Progress is the realization of Utopias.

—Oscar Wilde, 1891[1]

Essential questions:

- How are utopian dreams and communities a reflection of the wider culture?
- How have utopias changed over time? Stayed the same?

When our minds are freed from everyday life, we dream of limitless possibilities.[2] *Utopia* is the word for these imaginary or real places of perfection or limitless possibility. Historical utopian dreams and communities illustrate the interplay of past, present, and future in the human imagination. They demonstrate how ideals reflect or distort what is real in our daily lives. The study of conceptions of utopia through time and of historical utopian communities allows students to examine their lives through the perspective of the past. At the same time, it inspires dreams for a better future.

Utopian dreams are organized into two categories. Utopias can be *places of escape* from the harsh realities of everyday life.[3] These utopian fantasies are alternative worlds where the poor are rich, hunger is replaced with plenty, rain with sunshine, work with leisure, fear with pleasure, slavery and oppression with freedom.

Alternatively, utopias of *social reconstruction* or social dreaming are critiques of society that question current forms of government, economy, or cultural norms.[4] They aim to improve an entire society. Some only exist in literature, others have become real communities.

Modern concepts of utopia draw from thousands of years of accumulated human experience, simultaneously telling a story of the past, present, and future. They intermingle new ideas with reimagined utopias from the ancient, medieval, early modern, and industrial eras.

In this chapter, the history of utopia from the ancient world to the twentieth century is examined with a focus on utopias of escape. The utopias in this chapter never existed; they were ideals and dreams.

Utopias of social reconstruction are the focus of the following chapter. The achievements and obstacles of real historical communities seeking to remake society are examined. Some looked back to an ancient past for inspiration; others tried to create entirely new relationships and communities.

The word *utopia* was invented in 1517 by Thomas More (1478–1535) as the title for a short book written in Latin that described an ideal social, legal, and political system.[5] More, a Renaissance humanist, created this new word with an ambiguous meaning from the Greek word *topos*, meaning "place" or "where," and a prefix that could mean "no," or "not," or a happy, fortunate place. Therefore, utopia could mean a happy, fortunate place or, alternatively, it could mean nowhere. More himself commented on the word's double meaning, comparing his sixteenth-century vision to the one described in Plato's *Republic*:

> "No-Place" was once my name, I lay so far;
> but now with Plato's state I can compare,
> perhaps outdo her (for what he only drew
> In empty words I have made live and new
> In men and wealth, as well as splendid laws):
> "The Good Place" they should call me, with good cause.[6]

More's *Utopia* described the discovery of an unknown island where the religious, social, and political customs were radically different from those in his own world. Utopia's quality of life and level of equality were unknown to Europeans in the sixteenth century. Poverty was non-existent in the planned economy. Cities were clean, health care free, food plentiful, and working days limited to six hours, allowing for leisure activities. The political system was somewhat democratic but would fall short if judged by modern standards. Utopia's hierarchical and patriarchal government enforced strict laws and harsh punishments for those disturbing the peace.

More's work, like many utopias, was simultaneously a product of the past, present, and future. More, like his contemporary Renaissance humanists, drew from thousands of years of Greek, Roman, and Christian traditions such as Plato's *Republic* (c. 380 BCE) and Augustine of Hippo's *City of God* (c. 413–426). Ancient and Renaissance ideals of rational humans and societies combined to become a future reality in More's *Utopia*.

More's *Utopia* does more than reflect the past and visualize a possible future. It also reflected the era in which he lived and was a critique of conditions in his own time. In More's sixteenth-century England, thousands of peasants were displaced from small farms in the shift toward enclosed, private estates. Vagrancy, unemployment, and poverty increased for the lower classes while the wealth of the upper classes grew.

More's interest in government and religion reflected his own experiences as a sixteenth-century Catholic, scholar, and statesman. He served in the English parliament and as Lord Chancellor, the highest government officer for Henry VIII. More witnessed the violence and turmoil of the early years of the English Protestant Reformation. Eighteen years after writing *Utopia*, More was accused of treason and beheaded during the drama of King Henry VIII's divorce and reformation of the Church of England.

Utopia described a world in which the problems of More's world were solved. Like previous and subsequent utopian literature, More's island was a Bizarro World, a world where reality is inverted or opposite.[7] Utopias can describe genuine hopes for the future or satirize the failures of the present. Some scholars argue More's work was primarily a satire in which he questioned if humans could really ever be rational and whether a good life could really exist on earth.[8]

Dystopia, a word first used in the 1950s, refers to the opposite of a utopia. It too conveys doubts and fears, questioning or satirizing contemporary society. In a dystopia, everything is as bad as possible.[9] Disasters occur, diseases spread, technology goes wrong, and life is a struggle—all reflections of the worst fears of the age. Dystopias fully recognize the negative qualities of human behavior, pleading for societal changes before it is too late. Utopias and dystopias are at opposite ends of a continuum, but both are rooted in an underlying desire for change, or reform—better possibilities in a near or distant future.

Utopian literary works proliferated after More. However, utopia as a concept existed long before More's sixteenth-century invention of the word. For over two thousand years, imagined utopias appeared in every art form—poetry, drama, music, painting, literature, and folklore. Literary descriptions of utopias often begin with a journey by sea, land, or air to an unknown place. Visitors travel to perfect islands, valleys, continents, under the sea, or into space to the Moon or distant planets or galaxies. They may travel through time to the past or the future.

Once there, the traveler meets primitive people living in a natural state or people thriving in advanced planned communities and model towns. The utopian traveler is usually guided by a local inhabitant who explains the social, political, economic, and religious organization. Typically, it is implied that the traveler will return home to share what he or she has learned.[10]

The utopian world is very different from the one the traveler knows back home. Sometimes the unique society is the perfect ideal to be modeled; other times both strengths and weaknesses are presented. Sometimes dystopian societies are

Figure 3.1. Maps depicting imagined geography are often included with descriptions of utopias. This map was included in a 1518 edition of Thomas More's ***Utopia***. Raphael Hythloday, the fictional explorer More credited with discovering this imagined perfect society, appears at the lower left of this image.
Woodcut, Ambrosius Holbein, 1518. (Courtesy Folger Shakespeare Library and Wikimedia Commons)

also visited to provide a contrast or continuum from worst to best, usually with the traveler's world falling somewhere in the middle.

The purposes of the creators of artistic and literary utopias vary. Sometimes the work can be clearly distinguished as either a utopia of escape or a utopia of social reconstruction. But in others, these two purposes merge. Authors might be calling for immediate drastic change or simply warning readers about a possible future. Some creators really meant for the ideal to be implemented in the real world for small groups or an entire society. Literary utopias can be satirical; pointing out the vices, abuses, or shortcoming of the author's own society. Others are simply fantasies, describing escapes from the real world.[11]

Ancient Utopian Dreams

The oldest descriptions of utopias in ancient cultures described and intermingled visions of ideal pasts, presents, or futures. Life in these distant places usually involved peace and unity among all groups of humans and the gods. Pain, hunger, war, punishment, and the daily burdens of physical labor are absent. Instead, life is secure; food, clothing, and entertainment are abundant; and humans have a painless death or gain immortality. Today, some are considered myth, others as religious belief.[12] Golden ages, arcadias, distant islands, the promised land, the millennium, and paradise or heaven all envision a better life.

Many of the oldest descriptions of utopias look to a golden age in a distant past, when life was believed to have been better and humans were at peace with one another and the gods. Backward-looking utopias are a form of societal nostalgia, a sentimental longing for another time or place in the past. Nostalgia usually refers to memories of an individual's lived past, but nostalgia can also be collective, expressed in a common form by a society. Nostalgia usually originates in a discontentment with the present. Golden ages and "good old days" are ideals in which the harsh reality and challenges of those long past times are conveniently forgotten.

Golden ages appear often in ancient literature. The Greek poet Hesiod, in *Works and Days* (c. 700 BCE), described the decline of humans since a long-past Golden Age of peace and harmony. He contrasted this idyllic existence to his own troubled world, an Iron Age, when human lives were full of work and misery (see source 1). The legendary poet Homer, probably writing in the late 700s or early 600s BCE, located his mythical Golden Age in the one thousand years before the Trojan War.

Greek poems and playwrights continued to echo these themes centuries later in descriptions of a better life either in a Golden Age of Kronos, the leader of the first generation of ancient Greek deities, or in the underworld. Telecleides, a Greek comic poet of the fifth century BCE, depicted the Golden Age satirically, implying this ideal never really existed and prosperity only comes with hard work. Telecleides's description was quoted by a Roman scholar six hundred years later (see source 2).

The ancient Romans reaffirmed the existence of a Golden Age. Ovid's *Metamorphoses* (c. 8 CE) described the decline of humans in Four Ages—from a Golden Age of near perfection through a decline in the Silver and Bronze Age, to the war-torn Iron Age of his own time.

Atlantis was another perfect place described in classical literature. Plato quoted the three-hundred-year-old work of Solon, who claimed to have translated Egyptian accounts of the lost civilization of Atlantis. According to Plato, Atlantis had been a wonderful and powerful nation, but the gods caused it to sink into the sea. Plato's contemporaries may have recognized Atlantis as a metaphor for a nation punished for its pride, or may have believed the civilization was real (see source 3). Either way, Atlantis reappears frequently in Western culture.

For example, Francis Bacon re-created Atlantis as a scientific utopia located in the Pacific Ocean in his work *New Atlantis* (1627). The myth was given new life in 1882 by Minnesota politician Ignatius Donnelly in his book *Atlantis: The Antediluvian World.* Donnelly claimed all ancient civilizations originated from those who escaped from Atlantis. His book was printed in numerous editions and inspired a new interest in the ancient city.[13] Even today, scholars speculate about whether a newly discovered ruin may be Atlantis. Modern books and films re-create and reinterpret this 2,400-year-old myth, over and over again.

The ancient Greeks and Romans also described utopias in distant lands that existed in the present or places one traveled to after death. Homer's *Odyssey* described fabled lands such as Libya where cheese, meat, and sweet milk were abundant for all; the island called Syria, where no one became sick and death in old age was painless; and Scheria, where orchards bloomed and produced fruit all year long.[14]

Figure 3.2. Arcadia, an idyllic rural paradise where only a few people live in harmony with nature, has appeared in art and utopias since ancient times. Note the Greek temple in the distance. In myth, Arcadia was the mythical home of the Greek god Pan. This print was a copy of Thomas Cole's painting *Dream of Arcadia* (c. 1838). Cole often depicted American scenery as pastoral, picturesque, or sublime to inspire emotions in the viewer.
Print, 1850, James Smillie, engraver after Dream of Arcadia *by Thomas Cole. (Courtesy of Library of Congress)*

The Elysian Fields, or Elysium, originally a Greek afterlife for heroes, sometimes merged with the Fortunate Isles or Islands of the Blest. Horace contrasted the political turmoil and violence during the period of transition between the Roman Republic and the Empire to the utopian Islands of the Blest (see source 4).[15] Both were located in distant places requiring long voyages through the western oceans. Details and locations of these paradises varied over time, but an idyllic existence always awaited those who arrived.

The geography of ancient utopias included cities, islands, and peaceful rural settings such as Arcadia. In ancient Greece, Arcadia was both an actual region in the Peloponnese peninsula as well as the mythical home of the god Pan, the god of shepherds, fields, and forest. Over centuries, Greek and Roman writers imagined Arcadia as an unspoiled wilderness, inhabited by shepherds living in harmony with nature. The theme continued to be revisited in Renaissance reinterpretations and in art and literature until the modern age. Even today, back-to-nature movements and idealizations of a country home or farm living are reminiscent of Arcadia visions of perfection.

Even in ancient times, many knew these ideal places were fictional, but writers continued to create, repeat, and revise accounts of imaginary journeys and destinations. The second century satirist Lucian wrote an account of his own imaginary journey, mocking similar mythical tales from his culture. He described his adventure on the Moon and encounters with the kings of the Moon and Sun, making it the earliest known science fiction work (see source 5).

Biblical Influences on Utopia

Biblical references have an enduring influence on descriptions of utopia in Western culture. Three traditions are especially relevant—paradise; the promised land, or "the land of milk and honey"; and the millennium. Each of these terms alternatively or simultaneously describes a specific place; a state of mind; or a time in the past, present, or future.

Paradise, an ideal place, is a word often associated with utopias. The word itself originated from ancient Persian and originally meant a walled garden. The term came to refer to the biblical Garden of Eden, an unspoiled natural paradise described in Genesis, the first book of the Bible: "The Lord God had planted a garden in the east, in Eden; and there he put the man he had formed. The Lord God made all kinds of trees grow out of the ground—trees that were pleasing to the eye and good for food."[16]

According to the Bible, the Garden of Eden continued to exist after the first humans, Adam and Eve, were expelled. This belief inspired explorers and the faithful throughout history to search the planet for this idyllic place.

Paradise also can refer to the biblical heaven, the ultimate afterlife destination for believers. In biblical texts, heaven is described as a city. Conceptions of this biblical city merged with other utopian cities such as the one described in Plato's *The Republic*. The idea of heaven as a city was reinforced in the fifth-century Christian theologian Augustine's influential work *The City of God*. Centuries of oral and written religious traditions mingled and merged with classical visions of arcadia, ideal cities, and golden ages.

The promised land is a second biblical reference with an enduring impact on utopia. In the Bible's Old Testament, God told Moses to lead the Israelites out of slavery in Egypt to "a good and spacious land, a land flowing with milk and honey,"[17] This land was also referred to as the promised land or Canaan.

American slaves often viewed a place of freedom as the promised land. Martin Luther King Jr. used the idea of the promised land as a key theme in his famous 1968 speech. He compared his vision for civil rights with the biblical challenges of Moses and the Israelites to find freedom. In his conclusion, King said, "I've seen the Promised Land. I may not get there with you. But I want you to know tonight, that we, as a people, will get to the promised land!"[18]

Finally, the doctrine of millenarianism influenced many Christian utopian plans or communities. This interpretation of the final days of humanity on Earth holds that Jesus (Christ) will return from heaven and rule on Earth for one thousand years. This period is referred to as the kingdom of heaven on Earth. Beliefs originated from the concluding chapter of the Bible's New Testament that stated, "They [*Christian martyrs*] came to life and reigned with Christ a thousand years. . . . They will be priests of God and of Christ and will reign with him for a thousand years.[19]

Millenarianism is often associated with the Apocalypse, or final destruction of the world, and the Last Judgement in which believers will be sorted for heaven and hell according to their actions. These events are believed to be precursory to the ultimate and eternal utopia—heaven. Interpretations of these end-of-time events vary widely over time and between Christian denominations.

Movements inspired by millenarianism began in the early years of Christianity, continued through the Middle Ages, and still exist in modern times. Millenarian beliefs and communities vary widely because interpretations of biblical texts and opinions on how and when the events will occur are numerous. Some groups, such as the Shakers discussed in the next chapter, believed the millennium had already begun.

Others predicted its coming in the future. For example, the medieval Franciscan Joachim of Fiore (c. 1135–1202) predicted the millennium would begin in 1260. He believed the world would become an ideal monastery where everyone sang praises to God. In 1259, anticipation of Joachim's expected millennium, along with famine and war, inspired groups of flagellants. These flagellants whipped themselves to destroy their own sinful nature, thus preparing the new era. The movement died in Italy when the millennium failed to arrive.[20]

Ancient classical and Christian utopia traditions often intermingled themes from what modern scholars characterize as the two types of utopias—utopias of reconstruction that envision the creation of a new society and utopias of escape, where the drudgery of daily life disappears.[21]

Some scholars of utopian literature have implied utopias of reconstruction are superior to utopias of escape. Utopias of reconstruction are portrayed as serious exemplars meant to educate and inspire men into action. Examples of these include works authored by the religious, academic, and political elite—Plato's *Republic*, Augustine of Hippo's *City of God*, and later, More's *Utopia*.

On the other hand, utopias of escape have been viewed as childish, selfish daydreams of idleness failing to provide viable solutions to the harsh realities of life. Utopias of escape are depicted as inappropriate endorsements of the baser nature of humans. Critics have labeled them "vaporous fantasies meant merely to amuse or titillate"; tales intended only to divert eighteenth-century literate ladies with the adventures of heroes and heroines; or "popular hope literature" intended for a passive audience.[22]

Creating a dichotomy between the written work of an elite minority and the oral, popular traditions of myth, legend, ballad, and folktale overlooks the similarities in the two. Themes from both merge and separate, appear and reappear, throughout time. Both types of utopia communicate historical insight into lived experience and dreams for a better life of individuals, differing cultural or socioeconomic groups, and their wider societies.

Utopias of Escape: The Land of Cockaigne

In the Middle Ages, the Land of Cockaigne was a popular dream, depicting a peasant's utopia of escape and echoing imagery from ancient myths. The pleasures of Cockaigne are reminiscent of the Golden Age, the Garden of Eden, the Promised Land, and even the Muslim paradise, or "garden of delights."[23] Food and drink were plentiful, holidays numerous, work forbidden, and sleep encouraged and even rewarded. The weather was always good, the grass was always green. Everyone stayed young, and relationships were easy and free from society's restrictive rules.

Stories about Cockaigne circulated in European oral tradition for centuries before they began to be written down in the Middle Ages. The exact origins of the land of Cockaigne are impossible to know. Popular oral traditions and written literary works influenced one another and similar imagery appeared in older sources. Countless oral versions probably existed and varied according to the time, place, and audience. In France, this mythical land of plenty was known as Pays de Cocagne, in Germany as Schlaraffenland, in Holland as Luilekkerland, in Norway as Oleana, in Italy as Paese di Cuccagna, in Spain as Cucafia, in Ireland as Cokaygne, and in England the Land of Cockaigne and Lubberland.

Only a small fraction of the oral versions and texts survive in writing. The oldest surviving French texts are from the thirteenth century; the earliest Dutch and English texts from the late thirteenth and early fourteenth centuries. As printing became more common, versions of Cockaigne were posted in broadside prints and popular plays, and referenced in essays, travel accounts, and other works.[24]

While surviving versions differ somewhat, five themes dominate the accounts of Cockaigne (see source 6). First, Cockaigne existed in the present, not in an idealized past or future. But it was hard to find and difficult to enter. Second, food and drink were plentiful and easy to obtain. Third, work was not required in Cockaigne. Instead, days were filled with leisure and pleasure. Fourth, those living in Cockaigne were free from the common problems of everyday life. Finally, the social order was topsy-turvy—opposite of the reality of the medieval and early modern world in which the masses of average people had little or no power over their daily lives.

Cockaigne echoed the topsy-turvy world of ancient pagan festivals such as Saturnalia and the Christian tradition of carnival. Saturnalia was a seven-day Roman festival celebrated in December with gift giving, parties, and celebrations. The second century satirist Lucian complained that the Golden Age was long past and the rich were not sharing their feasts with the poor as prescribed for the holiday. He reminded readers that during Saturnalia, "All men shall be equal, slave and free, rich and poor, one with another."[25]

During Saturnalia, slaves were allowed to relax and treat their owners as equals at feasts; in some cases, the masters served the slaves at the table. A mock king of the festivities was chosen to preside over the feasts and order people to do silly things. People dressed in unusual ways, inverting what was normally expected. Many of the customs of Saturnalia were similar to Carnival, the celebrations preceding the Christian season of Lent.

Carnival is a set of customs and celebrations of excess occurring before the season of Lent, the solemn forty days prior to Easter. During Lent, Christians are to repent of sins and deny daily pleasures such as meat. However, prior to Lent, medieval feasts, farces, masquerades, and ceremonies parodying the normal social order took place. Drunkenness and normally rude and excessive behavior were overlooked. Masquerades allowed people to act their worst without being identified. Comedic farces were performed with characters such as the lewd monk, the greedy bishop, the fat priest, the quack physician, the foolish lord, hen-pecked husband, and nagging wife.[26] These traditions continue today in celebrations like Mardi Gras in New Orleans.

While medieval versions of Cockaigne presented utopian visions for working people, versions from later centuries condemned laziness and warned readers to avoid the pleasures of Cockaigne. Eating, drinking, sleeping, and playing transformed into the sins of gluttony, drunkenness, idleness, greed, and lust. In the seventeenth and eighteenth centuries, a growing middle-class, or Protestant, work ethic valued religious purity, hard work, and accumulation of wealth. For example, in the seventeenth century, the playwright Ben Jonson and popular ballads were contemptuous of Lubberland, a country for idle good-for-nothings.[27] Benjamin Franklin warned that success in America required hard work and nothing was free. Early colonists used imagery from Cockaigne and Lubberland to satirize and condemn those looking for an easy path in life (see sources 7, 8, 9).

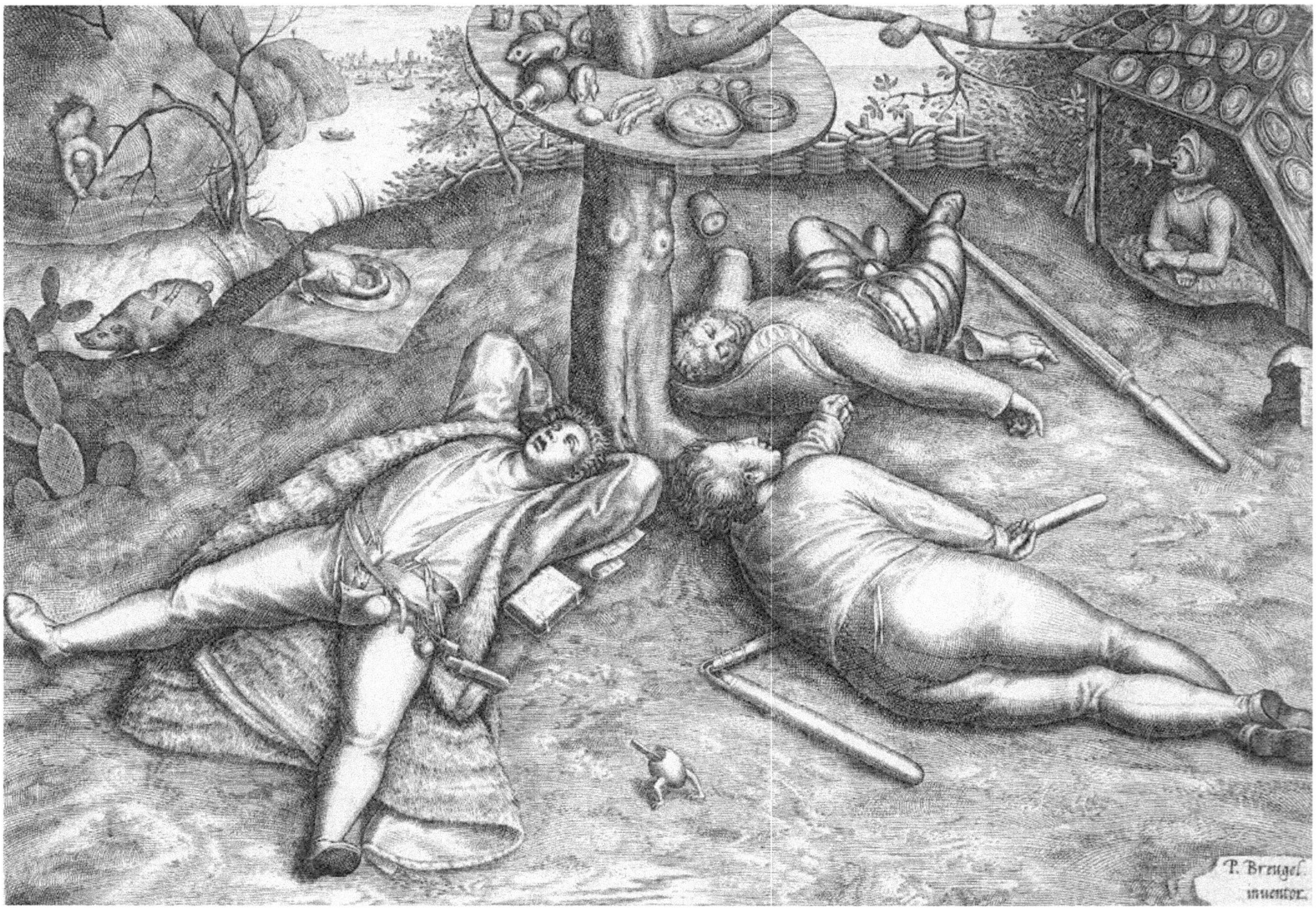

Figure 3.3. Cockaigne was a mythical paradise of plenty for hardworking people. This print was a copy of Pieter Bruegel's 1567 painting titled *Het Luilekkerland* ("lazy, luscious land") in Dutch, known in English as *Land of Cockaigne*. Some accounts of Cockaigne claimed one had to eat through a cloud of pudding to enter. This is depicted in the top-left corner. Pigs and fowl are already cooked and ready to eat. On the right, a bird flies into the mouth of a man resting in a house with a roof made of pies. The fence in the background is made of sausages. Food grows on trees above the resting clerk, peasant, and soldier.
Print, after c. 1570, attributed to Pieter van der Heyden after Land of Cockaigne *by Pieter Bruegel the Elder. (Courtesy of the Metropolitan Museum of Art)*

Utopias in the Era of Exploration

In the fifteenth century, the myths and reality of exploration and colonization in Africa, Asia, Australia, and the Americas mingled with the fabled Cockaigne and other travel tales. Ancient epics; religious pilgrim narratives; stories of a distant eastern kingdom ruled by the Christian king Prester John; and late medieval travel accounts such as those of Marco Polo (c. 1300) and John Mandeville (1499) combined centuries of myth and miraculous, eyewitness descriptions, and downright lies into an enlightening and entertaining soup of stories about faraway lands. Utopias often merged with real and imaginary travel literature.

As Europeans actually visited distant lands, the imaginary elements of travel literature began to disappear. However, imaginary voyages to islands, cities, or planets continued in utopian literature.

Many imagined utopias were located in the Americas. The potential of the New World inspired stories of noble savages in arcadian paradises and visions of golden ages before civilization corrupted humans. Old myths were superimposed on a new map. Thomas More's *Utopia* was set in the New World. He framed his work as a sequel to Amerigo Vespucci's widely circulated accounts published between 1502 and 1504. In More's work, the fictional Portuguese explorer Raphael Hythloday accompanied Vespucci, remained behind in Brazil, and discovered Utopia (see figure 3.1). "Hythloday" meant "nonsense-peddler."[28]

European explorers in the New World often described American abundance in biblical language. Christopher Columbus imagined he had found the Garden of Eden and a "new heaven and new earth." In 1612, John Smith described Virginia as a place where nature provided for all human needs, as well as pleasure and profit. Descriptions of the daily lives of Native Americans resembled the pleasures of Cockaigne—fish, game, and other foods were plentiful and just waiting to be harvested and eaten. Puritan William Bradford, who arrived in America on the *Mayflower*, wrote accounts of a new "land of promise" and wilderness paradise where all could eat and drink freely from a feast of wine, milk, spices, and honey.[29]

The qualities associated with ancient and medieval utopias became linked with America—a land of plenty, opportunity, and equality. The New World symbolized a new beginning for society and individuals of all social standing. Representations of America as a utopia are found in literature promoting immigration, travel accounts, ballads, and other popular literature, as well as immigrant stories and letters.[30] In the 1800s, Eastern European Jews were encouraged by letters from relatives and friends in the United States who described a "New Exodus" to a land of milk and honey. Hunger drove immigrants from Ireland and Italy to a place where work and food were available (see source 10).[31]

However, the tone and purpose of accounts describing the New World as a utopian paradise varied. Some were advertisements, encouraging new emigration for profit. Others were satirical or condescending, criticizing those who hoped for an easier life. Many were hopeful and even playful, reflecting the fantasies of those accustomed to poverty, hunger, and labor (see sources 7, 8, 9, 10).

Americans continued to dream of abundance and leisure in utopian lands of escape into the twentieth century. African Americans before and after the Civil War yearned for a promised land of freedom, alluding to the Israelite Exodus from Egyptian slavery to a promised land. In the face of poverty and oppression, African Americans imagined places like the medieval Land of Cockaigne where bread grew on trees and pigs ran around cooked and ready to eat (source 11).

Former slave Henry Green described the following timeless dream of an easier life when interviewed in the 1930s. The language has been standardized for easy reading:

> They told us that in Arkansas the hogs are just laying around already baked with the knives and the forks sticking in them ready to be eat, and that there was fritter ponds everywhere with them fritters a-frying in them ponds of grease, and that there was money trees where all you had to do was to pick the money off 'em like picking cotton off the stalk.[32]

The oral tradition of Diddie Wa Diddie (or Diddy-Wah-Diddy), an African-American mythical land of plenty, was the subject of Bo Diddley's 1956 song "Diddy Wah Diddy" The lyrics "I got a girl down in Diddy Wah Diddy; Isn't no town an' it isn't no city" references the oral tradition of a place "way off somewhere." This utopia is located at the end of a road that curves so much that a mule pulling a wagon of hay can eat off the back of the wagon as he goes. In Diddie Wa Diddie life is worry free, work is not required, and the food is plentiful and ready to eat. One can sit down and just wait for a big baked chicken to appear yelling "Eat me! Eat me!" with a knife and fork already stuck in its sides. Sweet potato pies appear and grow faster than they can be eaten.[33]

Poverty and hard times like the Depression also inspired utopias of escape. Depression-era folksongs such as "Franklin Roosevelt's Back Again," "No Depression in Heaven," and "There'll Be No Distinction There" communicated yearnings for a better life for working people now and in the afterlife.

In 1928, Harry "Haywire Mac" McClintock first recorded the song "Big Rock Candy Mountain," describing the ideal world of an American hobo. Springs of lemonade, lakes of whiskey and stew, handouts growing on bushes, and chickens laying soft-boiled eggs fill the hobo's stomach. The weather is always warm and dry. Policemen and watchdogs are not a threat, hard labor is not required in prison, and jails are easy to escape.[34]

In the late 1940s and 1950s, Al Capp's popular comic strip *Li'l Abner* portrayed the adventures of those living in the poor Southern mountain town of Dogpatch. His satirical, stereotypical portrayal of lazy hillbilly life included a lovable creature called the Shmoo. The Shmoo laid eggs, gave milk, and could be cooked in a variety of ways to produce meat that tasted like chicken or steak. They could be made into cloth, or buttons, or leather; reproduced quickly; and, best of all, "dropped dead, out of sheer joy, when anyone looks at 'em hungrily!!"[35]

We continue to imagine old and new utopian dreams. In the twenty-first century, we escape to utopias and dystopias in the past, present, and future in novels, movies, television shows, and video games. Utopian themes are prominent in modern marketing and advertising campaigns for goods and services. Lottery jackpots and vacations to exotic destinations filled with food, leisure, and entertainment are the modern equivalent of Cockaigne.

Figure 3.4. The Garden of Eden, paradise, the promised land, and the land of milk and honey are ideal places in the past, present, and future described in biblical texts. These names and the idyllic qualities of these locations are incorporated into utopian art, literature, and communities. This image depicts Adam and Eve in the Garden of Eden. It appeared in an early fifteenth-century manuscript of the history of the world from Creation through the Roman Empire.
"Adam and Eve in Paradise," Egerton Manuscript 912, f. 10, c. 1415, https://bit.ly/2AlYvW3 (Courtesy of the British Library)

Since ancient times, humans have imagined worlds where the challenges of daily life disappear. Ancient myths and peasants' dreams merge with the real and mythical allures of new worlds. In hard times, desires for better lives reemerge in topsy-turvy worlds portraying the opposites of hard realities. Utopias of escape provide hope, inspiration, and entertainment.

In the Classroom

Utopia is an interdisciplinary concept with special relevance to the humanities and social sciences. Political scientists, sociologists, psychologists, and other scholars examine how utopianism is related to social change, religion, political and economic thought, colonialism, globalization, revolution, and the individual.[36] Modern concepts of utopia are analyzed to better understand motivations for consumer spending, and conclusions are applied in the fields of marketing and advertising.

Utopias of Escape in the Classroom

The most engaging method to introduce the concept of utopia is to ask students to create their own utopia. Concentrating on a few specific themes related to a historical era or topic of study is the most meaningful experience. For example, daily life themes such as food or work might be highlighted by asking the following questions.

- What do you do all day in your utopia? Describe three or more activities you would do (or definitely *not* do) in your perfect world.

- Describe food, drink, and meals in your utopia. What do you eat and drink? How often? Where does the food come from? Does the food have unique qualities that don't exist in the real world?

After students have created their own utopias, introduce the essential questions, "How have utopias changed over time? How have they stayed the same?" And use selected primary source texts and images for comparisons and contrasts between the past and present.

For example, Land of Cockaigne texts and images help to focus discussion on utopias of escape. European medieval peasants rarely consumed meat, expensive and imported spices, and alcohols such as claret, sherry, and muscatel. Yet in Cockaigne, all are plentiful and free.

After chosen themes are explored in the historical text, ask students what their utopias say about the modern world. For example, a question to initiate the discussion related to the food theme might be the following:

- Are the qualities of food in your modern utopia different from those of the historical utopia? How? Why do these similarities and differences exist?

In a typical classroom, at least one student is likely to note that in modern utopias, people can eat anything but never gain weight. Ask students if this was a concern in the historical utopia (it was not) and explore why modern people might be concerned with weight gain (food is plentiful and obesity is considered undesirable for health and fashion reasons).

When compared to the preindustrial era, most modern lives are safer and easier. Ask students to closely examine their own lives and culture by considering if and how twenty-first-century boredom, disappointment, challenges, or tragedies are addressed in the modern dreams of escape.

Students can also be asked to create utopias of people on the opposite ends of the socioeconomic spectrum. For example, "Rock Candy Mountain" is a hobo's utopia. After listening to the song and reviewing the lyrics, ask students to imagine the utopia of an upper-class person or police officer from the same era.

Utopias of Social Reconstruction in the Classroom

Students also enjoy creating social reconstruction utopias in which cultural expectations, social relationships, government, and economy are reimagined. This is especially effective when small groups of students create a utopian version of school. The following will help to focus student work:

- Choose a name that reflects the nature of the school.
- Describe three problems that need to be addressed in your real school and how these problems will be solved in your utopian school.
- Describe the perfect day in your utopian school (schedule, classes, etc.).
- Describe how the humans and animals interact in this utopian environment.
- Draw a map of your perfect school, labeling elements as appropriate. Explain how individual elements improve upon elements in real school.

About half-way through the assigned work time, ask students to consider the following question, individually, in writing.

- It is likely that elements of your utopian school vision conflict with the ideas of others in your group. Describe the conflicting ideas. Why do you think these differences exist?

After students consider this question individually, ask them to explore, in small groups or as a whole class, the origins of conflicting views of utopia. The following questions can guide this discussion:

- What real-life school experiences (positive or negative) might contribute to differing conceptions of the perfect school?
- How do our individual experiences with peers, family, friends, or animals contribute to utopian dreams?

- If you were a teacher or a principal, what would a perfect school look like?
- If you were a young person trying to survive in a time or place where education was unavailable to you, what elements would be prominent in your utopian school?

Connections can be made to historical utopian communities. For example, ask students to consider the views of different groups of people living inside and outside the utopian communities described in the following chapter.

- Did all members of the Oneida Perfectionists, Rappites, or Shakers like or enjoy life within the community? Did all members support the redefined relationships between men, women, or races? Why or why not?
- Did motivations for joining these communities vary among the members? If so, what impact could that have on the group as a whole?
- How did the wealthy members of the community view the poor members that joined? Did economic equality really exist in these communities?
- Did African Americans or women in Shaker or Owenite communities feel as if they were treated equally?
- What did the neighbors of these communities think about the unique beliefs and practices of these groups?
- How would these groups be judged in American culture today?

Utopias and Geography

Utopias also provide a unique insight into both real and imagined geography. The remains of historical communities are mapped and studied by archaeologists and historians. Literary descriptions of utopias are often accompanied by maps. These imagined maps of perfect worlds are a form of mental mapping (see figures 3.1 and 3.5).

Mental maps combine objective knowledge and subjective perceptions to create impressions of real or imagined environments. They are influenced by direct exposure to real places, factual information, and indirect experiences communicated from other people or the media.[37]

Ask students to create maps and describe the physical characteristics of their utopias. For example, students can be asked:

- Describe the climate and weather in your utopia.
- Describe the physical geography of your utopia (rivers, oceans, mountains, etc.).
- Describe the human geography of your utopia (roads, buildings, etc. created by humans).

Ask students to compare and contrast their utopian mental maps with the geography, real and imagined, of their daily lives or historical utopias. For example, those living in cold weather imagine warm climates; those from the city wish for rural or wilderness paradises. Beaches are often prominent in modern utopias. Provide historical primary source texts or images describing or depicting utopias. Examples of modern print, television, or internet advertising for vacation destinations can also prompt discussion and analysis of the essential question: How are utopian dreams and communities a reflection of the wider culture?[38]

The Primary Sources

The primary source texts and images provided below can be used independently or in sets in relevant lessons or instructional units. The essential questions provided at the beginning of the chapter focus student attention on the themes of continuity and change in utopian dreams over time.

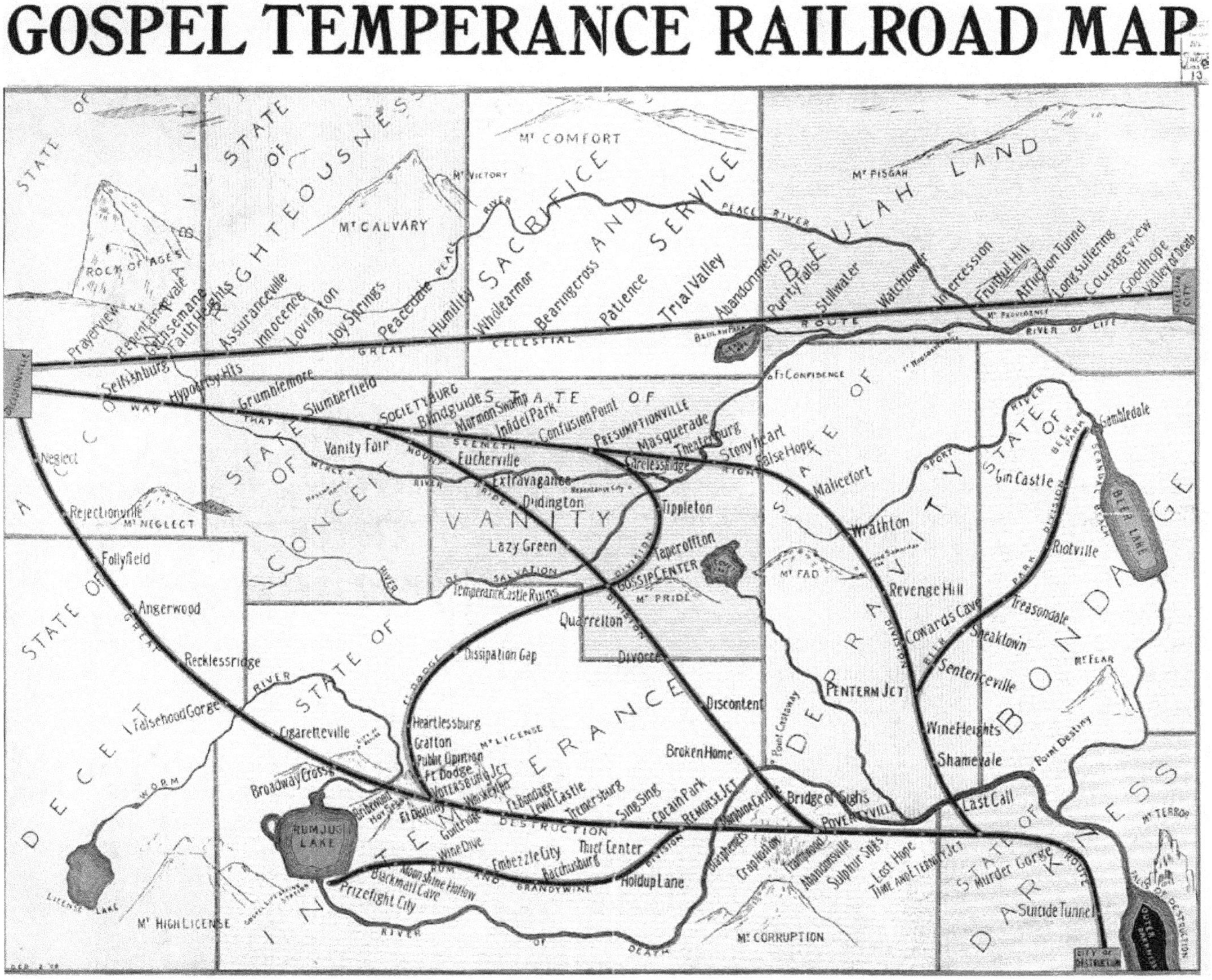

Figure 3.5. Spiritual progress is often depicted as an allegorical journey from lands of sin and despair to utopian promised lands of earthly and heavenly salvation. Dante's *Divine Comedy* (1320) and John Bunyan's *The Pilgrim's Progress* (1678) are examples of spiritual journeys through imagined geography. This map was created and distributed to encourage abstinence from alcohol. The Great Destruction Route beginning in the lower right corner and the Great Celestial Route ending in the top left corner are depicted in detail on the allegorical Temperance railroad.

Print, G. E. Bula, "Gospel Temperance Railroad Map," 1908. (Courtesy of Library of Congress)

Source 1

The Golden Age—eighth century BCE.

In the following excerpt from Works and Days, *the Greek poet Hesiod described a long-ago golden age. The overall purpose of this work was to describe a farmer's life and instruct readers how to be honest and hard-working persons. Historians are able to learn about ancient religious and moral beliefs as well as glean information about agriculture and country life.*

In the beginning, the immortals
who have their homes on Olympus
created the golden generation of mortal people.
These lived in Kronos' time, when he
was the king in heaven.
They lived as if they were gods,

their hearts free from all sorrow,
by themselves, and without hard work or pain;
no miserable old age came their way;
their hands, their feet, did not alter.
They took pleasure in festivals,
and lived without troubles.
When they died, it was as if they fell asleep.
All goods were theirs.
The fruitful grain land yielded its harvest to them of its own accord;
this was great and abundant, while they ate at their pleasure.[39]

Source 2

The Golden Age—fifth century BCE to third century CE.

Telecleides (c. 400s BCE) was a Greek comic poet and playwright. In this excerpt, the author describes a golden age of plenty, but is ridiculing those who believe such a land really existed.

This excerpt is from The Amphictyons; *only the titles and fragments of his six plays survive. This excerpt survived because it was quoted six hundred years later, during the Roman Empire, in* The Deiphnosophists (The Banquet of the Learned) *by the Greek scholar Athenaeus (c. 200 CE). In this work, nearly 800 Greek and Roman writers were quoted. In this excerpt, a group of Roman scholars of medicine, music, literature, and philosophy were quoting previous works about food and banqueting while at a banquet. Historians use compilations such as this to learn about lost manuscripts and their authors and gain insights into the ancient culture.*[40]

I will, then, tell of the life of old which I provided for mortals. First, there was peace over all. . . . Earth produced no terror and no disease; on the other hand, things needful came of their own accord. Every torrent flowed with wine, barley-cakes strove with wheat-loaves for men's lips, beseeching that they be swallowed. . . . Fishes would come to the house and bake themselves, then serve themselves on the tables. A river of broth, whirling hot slices of meat, would flow by the couches; conduits full of piquant sauces for the meat were close at hand for the asking, so that there was plenty for moistening a mouthful and swallowing it tender. On dishes there would be honey-cakes all sprinkled with spices, and roast thrushes served up with milk-cakes were flying into the gullet. The flat-cakes jostled each other at the jaws and set up a racket, the slaves would shoot dice with slices of paunch and tidbits. Men were fat in those days and every bit mighty giants.[41]

Source 3

Plato's description of Atlantis, 360 BCE

According to Plato, Atlantis was a wonderful and powerful nation, but the gods caused it to sink into the sea. Plato's contemporaries may have recognized his description as a metaphor for a nation punished for its pride, or they may have believed existed in the past.

They were furnished with everything which they needed, both in the city and country. Because of the greatness of their empire many things were brought to them from foreign countries, and the island itself provided most of what was required by them for the uses of life. . . . They dug out of the earth . . . **orichalcum** . . . being more precious in those days than anything except gold. There was an abundance of wood for carpenter's work, and . . . tame and wild animals. Moreover, there were a great number of elephants . . . all other sorts of animals, both for those which live in lakes and marshes and rivers, and also for those which live in mountains and on plains . . . whatever fragrant things there now are in the earth, whether roots, or herbage, or woods, or essences which distill from fruit and flower, grew and thrived in that land; also the fruit . . . which is given us for nourishment and any other which we use for food . . . drinks and meats and ointments, and good store of chestnuts and the like, which furnish pleasure and amusement, and are fruits . . . and the pleasant kinds of dessert, with which we console ourselves after dinner, when we are tired of eating—all these that sacred island which then beheld the light of the sun, brought forth fair and wondrous and infinite abundance. With such blessings the earth freely furnished them; meanwhile they went on constructing their temples and palaces and harbors and docks.[42]

orichalcum—probably reference to an ancient metal alloy, probably bronze or brass.

Source 4

Islands of the Blest—first century BCE.

Horace was a poet living during the chaotic years of the late Roman Republic. In the following excerpt, he contrasted the violent political turmoil of his time with a description of a utopian escape, the islands of the blest.

. . . . but hurry away, beyond the Etruscan coast,
Wide spreading Ocean awaits us: let us seek the fields,
the happy fields and the *islands of the blest,*
where the earth is not plowed, but yearly it yields the grain,
and the vine is not trimmed, but forever flourishes,
and the branch of the olive never fails to blossom,
and the black fig, ungrafted adorns its own tree,
honey drips from the hollow oak, from the lofty hills
the light-stepping spring come splashing down.
There the goats need no orders to come to the milking pails,
and the flock returns gladly with swelling udders,
and the bear does not growl as he circles the sheepfold at evening,
and the earth does not swell up with vipers,
and we shall wonder at greater blessings: the rainy Eastwind
does not wash away crops with a flood of showers,
and the fertile seeds are not scorched in the dried-up clods,
for heat and cold are controlled by the king of the gods.
No disease is in fact the flock, no raging heat
from a star can dry up the herd with drought.
. . .
Jupiter set the shores apart for a God-fearing people
when he debased the Golden age with bronze.[43]

Source 5

Lucian's Utopian Voyage—second century CE

The Greek satirist Lucian (125 CE–after 180 CE) wrote an account of his own imaginary journey, mocking similar mythical tales of perfect lands. He described his encounters with the kings of the Moon and Sun, making it the earliest known science fiction work. He claimed he was swallowed by a whale and visited the Isles of the Blessed. He promised a sequel describing a voyage to a distant continent. This following excerpt is from the introduction of his tale.

I tell all kinds of lies in a plausible and specious way, but also because everything in my story is more or less comical parody of one or another of the poets, historians and philosophers of old, who have written much that smacks of miracles and fables. I would cite them by name, were it not that you yourself will recognize them from your reading. One of them **Ctesias** . . . wrote a great deal about India and its characteristics that he had never seen himself nor heard from anyone else with a reputation for truthfulness. **Iambulus** also wrote much that was strange about countries in the great sea: he made up a falsehood that is patent to everybody, but wrote a story that is not uninteresting for all of that. Many others, with the same intent, have written about imaginary travels and journeys of theirs, telling of huge beasts, cruel men and strange ways of living.

Their guide and instructor in this sort of charlatanry is Homer's Odysseus, who tells Alcinous and his court about winds in bondage, one eyed men, cannibals and savages; also about animals with many heads, and transformations of his comrades wrought with drugs. . . . Well, on reading these authors, I did not find much fault with them for their lying, as I saw that this is already a common practice even among men who profess philosophy. I did wonder, though, that they thought they could write untruths and not get caught at it. Therefore, as I myself, thanks to my vanity, was eager to hand something down to posterity, that I might not be the only one excluded from the privileges of poetic license, and as I had nothing true to tell, not having had any adventures of significance, I took to lying. But my lying is far more honest than theirs, for though I tell the truth in nothing else, I shall at least be truthful in saying that I'm a liar.[44]

Iambulus (third century BCE) an ancient Greek merchant and probably the author of a tale about a place called Islands of the Sun.

Ctesias (fifth century BCE) wrote *History of the India* that he claimed was based on stories gathered while living in Persia. Lucian recognized the stories as myths and lies.

Source 6—Land of Cockaigne

While surviving versions of medieval and early modern Cockaigne or Lubberland differ somewhat, five key themes are outlined below along with excerpts of several different versions. Readers are encouraged to explore the complete translations cited in the footnotes.

1. Cockaigne existed in the here and now, not the past, the future, or after death. It was distant and hard to reach. In one version, to get to Cockaigne, one had to spend seven years up to the chin in pig manure to be admitted. In other words, only those that had lived and worked like peasants were admitted.[45]

Those who made their way there found it better than the Christian heaven. According to the version below, heaven was somewhat boring, and only fruit and water were consumed. On the other hand, in Cockaigne food and drink were limitless.

Far out to sea and west of Spain
There is a country named Cockaygne.
No place on earth compares to this
For sheer delightfulness and bliss.
Though Paradise is fair and bright,
Cockaygne is a finer sight.
In Paradise what's to be seen
But grass and flowers and branches green?
Though paradisal joys are sweet,
There's nothing there but fruit to eat;
No bench, no chamber, and no hall [*rooms for drinking and feasting*],
No alcoholic drink at all.
. . . . .
But Cockaygne offers better fare,
And without worry, work, or care;
The food is good, the drink flows free
At lunchtime, suppertime, and tea.
. . . . .
There are rivers great and fine
Of oil and milk, honey and wine;
Water's uses there are few—
For washing in, and for the view.[46]

2. Food and drink were plentiful and free for everyone. The types of food in various versions of Cockaigne varied by culture. In the medieval English version quoted below, meat pies, puddings (dense steamed breads), and sweet pastries seasoned with expensive spices were featured. In the real medieval world, all of these foods were sparse or absent in a peasant's diet. Vegetables aren't mentioned; a reversal of the peasants' diet that depended heavily on vegetables and grain porridges or stews.

An Irish version of Cockaigne described a fort beyond a lake made of butter, white bread, bacon, and cheese.[47] Scandinavian versions featured rivers of sour cream and mountains of porridge; the French preferred trees of butter, rocks of melted cheese, and pigs stuffed with chestnuts. Italy's Paese de Cuccagna featured a cheese mountain with the cauldron on top bubbling over with pasta, rivers of fine wine, and an abundance of meat. Later, Mexican tales told of tortilla hills, fountains of olive oil, and sopaipilla trees.[48]

Made with rich fillings, fish and meat,
The tastiest a man could eat.
Flour-cakes are the shingles all
Of cloister, chamber, church, and hall.
The nails are puddings, rich and fat—
Kings and princes might dine on that.
There you can come and eat your fill,
And not be blamed for your self-will.
. . . . .
The geese when roasted on the spit
Fly to the abbey (believe it or not)
And cry out "Geese, all hot, all hot!"
With garlic in great quantity,
The best-dressed geese a man could see.
The larks are known to do the same—
Land in your mouth, well-cooked and tame,
Freshly stewed and nicely done,
Sprinkled with cloves and cinnamon.[49]

A description of Lubberland claimed,

Hot roasted pigs will meet ye,
They in the streets run up and down,
Still crying out, Come eat me
Likewise, he says, At every feast,
The very fowls and fishes,
Nay from the biggest to the least,
Comes tumbling to the dishes.[50]

3. In Cockaigne "*Those who longest sleep, earn the most.*"[51] Labor was not required and work-free holidays multiplied; the opposite of daily life in the pre-industrial era requiring constant hard work. The reality of medieval life was work all year and every day. Water had to be carried; wood chopped for fuel; food planted, harvested, preserved, and cooked; fibers spun, woven, and sewn into clothes. But in Cockaigne, food, clothing, houses, and land were free for the taking.

Nice clothes there are mighty cheap,
In front of each door lies a heap.
All may, to their own liking, choose
some stockings and a pair of shoes.
Those who wish, don new attire.[52]
. . . . .
You'll never hear a sharp retort,
Or see a snake, or wolf, or fox,
Horse or gelding, cow or ox,
Never a sheep or goat or pig—
And so, of course, no dung to dig[53]

4. Not only was life filled with leisure, but the inhabitants of Cockaigne did not suffer from pain, blindness, sickness, or insects. Medicine, ointments, and balms were free or flowed like water from springs. In real life, disease, accidents, and illnesses were common and treatments were few. In some versions, a fountain of youth flowed, enabling residents

to stay young and healthy. In the following excerpt, the Jordan River is a biblical reference to the Middle Eastern river the Israelites were believed to have crossed to enter the Promised Land.

A Jordan [*river*] runs through that very region,
The number of people who go there is legion.
For when its water touches their tongue,
Old folk all start turning young.[54]

The weather in this paradise was always good; every day was like a spring day. In the real world, bad weather meant failed crops, famine, hunger, and starvation.

There's no fly or flea or louse
In clothes, in village, bed, or house;
There's no thunder, sleet, or hail,
Or any nasty worm or snail,
No storm, wind, rain of any kind.[55]

5. Cockaigne inverted the medieval social order as well as the routines of daily life. In most versions, Cockaigne was reserved for common people; the rich could not enter. In some versions, the rules of the Catholic Church or the local lord disappeared. In Cockaigne, peasants dressed and ate like kings and princes of the real medieval world.

Those who wish, don new attire,
Whether they be knight or squire.[56]

Crime and punishment ceased to exist because everyone in Cockaigne freely shared in the abundance.

No hate or envy, truth to tell.
Things found lying around, unretrieved,
One take without a by-your-leave
For one's own gain and no confessions;
One treats them as one's own possessions.[57]

In Lubberland . . .

There is no law nor lawyer's fees
All men are free from fury,
For ev'ry one do's what he please,
Without a judge or jury:
The summer-time is warm they say,
The winter's ne'er the colder,
They have no landlords' rent to pay
Each man is a free-holder.[58]

Priests didn't forbid gluttony or insist upon marriage in Cockaigne. In an English edition, large parts of the poem describe a topsy-turvy monastery where the monks and nuns break all the rules of poverty, worship, order, and celibacy imposed in the real medieval world.

There you can come and eat your fill,
And not be blamed for your self-will[59]
. . . . .
Neither men nor women offer excuses,
There is not one who refuses
To sleep with another tenderly.[60]

Source 7

The New World was promoted in broadside ballads that circulated in England for several centuries beginning in the early 1600s. The songs were so popular they inspired satirical responses such as the one below, which probably originated in the 1630s. Religious frauds were encouraged to go to America so England and her church could be purified. An easy life was promised to sinners and prisoners in a land where milk flowed in rivers and streams and honey grew on trees.[61] *The original language has been simplified.*

A Proper New Ballad Called The Summons to New England
There milk from springs, like rivers, flows,
And honey upon hawthorn [*trees*] grows;
Hemp, wool, and flax, there grows on trees,
The **mould** [*top soil*] is fat, and cuts like cheese;
All fruits and herbs grow in the fields,
Tobacco is good plenty yields;
. . . .
There's venison of all sorts great store,
Both stag, and buck, wild goat, and boar,
And all so tame, that you with ease
May eat your fill, take what you please;
There's beavers plenty, yea, so many,
That you may buy two skins for a penny.
. . . .
There twice a year all sorts of grain
Doth down from heaven like hailstones rain;
You never need to sow nor plough,
There's plenty of all things enough;
Wine sweet and wholesome drops from trees.[62]

Source 8

William Byrd II was an upper-class Virginia planter. This excerpt is from The History of the Dividing Line Betwixt Virginia and North Carolina *(1728), his account of a surveying expedition to determine the boundary between the two colonies. He contrasted the natural wonders he saw to the laziness of the working-class people who had settled there.*

Surely there is no place in the world where the inhabitants live with less labor than in North Carolina. It approaches nearer to the description of Lubberland than any other, by the great felicity of the climate, the easiness of raising provisions and the slothfulness of the people. . . . The men, for their parts, just like the Indians, impose all the work upon the poor women. They make their wives rise out of their beds early in the morning, at the same time that they lie and snore, till the sun has risen one third of his course, and dispersed all the unwholesome damps. Then, after stretching and yawning for half an hour, they light their pipes, and, under the protection of a cloud of smoke, venture out into the open air; though, if it happens to be never so little cold, they quickly return shivering into the chimney corner. When the weather is mild, they stand leaning with both their arms upon the corn field fence, and gravely consider whether they had best go and take a small heat at the hoe: but generally find reasons to put it off till another time. Thus they loiter away their lives, like **Solomon's sluggard**, with their arms across, and at the winding up of the year scarcely have bread to eat. To speak the truth, it is a thorough aversion to labor that makes people file off to North Carolina, where plenty and a warm sun confirm them in their disposition to laziness for their whole lives.[63]

Solomon's sluggard—a reference to a lazy man described in the Bible's Old Testament book of Proverbs thought to be written by King Solomon.

Source 9

In 1782 Benjamin Franklin, in an essay for those considering a move to America, warned readers they would not find a life free from work.

> If he [*the immigrant*] does not bring a fortune with him, he must work and be industrious to live. One or two years residence give him all the rights of a citizen; but the government does not . . . hire people to become settlers, by paying their passages, giving land, Negroes, utensils, flocks or any other kind of compensation whatsoever. In short, America is the land of labor, and by no means what the English call *Lubberland*, and the French *Pays de Cocagne*, where the streets are said to be paved with half-peck loaves, the houses tiled with oatcakes, and where the fowls fly about ready roasted, crying, *Come eat me!*"[64]

Source 10

Excerpt from Norwegian Emigrant Song, "The Ballad of Oleana," 1853.[65]

I'm off to Oleana, I'm turning from my doorway,
    No chains for me, I'll say good-by to slavery in Norway.
They give you land for nothing in jolly Oleana,
    And grain comes leaping from the ground in floods of golden manna . . .
The crops they are gigantic, potatoes are immense, Sir,
    You make a quart of whisky from each one without expense, Sir.
And ale as strong and sweet as the best you've ever tasted,
    It's running in the foamy creek, where most of it is wasted.
The salmon they are playing, and leaping in the brook, Sir,
    They hop into your kettle, put the cover on, and cook, Sir.
And little roasted piggies, with manners quite demure, Sir,
    They ask you, Will you have some ham? And then you say, Why, sure, Sir.
The cows are most obliging, their milk they put in pails, Sir,
    They make your cheese and butter with a skill that never fails, Sir.
The calves are very helpful, themselves they skin and kill, Sir,
    They turn into a tasty roast before you drink your fill, Sir.
The hens lay eggs colossal, so big and round and fine, Sir,
    The roosters act like eight-day clocks, they always tell the time, Sir.
And cakes come raining down, Sir, with chocolate frosting coated,
    They're nice and rich and sweet, good Lord, you eat them till you're bloated . . .
I'm off to Oleana, to lead a life of pleasure,
    A beggar here, a count out there, with riches in full measure.
I'm coming, Oleana, I've left my native doorway,
I've made my choice, I've said good-by to slavery in Norway.
Ole—Ole—Ole—oh! Oleana!
Ole—Ole—Ole—oh! Oleana!

Source 11

John Henry was a mythical black workingman's hero, the subject of songs and folk stories. Everything John Henry did was larger than life. The excerpt below is a John Henry story documented in the 1920s and thought to be from North Carolina and Georgia. The language has been standardized for easy reading.

> One day John Henry left rock quarry on the way to camp and had to go through woods and fields. Well, he met a big black bear and didn't do nothing but shoot him with his bow and arrow and the arrow went clean through bear and stuck in a big tree on the other side. So, John Henry pulls the arrow out of the tree and pull so hard he falls back against another tree which

is full of flitterjacks and the first tree is full of honey, and in pulling the arrow out of one he's shaken down the honey, and in falling against the other he is shaken down flitterjacks. Well, John Henry set there and ate honey and flitterjacks. And after a while when he went to get up, a button popped off his pants and killed a rabbit more than 100 yards on the other side of the tree. And so up jumped a brown baked pig with a sack of biscuits on his back. And John Henry ate that too.

So John Henry gets up to go on through woods to camp for supper, because he . . . mighty hungry for supper. John Henry sees a lake down the hill and thinks he'll get a drink of water, 'cause he's thirsty, after eating honey and flitterjack and brown roast pig and biscuits. And so he goes down to get a drink of water and finds a lake is full of honey, and out in the middle of that lake is a tree full of biscuits. And so John Henry don't do nothing but drink that lake of honey dry. And he ate the tree full of biscuits too.[66]

Notes

1. Oscar Wilde, *The Soul of Man under Socialism* (1891), 40, http://www.gutenberg.org/files/1017/1017-h/1017-h.htm
2. Adapted from the following quote by Hal Rammel, "Liberated from the everyday, we dream of the world's limitless possibilities, the pleasures of life, and the bountiful earth, one day free for all. No dream calls us more urgently." In *Nowhere in America, The Big Rock Candy Mountain and Other Comic Utopias* (Urbana: University of Illinois Press, 1990), 144.
3. Lyman Tower Sargent, "The Three Faces of Utopianism Revisited," *Utopian Studies* 5, no. 1 (1994): 4, http://www.jstor.org/stable/20719246.
4. Ibid., 3.
5. *Oxford English Dictionary Online*, s.v. "utopia, n.," http://www.oed.com/.
6. Thomas More, "Six Lines on the Island of Utopia, written by Anemolius, Poet Laureate, and Nephew to Hythloday by his Sister" in *Utopia*, ed. George M. Logan, trans. Robert M. Adams, 3rd edition (Cambridge: Cambridge University Press, 2016), 123.
7. Bizarro World was a fictional planet introduced by DC Comics in the 1960s as the opposite of Superman's Earth.
8. Gregory Claeys, *Searching for Utopia: The History of an Idea* (New York: Thames & Hudson), 58–69.
9. *Oxford English Dictionary Online*, s.v. "dystopia, n."
10. Fátima Vieira, "The Concept of Utopia," in *Cambridge Companion to Utopian Literature*, ed. Gregory Claeys (Cambridge: Cambridge University Press, 2010), 3–27, doi:10.1017/CCOL9780521886659.001; Claeys, *Searching for Utopia*, 12.
11. Lyman Tower Sargent, *Utopianism: A Very Short Introduction* (Oxford and New York: Oxford University Press, 2010), 8.
12. Sargent, "The Three Faces of Utopianism Revisited," 10.
13. John D. Hicks, "The Political Career of Ignatius Donnelly," *Mississippi Valley Historical Review* 8, nos. 1–2 (June–September 1921): 101, http://www.jstor.org/stable/1889278.
14. Gorman Beauchamp, "The Dream of Cockaigne: Some Motives for the Utopias of Escape," *Centennial Review* 25, no. 4 (Fall 1981): 352–53, http://www.jstor.org/stable/23739084.
15. Ibid., 352–53.
16. Genesis 2:8–9 (NIV).
17. Exodus 3:8 (NIV).
18. Martin Luther King Jr., "I've Been to the Mountaintop" speech, Memphis, Tennessee (April 3, 1968), accessed June 2018, https://www.americanrhetoric.com/speeches/mlkivebeentothemountaintop.htm.
19. Revelation 20:4–6 (NIV).
20. Norman Cohn, *The Pursuit of the Millennium* (New York: Oxford University Press, 1970 edition), 108–9, 129.
21. Sargent, "The Three Faces of Utopianism Revisited," 3–4.
22. Frank E. Manuel and Fritzie P. Manuel, *Utopian Thought in the Western World* (Cambridge, MA: Belknap Press of Harvard University Press, 1979), 7–9; Lewis Mumford, *The Story of Utopias* (New York: Boni and Liveright, 1962), 16–21, https://archive.org/details/storyutopias00mumfgoog/page/n32.
23. Dorothee Metlitzki, *The Matter of Araby in Medieval England* (New Haven, CT: Yale University Press, 1977), 210–11.
24. Herman Pleij, *Dreaming of Cockaigne: Medieval Fantasies of the Perfect Life* (New York: Columbia University Press), 3–4; Luisa Del Giudice, "Mountains of Cheese and Rivers of Wine: Paesi di Cuccagna and Other Gastronomic Utopias," in *Imagined States, Nationalism, Utopia, and Longing in Oral Cultures*, ed. Luisa Del Giudice and Gerald Porter (Logan: Utah State University Press, 2001), 12, http://www.jstor.org/stable/j.ctt46nxsn.4; Rammel, *Nowhere in America*, 10–16, 31–39.
25. Cronosolon, "First Table of Laws," Internet Sacred Text Archive (accessed June 2018), http://www.sacred-texts.com/cla/luc/wl4/wl423.htm
26. Rammel, *Nowhere in America*, 40–56.
27. A. L. Morton, *The English Utopia* (London: Lawrence & Wishart, 1922), 24–26; Karma Lochrie, *Nowhere in the Middle Ages* (Philadelphia: University of Pennsylvania Press, 2016), 10.

28. Thomas More, *Utopia*, 1516, Book I, Open Utopia edition, accessed July 2018, http://theopenutopia.org/full-text/book-i-of-utopia/.
29. Etta M. Madden and Martha L. Finch, "Introduction," in *Eating in Eden: Food and American Utopias*, ed. Etta M. Madden and Martha L. Finch (Lincoln: University of Nebraska Press, 2006), 5.
30. Rammel, *Nowhere in America*, 17–27; Del Giudice, "Mountains of Cheese and Rivers of Wine," 48–50.
31. Madden and Finch, "Introduction," 6.
32. Henry Green, Interview. Federal Writers' Project: Slave Narrative Project, Vol. 2, Arkansas, Part 3, Gadson-Isom (1936), 99–100, Library of Congress, https://www.loc.gov/resource/mesn.023/?sp=99.
33. Benjamin A. Botkin, "Mythical Places of the Florida Negro," in *A Treasury of Southern Folklore* (New York: Crown Publishers, 1949), 479.
34. Harry McClintock, "Big Rock Candy Mountain," accessed June 2018, https://genius.com/Harry-mcclintock-big-rock-candy-mountain-lyrics.
35. Al Capp, *The Short Life and Happy Times of the Shmoo* (Woodstock, NY: Overlook Press), 12.
36. Peter Fitting, "A Short History of Utopian Studies," *Science Fiction Studies* 36, no. 1 (March 2009), 121–31, http://www.jstor.org/stable/25475211; Sargent, *Utopianism, A Very Short Introduction*, 7.
37. National Geography Standard 2, National Geographic Society, https://www.nationalgeographic.org/standards/national-geography-standards/2/.
38. Cynthia Resor and S. Kay Gandy, "Dreaming of a Better Life: Utopia as a Focus for Thematic, Interdisciplinary Instruction," *Clearing House: A Journal of Educational Strategies, Issues and Ideas* 87, no. 1 (204): 1–8, doi: 10.1080/00098655.2013.813432.
39. Hesiod, *Works and Days*, trans. Richmond Lattimore (Ann Arbor: University of Michigan Press, 1959), 31–33.
40. John Paulas, "How to Read Athenaeus' 'Deipnosophists,'" *American Journal of Philology* 133, no. 3 (Fall 2012): 403–39, http://www.jstor.org/stable/23269874.
41. Athenaeus, *The Deipnosophists of Athenaeus of Naucratis*, trans. Charles Burton Gulick (London: William Heinemann, 1929), excerpted in "Learning Dreamers and Dissenters," British Library, accessed June 2018, http://www.bl.uk/learning/histcitizen/21cc/utopia/perfection1/athenaeus1/perfect.html.
42. Plato, *Critias* (360 BCE), trans. Benjamin Jowett (New York: C. Scribner's Sons, 1871), http://classics.mit.edu/Plato/critias.html.
43. Horace, "Epode 16," in *The Odes and Epodes of Horace*, trans. Joseph P. Clancy (Chicago: University of Chicago Press, 1960), 224–25.
44. Lucian, "A True Story," trans. A. M. Harmon, vol. 1 (Cambridge, MA: Harvard University Press, 1913), 251–53.
45. "The Land of Cockaygne," Harley Manuscript 913, ff. 3r–6v, British Library, lines 180–82, accessed June 2018, http://www.soton.ac.uk/~wpwt/trans/cockaygn/coctrans.htm.
46. Ibid., lines 1–12, 17–20, 45–48.
47. "Aislinge Meic Con Glinne," Corpus of Electronic Texts Edition: T308002, Electronic edition compiled by Beatrix Färber, accessed June 2018, https://celt.ucc.ie//published/T308002/index.html.
48. Del Giudice, "Mountains of Cheese and Rivers of Wine," 12.
49. "The Land of Cockaygne," Harley Manuscript 913, lines 55–62, 102–10.
50. "An Invitation to Lubberland" (Printed for J. Deacon, at the Angel in Gilt-spur-street, c 1685), EBBA 30687. British Library, Roxburghe, accessed June 2018, https://ebba.english.ucsb.edu/ballad/30687/xml.
51. "The Land of Cokaygne," line 18, accessed June 2018, https://web.archive.org/web/20050207153710/http://www.thegoldendream.com/landofcokaygne.htm.
52. Pleij, *Dreaming of Cockaigne*, 34, lines 47–50.
53. "The Land of Cockaygne," Harley Manuscript 913, lines 30–35.
54. Pleij, *Dreaming of Cockaigne*, 35, lines 89–94.
55. "The Land of Cockaygne," Harley Manuscript 913, lines 37–42.
56. Pleij, *Dreaming of Cockaigne*, 34, lines 51–52.
57. Ibid., 35, lines 70–74.
58. "An Invitation to Lubberland."
59. "The Land of Cockaygne," Harley Manuscript 913, lines 61–62.
60. Pleij, *Dreaming of Cockaigne*, 39, line 105.
61. Rammel, *Nowhere in America*, 19.
62. "A Proper New Ballad Called The Summons to New England," in *An American Garland, Being a Collection of Ballads Relating to America*, ed. C. H. Firth (Oxford: B. H. Blackwell, 1915), 27–30, https://archive.org/details/anamericangarlan00firtiala/page/n5.

63. William Byrd and Edmund Ruffin, *The Westover Manuscripts: Containing the History of the Dividing Line Betwixt Virginia and North Carolina; A Journey to the Land of Eden, A.D. 1733; and A Progress to the Mines* (Petersburg, VA: Edmund and Julian C. Ruffin, 1841), 27 (accessed April 2018), https://docsouth.unc.edu/nc/byrd/byrd.html.

64. Benjamin Franklin, "Information to Those Who Would Remove to America," in *The Works of the Late Dr. Benjamin Franklin: Consisting of His Life Written by Himself, Together with Essays, Humorous, Moral, and Literary, Chiefly in the Manner of the Spectator* (New York: John Tiebout, 1799), 91, accessed April 2018, https://play.google.com/store/books/details?id=l10zAQAAMAAJ&rdid=book-l10zAQAAMAAJ&rdot=1.

65. Theodore C. Blegen, trans., "The Ballad of Oleana," in *Norwegian Emigrant Songs and Ballads*, vol. 14 (London: H. Milford, 1936), 117, from Norwegian-American Historical Association Online, http://www.stolaf.edu/naha/pubs/nas/volume14/vol14_5.htm.

66. Howard Washington Odum and Guy Benton Johnson, *Negro Workaday Songs* (Chapel Hill: University of North Carolina Press, 1926), 239–40, https://archive.org/details/negroworkadayson00odum/page/n7.

CHAPTER FOUR

Utopian Communities

So this is Utopia, is it? Well? I beg your pardon; I thought it was Hell.

—Max Beerbohm[1]

Essential questions:

- How can one person's utopia become another person's dystopia?
  - Is your utopia the same as my utopia? Is your utopia my dystopia?
- What is most important in utopian communities?
  - the rights or freedom for individuals?
  - the survival of the community?
  - achieving the utopian goals of the community?

Utopias are not just fantasies. Throughout history, utopian dreams have inspired real communities. The inspiration, organization, membership, and goals are unique to each group. But all are products of the wider social, economic, and political circumstances of their era. Their creators are inspired by visions of past golden ages, societal transformation, or radical reforms. However, founding ideals often recede as problems arise from inside and outside the community. Some utopian communities overcome the challenges; most fade, and members scatter. A few become dystopias.

Words describing these communities have unique connotations. Nouns include cult, sect, phalanx; common adjectives are alternative, collective, communal, socialist, or communist. These descriptors have subjective meanings, condoning or criticizing the community. Therefore, the term *intentional community* best describes these real-world utopias. An intentional community is a group of five or more adults, with or without their children, who come from more than one nuclear family. They choose to live together because of shared values, goals, vision, or for some other mutually agreed upon purpose."[2]

Numerous intentional communities have existed over time. Therefore, six intentional communities are the focus of this chapter: the English Diggers, the German-American Rappites, the Shakers, the Oneida Perfectionists, and two Owenite communities in New Harmony, Indiana, and Nashoba, Tennessee. These groups were chosen to illustrate four key themes.

The inspirational vision of the community is the first theme. Most utopian communities established prior to the nineteenth and twentieth centuries focused upon religious beliefs and practices. With the Industrial Revolution and the development of modern science, more utopian communities were secular; many inspired by advances in science and technology. Second, intentional communities developed differing approaches to economic organization and property ownership, but many in the nineteenth century adopted a communitarian philosophy.

Figure 4.1. Shakers at Pleasant Hill, Kentucky, late 1800s. The Shaker village at Pleasant Hill in central Kentucky was established in 1806, one of the twenty-one communities established by the Shakers. Membership at this village peaked at around five hundred in the 1820s. By the time this photograph was taken, the declining membership was made up of the aged and younger members who had been adopted by the community. In 1910, the twelve remaining Shakers deeded what remained of their property to a local landowner in exchange for providing care for them until their deaths. The last Shaker at Pleasant Hill died in 1923.
Photograph, Shakers at Pleasant Hill, Kentucky, late 1800s. (Courtesy of Archives of Shaker Village at Pleasant Hill, Kentucky)

The third and fourth themes are discussed later in this chapter, after brief histories of these six communities. Third, the communities redefined and reinterpreted roles and relationships between people of different races and males and females. Free or enslaved African Americans were welcome in some, but their roles in the community may have been little different from the wider culture. Marriage was condoned in some communities, condemned or completely redefined in others.

Finally, utopias as places on the map are explored. The formation of these communities was inspired by utopian visions of the New World. Nineteenth-century American utopian communities influenced each other and the attitudes of the wider communities around them. And the remains of their communities still exist, many as historical sites open to visitors.

Theme One: Religious or Secular Inspirational Visions

Four of the communities to be examined—the Diggers, Shakers, Rappites, and Oneida Perfectionists—were inspired by religious traditions. Each group interpreted biblical scriptures and Christian doctrine differently than the mainstream Christian practices of their era did.

The seventeenth century English Diggers originated in the era of the English Civil War when religious conflicts between Catholics and diverse types of Protestants were inseparable from politics. While the Digger manifesto was presented in very Christian terms, their goal was an economic utopia for the working poor of England (see source 1).

The nineteenth-century American Shakers originated from the English Quaker tradition. The Quakers and the Shakers were two of the many dissenting religious groups wishing to separate from the state-sponsored Church. Early Quakers were contemporaries of the Diggers. Ann Lee, originally a Quaker and a founding Shaker, was arrested and jailed for her religious activities in England. The Shakers, like the Rappites, left Europe for a new world of religious freedom.

The Rappites, also radical Protestants, were Pietist Germans who disagreed with the theology and practice of Lutheranism. Pietists stressed practices and especially devout behavior that conflicted with the doctrines of state religions, both Catholic and Protestant, of Europe. Other groups with a similar background also migrated to America, including the Moravians and the Community of True Inspiration or Amana Colony. The Amish, Mennonites, and Hutterites also have Central European roots and migrated to America, but their beliefs originated in the sixteenth century Anabaptist traditions.

The Diggers, Shakers, and Rappites were products of European political and religious conflicts between Catholics and diverse types of Protestants. All three groups, as well as the Oneida Perfectionists were inspired by biblical descriptions of communal societies of first-century Christians.

The nineteenth-century Oneida Perfectionists followed the unique Christian doctrines of John Humphrey Noyes. This group illustrates the diversity of Christianity and the impact of one powerful and charismatic leader. Religious communities throughout history have interpreted Christian texts in distinct and often conflicting ways. For example, the Shakers and Rappites rejected the mainstream Christian doctrine of the Trinity or God as three beings, the Father, Son, and Holy Ghost. Both groups were dualists, believing God was male and female. This divergent belief influenced the roles of women in these communities.

Beliefs in Christian perfectionism also inspired many utopian societies. Perfectionism in this context holds that an individual or community can achieve spiritual perfection by improving inner faith and outward conduct. Practices such as celibacy, poverty, abstaining from certain foods or drinks, or living separately from the wider society are common practices. Catholic monastic communities and many of the radical Protestant sects formed during the Reformation shared this conviction. The ideals of Christian perfectionism were prominent in many American utopian communities.

In contrast to religious communities, the short-lived communities of New Harmony, Indiana, and Nashoba, Tennessee, were inspired by the beliefs of Robert Owen, a wealthy British industrialist. Owenite communities were distinctly secular, promoting free thought and often rejecting religion entirely. The Owenites were one of many groups in the nineteenth and twentieth centuries who rejected what they saw as the restraints of their contemporary societies – religion, marriage, and traditional sex and gender roles.

Other secular communities were inspired by the writings of the French utopian Charles Fourier (1772–1837) who promoted radical rejection of the existing economic, religious, and social order. Fourier inspired at least thirty nineteenth century Phalanxes or Associationist communities in the United States.

Theme Two: Economic Organization and Property Ownership

All of the groups highlighted below were communitarian. This method of economic organization and property ownership has been referred to by various names over time—communal, cooperative, socialist, or communist. In its most basic form, all members own the property and industries of the community. Economic benefits are distributed in an equal or equitable manner to members. The core philosophy of this economic organization is the belief that solving the problems of the wider society requires a *collective* approach. Nineteenth-century communitarians believed if a small, voluntary group demonstrated to the world a better way to live and work, people in the wider society would choose to follow their example.

Not all communitarian societies have utopian visions or willing participants. Some were created simply for survival in a harsh world, such as the early years in Virginia's Jamestown settlement. In Communist China and the Soviet Union, many were compelled to participate against their will in collective farms or communes.

The communitarian approach to remaking society contrasts with two other approaches. First, individualism is a theory of reform holding that each individual must improve himself or herself for the wider society to gradually improve.

This approach to reform was held by many nineteenth-century evangelical reformers such as the famous minister and founder of the American Temperance Society Lyman Beecher (1775–1863). Communitarians, in contrast, advocated an immediate and drastic, but peaceful, remaking of society by the wider communities, not just individuals.

Communitarians also rejected another path to social change—revolution. Revolution is a sudden and often violent overthrow of the existing social order. The violence and class conflict of the French Revolution (1789–1799) frightened nineteenth-century Americans. Furthermore, change through revolution is often forced upon many. Communitarians such as Shakers and the followers of Robert Owen insisted people must voluntarily adopt the new social order for success to be achieved.

The communal societies discussed below predate the revolutionary, socialist, or communist theories of Karl Marx (1818–1883) and Friedrich Engels (1820–1895). Modern, often negative, perceptions of communism and class struggle originated in the late nineteenth and early twentieth centuries. The oppressive, communist governments of the Soviet Union and China have colored modern views. However, before the late nineteenth and twentieth centuries, communal societies were viewed in a much more positive manner because of their historic associations with Christianity and medieval tradition.[3]

Christian traditions influenced most utopian societies in Western culture before the late nineteenth century. Biblical visions of Heaven, the promised land, and the millennium appeared consistently in European and American utopian experiments. Inspiration for collective sharing of economic resources was inspired by biblical descriptions of first-century Christian communities. The New Testament of the Bible suggested the earliest Christians established small communities in which goods were owned in common and shared among all members. The following verses from Acts appear frequently in the documents of communal societies.

> All the believers were one in heart and mind. No one claimed that any of their possessions was their own, but they shared everything they had. With great power the apostles continued to testify to the resurrection of the Lord Jesus Christ. And God's grace was so powerfully at work in them all that there were no needy persons among them. For from time to time those who owned land or houses sold them, brought the money from the sales and put it at the apostle's feet, and it was distributed to anyone who had need.[4]

> All the believers were together and had everything in common. They sold property and possessions to give to anyone who had need.[5]

Communism was also perceived as a positive experience practiced in a golden era located in the medieval past. Medieval communes were seen as places of freedom for rural peasants. Communes were self-governing towns that had made an agreement, or charter, with the local lord or king. This legal document established individual and economic freedoms for the inhabitants of the towns. In medieval communes and guilds, the citizens and members took oaths of mutual protection and assistance. Even medieval peasants were guaranteed certain rights to the land they cultivated.

Over the sixteenth and seventeenth centuries as a changing economy eroded these communal forms of mutual assistance, their existence in the past was idealized. The negative impact of industrialization on rural and village life in England and America caused many to nostalgically yearn for the idyllic golden age in the past. The realities of medieval inequality and poverty were conveniently forgotten.[6]

The Diggers or True Levellers

One hundred thirty-three years after Thomas More described his imagined model society, groups of English working people created their own real, but short-lived utopias. In 1649, the Diggers started cultivating unused land, hoping to provide economic support for the working poor of the nation. All were invited to join the effort; all who joined were promised food, drink, and clothes.

This movement took place toward the end of thirty years of bad harvests and rising food prices in England. The cost of living and taxes rose but wages of working people did not. The violent political and religious turmoil of the English Civil War (1642–1651) made already bad conditions even worse. When the armies were disbanded, soldiers joined the throngs of unemployed peasants who had lost their traditional rights to land through the enclosure of small holdings into the large estates of wealthy landowners.

The Diggers were not a single united group, but one of many movements protesting the conditions of the time. They referred to themselves as the "True Levellers" to distinguish themselves from the politically motivated Levellers who supported popular sovereignty, extended suffrage, equality before the law, and religious tolerance.

The most famous of these nine documented groups was established on St. Georges Hill near London, led by the commoner, Gerrard Winstanley. The English Civil War had bankrupted his tailoring business in London. Winstanley and fourteen coauthors published a pamphlet entitled *The True Levellers Standard Advanced* (1649) explaining their communal vision (see source 1).

The Diggers proposed that all of the uncultivated common land in England be improved through the application of manure (used as fertilizer) and farmed. They believed this effort would produce enough food to feed the unemployed and working poor of England. Through this communal effort and subsequent increase in food production, begging and crime could be ended and the price of land and cost of living reduced. The Diggers argued their effort could ultimately make England the wealthiest of nations.

The True Levellers Standard Advanced looked back to many centuries of utopian dreams, biblical traditions, and medieval customs protecting peasants' rights to the land. The text refers to the beginning of creation in the Garden of Eden when all were equal, the Promised Land of the Israelites, as well as the Golden Era of Saxon rule before the foreign Norman Conquest of 1066. They grafted contemporary radical Protestant views of economic equality onto the model of communism supplied by first century Christians.

Sadly, the Diggers' efforts to create a better life for working people ended in less than two years. The participants at St. George's Hill were harassed by the local lord and sued in court, and forced to abandon their efforts.[7]

The Shakers, or the United Society of Believers in Christ's Second Appearing

The Shakers began under the leadership of a former English Quaker, Ann Lee (1736–1784) in late eighteenth-century England. In 1776, their first communal village was established in Watervleit, New York. Over the next century, twenty villages were established in Maine, New Hampshire, Massachusetts, New York, Connecticut, and the frontier states of Ohio and Kentucky. Membership peaked at around six thousand members in the years prior to the Civil War. Membership declined after the war, and most of the villages closed in the late nineteenth and the early twentieth centuries. As of the publication of this book, only two living Shakers reside in Sabbathday Lake, Maine, the last active community.

The Shakers were millennialists, believing Jesus's one-thousand-year reign on Earth had already begun. The Shaker belief in the dual nature of God as male and female translated into communities where men and women were equal in matters of both religion and governance. Each Shaker community was led by men and women holding equal power and responsibilities. But the Shakers were not governed democratically. A clear hierarchy was established within and among the communities, with the ultimate authority centered in New Lebanon, New York. Female and male leaders were appointed, not elected.

Although men and women were considered equal, Shakers practiced strict segregation of the sexes. Male and female members worked, ate, and slept separately. Work duties were separate, but equal. Women worked at traditionally female occupations of food preparation and preservation, sewing, and cleaning; men performed traditionally male duties of farming and manufacturing. Celibacy, a perfectionist practice modeled upon the example of an unmarried Jesus and other biblical scriptures, was required.

The Shakers actively recruited new members. Adults seeking to join were required to deed their property to the community to be held in common by all. Married couples seeking to become Shakers agreed to live as brother and sister upon becoming Shakers, and their children were legally indentured to and raised by the community. Shaker communities also accepted foundlings, orphans, and children indentured to the society by non-Shaker parents. At age twenty-one, those raised in the village were allowed to officially join the community or depart.[8]

Shaker communities were especially appealing to nineteenth-century women. In the peak years, female members outnumbered male members. By the early twentieth century, women made up from 83 to 88 percent of membership in the remaining Shaker villages.[9] Women chose to join for religious reasons, as well as for economic and personal security. Women with children who became Shakers could be certain their children were fed and clothed until they became adults, even if both parents died. In an era when married women faced the often-deadly complications of childbirth, the celibate Shaker lifestyle provided a welcome alternative for many.[10]

The Shakers welcomed converts of African descent and created some of the earliest American interracial communities. At least nine black members lived in the northeastern villages, but the two communities in Kentucky, a slave state until after the Civil War, had the highest populations of people of African descent. Some became Shakers, others were temporary residents or were employed by the Shakers. Full integration and participation of black Shakers varied over the history of the group and from village to village.

At the Pleasant Hill community in central Kentucky, at least nine black community members had been enslaved before or at the time of their arrival. Those arriving as slaves to Shaker villages were freed through various means. An additional ten men and women of African descent living in the village were free upon arrival.[11]

The life of African American Shaker Justinian Cartwright at the village of South Union, Kentucky, illustrates the complicated relationships between races in utopian communities. In 1807, Cartwright was around seven years old when he arrived in the western Kentucky Shaker village. He was one of several enslaved people brought by owners interested in becoming Shakers. All young people in Shaker villages learned a trade; Cartwright worked in the blacksmith's shop alongside his owner's son.

By age nineteen, Cartwright was legally freed by the Shakers and chose to follow the Shaker faith and become a full member of the community. According to the journals of the village, he and a white Shaker, Lucinda Smith, had a child in 1829. He confessed he had broken the rule of celibacy, asked forgiveness, and chose to continue as a Shaker. However, in 1835, he and Lucinda and their child left the village and moved to New Harmony, Indiana.[12] While the Owenite experiment in New Harmony had officially closed eight years before the Cartwright family arrived, New Harmony continued to be a center for liberal thought and education. This may have influenced Cartwright's choice to move.

John Humphrey Noyes and the Oneida Community

The Oneida Community, also called the Oneida Perfectionists, was founded by charismatic John Humphrey Noyes in New York in 1848. Noyes's theology was similar to other contemporary religious communities based on biblical communism and Christian perfectionism. The group, like the Shakers, believed Jesus had already returned to Earth and established his millennial kingdom. Noyes's theology was also dualist, but the two aspects of God were defined as a male father and son, not an equal male and female as interpreted by the Shakers.

Noyes's philosophy of complex marriage rejected established marriage traditions of his era. Noyes argued traditional marriage was a form of selfish love competing with the individual's love for God and community. But, unlike the Shakers, he did not believe celibacy was the answer. Instead, all adult members of his community were married to each other. Theoretically, individuals were allowed to choose consenting sexual partners based on mutual attraction. Marriage and children, as well as the community's financial resources, were communally shared (see figure 4.3).

Noyes's writing portrayed his community as an egalitarian, free-love utopia. In reality, Noyes was an authoritarian and paternalistic leader. His approval was required for the relationships in his complicated system of free love, thus limiting individual choice. Noyes was not a feminist. In his theology, men were superior to women, just as God was superior to the son, Jesus. He often criticized the women's rights movement of his era, noting problems could be remedied by changing relations between the sexes rather than granting women the right to vote.

Oneida Community women may have had more personal freedoms than those in the wider culture. They cut their hair short and wore a Bloomer-type outfit with shortened skirts and full pants to allow for easier movement. Within the community, men and women shared work and chores, but men dominated the income-producing work and financial decisions. Boys were educated to the college level, while girls ended formal schooling at age twelve.[13]

At its peak in the 1870s, the Oneida community had around three hundred members sustained by various business ventures, including the sale of traps used by hunters and table cutlery. The community ended in 1880 due to internal conflicts over leadership and practices. Most of its members formed a joint-stock company based on the community's economic assets. This organization was the forerunner of Oneida Limited, the modern manufacturer of tableware.[14]

The Harmony Society or the Rappites

The Harmony Society, also referred to as the Rappites, was founded in 1805 in western Pennsylvania. This religious society was one of the many German Pietist groups breaking from the Lutheran Church in Europe in the seventeenth and eighteenth centuries. The original village consisted of over three hundred German immigrant families, followers of George Rapp (1757–1847), who sought a new location to practice their faith.

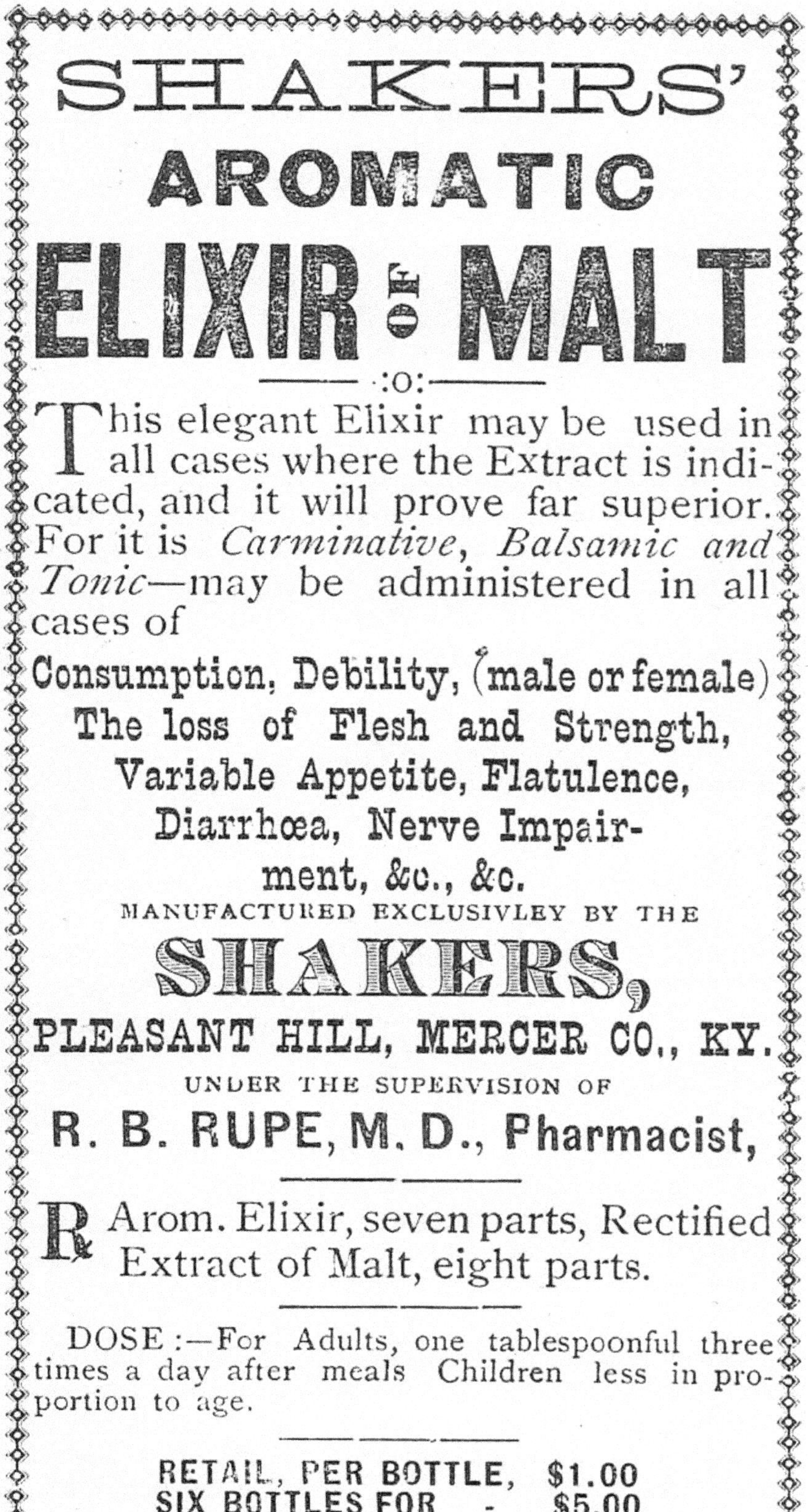

Figure 4.2. The Shakers grew, processed, and sold dozens of botanical ingredients used in nineteenth-century medicines. Of the sixty-four plants recommended by Samuel Thomson, at least sixty were sold by the Shakers. Several Shaker communities also sold their own unique remedies. In 1879, in an effort to solve financial problems, the Pleasant Hill Shakers were convinced to make and sell Aromatic Elixir of Malt by what was probably a trio of swindlers. They invested in the scheme, but sales were disappointing.

Label of Aromatic Elixir of Malt, Pleasant Hill Shakers, late 1800s. (Courtesy of Archives of Shaker Village at Pleasant Hill, Kentucky); J. Worth Estes, "The Shakers and Their Proprietary Medicines," Bulletin of the History of Medicine *65, no. 2 (Summer 1991): 162–84.*

All property in their six-thousand-acre settlement was held in common, modeling the communities of first-century Christians. Members lived according to strict religious rules. Celibacy was recommended but marriages were allowed. The Rappites believed Jesus would return in their lifetimes to begin the era of the Millennium.

While women were not equal by modern standards, the Rappites allowed women more rights than the wider nineteenth-century American society. Women had equal property rights, and although they could not hold leadership positions, they were allowed to vote in community elections. Women could choose to marry or remain celibate, and they had the same right as men to leave their spouses or the Society. Boys and girls were educated. But women did perform all of the traditionally female work in addition to working in the communities' industries and farms.[15]

The Rappites were financially successful, investing their communal labor and resources in farming, mills for grain and hemp, and the manufacture of textiles, shoes, hats, and other products for sale. Their location near the Ohio River enabled them to distribute their products to a wide market. Like the Shakers and the Oneida Community, the Rappites lived separate from the outside world for religious purposes, but also recognized that their long-term success required economic interaction with the wider community.

In 1815, the group sold their holdings in Pennsylvania, purchased twenty thousand acres on the Wabash River in southern Indiana, and created a new village, named Harmony. The group continued to prosper, new German immigrants joined, and their numbers grew to a thousand. In 1825, after ten years in Indiana, they sold the entire village to Robert Owen and moved back to western Pennsylvania. The Rappites built a third village there, named Economy, on the Ohio River.

As was the case with many communal societies, disputes arose over communal property ownership, religious practices, and leadership. But despite these challenges the Harmony Society continued to exist until 1905. Its final dissolution was a result of financial problems and internal disputes.[16]

Robert Owen and New Harmony

Robert Owen (1771–1858) was a British factory manager and owner turned reformer. He contributed a secular vision to the nineteenth-century communitarian movement. Most early nineteenth-century communities, such as the Shakers, Rappites, and Oneida Perfectionists, were founded on unique religious doctrines and had hierarchical systems of government. Owen was similar to these groups in that he believed economic success could be achieved through a communal economy.

However, Owen envisioned a secular and more egalitarian society. Owen believed the key to the success was quality education starting from a very young age. Through education, Owen believed the three oppressive elements of the contemporary culture could be destroyed—ownership of private property, irrational systems of religion, and the strict conventions of marriage (see source 3).

Robert Owen's vision for a cooperative community originated from his experiences improving conditions for workers at his textile factories in New Lanark, Scotland. Before coming to America, Owen had implemented numerous reforms over twenty-five years at New Lanark, one of the largest cotton-spinning complexes in Britain. Owen improved housing and provided a school for the children of millworkers and educational opportunities for the adults.

New Lanark's village store became an early example of the consumer cooperative. Consumer cooperatives are businesses owned by the members with the goal of serving the needs of members first, rather than merely making a profit. At New Lanark, the cooperative store provided quality goods to workers and profits funded additional innovations in the community.

Owen was searching for an opportunity to put his ideas into practice outside his Scotland factories. In 1820, he wrote to George Rapp, requesting information about the Rappites and sharing information about his own philosophies (see source 2). In August 1824, a representative of the Rappites traveled to Scotland and offered to sell the Indiana community, fully equipped for community life for about seven hundred people, to Owen. The property had much more acreage and was just a quarter of the price Owen had estimated he would need to establish a community in Britain. Seven weeks later, he was on a ship to the United States.[17]

In America, he hobnobbed with politicians, reformers, and intellectuals on the East Coast to publicize and promote his venture and even addressed the United States Congress. Like many other utopian visionaries, he visited the Shakers to observe their community. By December, he reached Harmony, Indiana, and officially purchased the village. Then he went back to the eastern United States to publicize his new community and recruit members. He returned to New

Harmony in April 1825, stayed until June, and departed for London, leaving his son, William Owen, in charge. Owen left without giving clear instructions on how to organize the community.

Owen returned six months later, in January 1826, with a group of scientists, educators, and artists to carry out his vision of improved education. But disputes over how to best govern the community, how to organize work responsibilities, the role of religion, and how to admit new members overcame Owen's cooperative vision. By 1827, the communal experiment officially ended, even though many of its members continued to live in the community. Owen left New Harmony permanently in June 1827, just two years after the experiment began. New Harmony was the best known of sixteen communities established between 1825 and 1829 based upon Owen's socialist vision.

Owen returned to England after spending a large part of his fortune on the American experiment. He helped to found early British trade unions and cooperative societies offering grocery, insurance, education, and other services to their consumer owners.

Nashoba, Fanny Wright's Owenite Community

Fanny Wright's Nashoba was one of the communities inspired by Robert Owen's secular communitarian ideals. Her short-lived settlement in the western Tennessee wilderness added radical new elements. Wright hoped to end slavery in the United States. Community members ignored societal condemnation of interracial and premarital relationships between men and women. In the twenty-first century, Nashoba appears to be an interracial utopian community far ahead of its time, but the reality may have been much different.

Wright was inspired by visits to Owen's New Harmony and impressed by the economic success of the Rappite and Shaker communities. She visualized a model farm where slaves worked cooperatively to earn money to buy their freedom while being educated for their future lives. She believed the economic success of this farm would provide enough profits to purchase the freedom of its slave members and pay the bills to transport the former slaves to a foreign colony such as Liberia or Haiti. She hoped this economic model would prove to be so financially feasible that it would be adopted and practiced across the nation, thus ending slavery.

Wright purchased a large tract of land on the Wolf River in Shelby County, Tennessee, near Memphis, in the fall of 1825 and officially founded the community of Nashoba in 1826. Instead of the one hundred slaves she visualized, the community only had fifteen enslaved people and a handful of white and free black residents. Wright and Robert Dale Owen, a son of Robert Owen, traveled to England to solicit donations and volunteers.

In Wright's absence the community suffered public scandal when its white leader, James Richardson, publicized his relationship with a free black woman living in the community. The article, published in an antislavery newspaper, also revealed the slaves were beaten and denied access to their children in an effort to "reform" their work habits and attitudes.[18]

Meanwhile, in England, Wright managed to recruit Frances Trollope, who arrived in late 1827 with her children, intending to join the community. But Trollope left disappointed after spending only ten days in Nashoba (see source 4). In early 1828, Wright tried to salvage the reputation of the community by publishing an explanation of her vision. Her views of slavery were already controversial in the South, but her published condemnation of marriage and promotion of interracial relationships just made the situation worse. Wright revealed that marriage was not recognized in her community, women and men could freely choose their partners, black and white children were educated together, and the mixing of black and white people was acceptable.[19]

By the summer of 1828, Wright abandoned her utopian Nashoba. The enslaved residents remained in Nashoba and in slavery two more years. In 1830, Wright arranged for these eighteen adults and sixteen children to be freed and transported to Haiti.

The enslaved residents in Nashoba were never treated as equals. Communal labor could not support the community without the large donations that failed to materialize. Too much work, too few people, and not enough money were problems within the community. In addition, radical ideas turned the public against Nashoba.

However, Wright's memorable career did not end with Nashoba. She and Robert Dale Owen became coeditors of the activist newspaper the *New Harmony Gazette* (later renamed *Free Enquirer*) and continued to spread Owenite ideas in America. Her life and opinions on marriage, women's rights, and race were scandalous when measured by early nineteenth-century standards. "Fanny Wrightism" became a derogatory reference invoked as a warning against freethinking, especially by those advocating traditional roles for women (see chapter 2, source 3).[20]

Figure 4.3. Redefined family relationships required redefining family homes. The Mansion House was constructed in 1861 to meet the needs of the unique social structure of the Oneida Community. This double image is a stereograph, a card created to view through a stereoscope. These popular devices created a three-dimensional image for a viewer. Viewing images of famous landmarks, distant locations, major events, and entertaining scenes was a popular pastime in the late nineteenth century.
Stereograph, Oneida Community, between 1860–1930. (Courtesy of Library of Congress)

Theme Three: Reinterpreting Roles and Relationships in Utopia

Utopias redefine the real world. Governments, economies, religion, societal expectations, and individual roles are often discarded, reimagined, or turned upside down. In the eighteenth- and nineteenth-century communities described above, the rights, responsibilities, and expectations of workers, women, and people of color were redefined. Some communities allowed men and women to associate with each other in ways not common in the wider society. Others promised freedom and equality for black members. The conventional views that women and the enslaved should work for free but men should be paid were called into question. The labor of all was seen as equal for the success of the community.

The reevaluation of male-female relationships of these communities ranged from celibacy to free love. These practices provided both advantages and disadvantages for community members, especially for the women.

Celibate Shaker women and Oneida Community women who chose not to have children avoided health problems and risk of death associated with childbirth. Throughout history, complications of pregnancy and childbirth were the leading cause of death for women.[21] Most nineteenth-century women in the wider society gave birth numerous times. They were also responsible for the heavy burdens of child care, household labor, and other work needed for the survival of the household. Women in communitarian societies had distinct advantages in these areas. Children were cared for and educated with community resources. Because the chores of daily life were shared by all within the community, women had more free time for leisure or to pursue individual interests.

Women were assumed to be equal to men, in varying degrees, in many of these communities. Women gained opportunities to be more than a wife, mother, and housekeeper. The Shakers and the Nashoba community were founded by women. The Shakers gave women equal roles in spiritual matters, governance, and the work of the community. Education of both boys and girls was an important part of these American communities.

The Owenites championed equality of the sexes, and Robert Owen criticized a social order in which women were viewed as property and were forced to marry for financial support. Official statements and publications of the Owenites proclaimed that education and work for males and females should be equal. Owenites and Rappite women were allowed to vote. Owenite and Oneida women wore practical clothing allowing for freedom of movement.

On the other hand, these ideals were not always the daily reality. While both the Nashoba and Shaker communities welcomed enslaved and free African American members, white members struggled to overcome nineteenth-century attitudes toward race. In Nashoba, slaves continued to be treated as slaves, even though the goal was freedom.

The Owenites often failed to reject nineteenth-century assumptions about the opposite natures of men and women. In New Harmony schools, education was supposed to be equal, but boys prepared for traditional male jobs outside the home while girls' education focused on teaching "female employments" such as sewing, cooking, and washing.

In New Harmony, an "equal" workload meant women often worked two jobs—one in the traditionally male occupations for the economic benefit of the community, the other as a household laborer. In the spirit of equality, employing household servants was not allowed.[22] Upper-middle- and upper-class wives at New Harmony, accustomed to more leisure time and servants who performed the domestic chores, were especially dissatisfied.[23]

In the Oneida Community, Noyes claimed men and women were equal. But in reality, a small group of men chosen by him made the major decisions for the community, allowing only older and more spiritual women to advise. The freedom to choose sexual partners was not as it appeared; Noyes orchestrated these choices with strict rules, from which he often benefited.[24]

Many communities struggled to deal with unhappy wives and husbands. Some were unwilling members of the community who had no choice but to remain when their spouse joined. Spouses refusing to join might be abandoned, which was especially problematic for women.

Mary Dyer was a disillusioned and unwilling Shaker who followed her husband to the Enfield, New Hampshire, community. She subsequently left her husband and the community but was forced to leave her children behind. Despite years of legal battles and public criticism, she never regained custody of her children (see source 5). Most of the female members of the Owenite experiments had little choice in joining the community; they came with husbands who made the decision for the entire family.

The maxim that one person's utopia is often another's dystopia applies to most intentional societies to some degree. Most declare and publicize lofty goals. Some communities achieve those ideals for at least some of their members. Others groups become abusive or deadly. For example, Jim Jones, leader of the Peoples Temple, and David Koresh of the Branch Davidians promised a panacea to the world's problems. But both exploited and oppressed their followers and ultimately led to over nine hundred deaths in Guyana in 1978 and seventy-six deaths in Waco, Texas, in 1993.

Theme Four: Utopias and Geography

Utopias are places, imaginary or real. The intentional communities described above and the imagined utopias described in the previous chapter demonstrate themes of geography, particularly the themes of location, place, movement, and interaction with the environment.

Promises of freedom and plenty in the New World made America attractive to settlers looking to fulfill utopian dreams. America became the embodiment of an unspoiled arcadia, earthly paradise, and promised land. Like Cockaigne, food was plentiful and work, relationships, and social classes could be redefined. Land was plentiful and cheap in comparison to Europe. The American Constitution guaranteed new religious and political freedoms.

Many migrated to establish religious communities in a new location. The Rappites, along with many other groups not discussed above—the Hutterites, Moravians, Amish, Mennonites, members of the Zoar Village and the Amana Colonies—emigrated from Europe to practice their faith. A small group of English Shakers arrived in 1776 and began recruiting new members in the same year that old political traditions were overturned.

The American Constitution also allowed for the growth of secular communities. Robert Owen and Fanny Wright, both from Britain, established secular communities on America's frontier. Rugby, Tennessee, was founded in 1880 by English author Thomas Hughes for the younger sons of Britain's upper-class families who were not allowed to inherit the family's resources (see figure 4.4). The philosophies of Frenchmen Charles Fourier and Étienne Cabet were put into practice by Americans in secular Associationist and Icarian communities.

Americans also created their own, unique communities across the United States. American John Humphrey Noyes was just one of many American utopian visionaries. Brook Farm and Fruitlands in Massachusetts were founded by

American transcendentalists. The 1888 novel *Looking Backward: 2000–1887* by American Edward Bellamy inspired socialist experiments in growing cities.

As the frontier moved west, so did visionary communities. Joseph Smith, the founder of Mormonism, established new forms of religious practice and new communities. The Mormons moved west as followers increased and criticism from the wider culture grew. American counterculture communities, many with California origins, such as The Farm, thrived in the 1960s and 1970s.

The successes and failures of all of these communities depended upon where they settled. Economic success depended on the natural resources of the area and access to transportation routes. Interaction with other communities and the wider world encouraged the spread of their ideas, recruitment of new members, and the growth and transformation of the societies. Community members traveled throughout the United States and Europe to visit each other, sell their products, defend their practices, and attract new members.

Figure 4.4. Men and women of the Rugby Community in front of the Rugby Lawn Tennis Association clubhouse, 1880s. Rugby, Tennessee, was founded in 1880 for the younger sons of Britain's upper-class families. Its founder, author Thomas Hughes, intended for the community to be a cooperative, agrarian community with cultural opportunity, religious freedom, and strict temperance. Around three hundred people lived in the community at its height in the mid-1880s. But the lack of interest in farming by members along with a typhoid epidemic and other factors caused the community to decline by 1900. Historic Rugby welcomes visitors today. Like many other historic communitarian sites, the village is dedicated to preservation and education.

Photograph, "Men and Women of Rugby Community, Tennessee, 1880s." (Courtesy of Historic Rugby Inc., www.historicrugby.org/)

Members unhappy with a utopian community departed for the outside world or joined other communities, spreading ideas across the map. For example, brothers John and Richesson Whitbey became Shakers at the Pleasant Hill, Kentucky, village in 1817 and 1816, respectively. While a Shaker, John was inspired by the ideas of Robert Owen and advocated for unwelcome changes in his Shaker community. He and his brother left the Shakers in 1825 and joined the New Harmony community. John published an account criticizing the Shakers (see source 6). Richesson Whitby subsequently left New Harmony to join the Nashoba community and married Fanny Wright's sister Camilla.[25]

Promoters, detractors, and tourists journeyed among the various communities reporting what they saw in letters and published accounts. Nationally distributed newspapers and magazines published stories about these experiments, both positive and negative (see sources 5, 6, 7, 8). Utopian societies need the acceptance of their neighbors to survive. As stories of real and fabricated abuses spread, public opinion could turn against an intentional community, as with Fanny Wright's Nashoba or Joseph Smith's Mormon community in Nauvoo, Illinois, in 1844.

Conclusion

The Land of Cockaigne was an imaginary world. Working people temporarily imagined a world turned upside down where instead of work, hunger, and poverty, they were rewarded for idleness with endless food, drink, and entertainment. But these dreams did little to change religious, social, or political realities.

The seventeenth-century English Diggers, nineteenth-century American communities described above, and many others took action, hoping to permanently remake the wider society around them. The Diggers rejected a society that ignored hungry, unemployed, and displaced working people and proposed a solution to end poverty. Other groups rejected established religions, followed unique theologies, allowed any faith, or promoted atheism. They all rejected or redefined elements of their wider culture.

In the late nineteenth century, the growth of industrial capitalism, the development of new technology, and the shift in focus away from community ideals and toward the individual changed the nature of utopian experiments. Karl Marx's reinterpretation of communism as a class struggle overshadowed early nineteenth-century socialist ideals.

Communism was violently imposed on entire nations by Joseph Stalin and Mao Zedong in the Soviet Union and China in the twentieth century. Adolf Hitler envisioned and imposed a new society in Nazi Germany and destroyed over six million people he wanted to exclude from his new world order. Utopian dreams became dystopias; millions died through famine, genocide, and war.

A renewed interest in small-scale utopian communal living took place in the 1960s. Counterculture or hippie communes rejected twentieth-century expectations of marriage, gender, nuclear family, consumerism, and mainstream middle-class culture. In the 1980s, the New Age movement turned away from attempts at communal living. Instead, the focus was on the individual and renewing the self rather than a whole society. Old concepts that focused on individual spiritual renewal from Eastern religions and astrology were revived, modified, and combined with modern psychology.[26]

In the twenty-first century, the concept of utopia has been embraced by the marketing and advertising industry. Products and experiences are hawked to consumers, promising to make life better and dreams come true. Literary utopias have been abandoned in favor of dystopias of worldwide epidemics, war, climate disasters, asteroid collisions with Earth, domination by machines and computers, totalitarian governments, and zombies—all reflecting our fears instead of our dreams.

In the Classroom

The themes illustrated in this chapter are equally relevant to modern culture. In the United States, tensions continue to exist among religious denominations and between religious and secular ideologies. The role of government in the economy and the distribution or redistribution of wealth are still hotly debated. And the ideals, goals, or rights of individuals or groups continue to merge with or diverge from perceived goals of the nation as a whole. These matters were debated in nineteenth-century media; those same debates continue today.

The histories of these groups, the essential questions of this chapter, and the primary sources below can prompt students to consider their stance on these enduring conflicts, the source of their opinions, and how these issues are portrayed in the modern and historical media.

Utopian societies also provide an excellent context to explore civic relationships, rights, and duties. Ask students to discuss how the goals of any community—classroom, school, family, city, or nation—can be successful or fall short of providing for the daily needs or fulfilling the hopes of all of its members. What are the responsibilities of the members of the community to effect change?

In the communities described above, the experience of some was dystopian, rather than utopian. Depictions of dystopia are far more prevalent in twenty-first-century popular culture than literary utopias or movements to establish utopian communities. *Fahrenheit 451* (1953), *Nineteen Eighty-Four* (1949), *The Handmaid's Tale* (1985), *The Giver* (1993), and *The Hunger Games* trilogy (2008–2010) are just a few published examples. Countless more dystopias are portrayed in television, movies, and video games.

Dystopian fears shift over time, reflecting anxieties of the age. Ask students to analyze the prevalent themes in their favorite accounts of dystopia. Invite students to examine how the destructive elements of dystopias reflect modern fears.

Finally, make the study of utopias place based. Locate intentional communities in your state or region. Explore the history of the communities' founding, members, growth, and decline. Analyze how geography impacted their stories. Investigate the archives, often housed on location or in nearby historical societies or university archives. If possible, organize field trips or encourage students to visit historical intentional communities.

Figure 4.5. The Shakers and other nineteenth-century communitarian societies generally welcomed visitors to their villages. Some visitors may have been interested in joining the community, others were tourists. The three women on the right in this photograph were visitors to the Pleasant Hill Shaker Village. Brooms were one of the products manufactured by the Shakers for sale to the public. Many historical utopians are historic sites today and continue to welcome visitors. Pleasant Hill is the largest restored Shaker village, with a restaurant, hotel, historic tours, and other activities.
Photograph, Shakers and guests at Pleasant Hill, Kentucky, late 1800s. (Courtesy of Archives of Shaker Village at Pleasant Hill, Kentucky)

The Primary Sources

A wealth of primary sources survive to reconstruct the history of nineteenth-century communitarian societies. Primary source analysis requires that the author, audience, purpose, and type of source be considered. However, students may struggle when considering what type of source is represented without additional information. The excerpts below represent five different categories of primary source material, each with unique characteristics. All of these sources, with the exception of source 2, appeared in the media of the nineteenth century. Nineteenth-century media literacy equates with twenty-first-century primary source analysis.

Sources 1 and 3 represent manifestos publicly declaring the motives or views of the founder or community. Such statements are usually intended to recruit new followers and reinforce the beliefs of current members. Descriptions of religious doctrines also belong in this category. Day-to-day reality or religious practice may have fallen short of these visionary statements.

Source 2 is an example of the many documents created or received by members of communities, providing an insider view of daily life in the community. Large collections of these documents survive in archives. Some have been transcribed and published by historians; many others are in their original, usually handwritten, format. Letters, journals, diaries, membership records, financial records, and many other documents represent the economic, legal, religious, social, and personal matters of the community as a whole and of the individuals within the community.

Sources 5 and 6 are published accounts of apostates. Apostates are community members who become disillusioned and leave the group. The accounts of apostates must be carefully scrutinized and compared to other surviving sources. Their authors may exaggerate or fabricate incidents to garner public support, turn public opinion against the community, or sell more copies of their work.

Sources 4 and 7 are examples of travel literature in which outsiders describe their visits to utopian communities. While these types of primary sources are valuable, their purposes must be considered. Authors of travel literature hoped to sell their books or articles or encourage more visitors to the sites described. Therefore, accounts may depict the ideal or entertaining qualities of a location and omit negative realities. Tourists are notorious for seeing what confirms their assumptions or the accounts of previous travelers to the same location, while ignoring the rest.

Source 8 is an example of a newspaper article that would be called an editorial today. Editorials are written to persuade, not just to present the facts. The author is very critical of several reform movements, inciting fear by claiming the entire society is threatened by their existence. The author contrasts "subversive" reforms with idealized depictions of the wider society's cultural expectations for men, women, and families. One can't assume all readers agreed with the author.

Source 1

Excerpt from *The True Levellers Standard Advanced* (1649) by Gerrard Winstanley and others.[27]

> Take notice, that England is not a free people, until the Poor without land have a free allowance to dig and labor the **Commons**, and so live as comfortably as the landlords that live in their **enclosures**. For the People have not laid out their monies, and shed their blood, that their landlords, **the Norman power**, should still have liberty and freedom to rule in tyranny through lords, landlords, hudges, hustices, bailiffs, and state servants. Instead, the Oppressed should be set free, prison doors opened, and the Poor people's hearts comforted by a universal consent of making the Earth a **common treasury**, that they may live together as one **House of Israel**, united in brotherly love into one spirit; and having a comfortable livelihood in the community of one Earth their Mother.

Commons—land belonging to the whole community.

enclosures—process in which traditional plots of land belonging to peasants were deeded to and controlled by one landowner, usually the local lord.

the Norman power—Winstanley negatively depicted the lords as foreign powers who ignored the egalitarian medieval traditions of England. He is referencing the transfer of power from English rulers to the foreign, Norman government of William the Conquerer in 1066.

common treasury—a biblical reference to early Christians who shared their economic resources.
House of Israel—a biblical reference used to describe England's working poor as God's chosen people.

Source 2

Excerpt from a letter to George Rapp from Robert Owen requesting information about the Harmony Society.[28]

New Lanark, August 4, 1820
The Rev. Mr. Rapp
Most Worthy Sir:

Having heard much of your society, and feeling a peculiar interest respecting it I am induced to solicit a correspondence with you, and the expectation of procuring a correct account of your establishment.

My first attention was called to it by some travels published in America by **Mr. Melish** who in 1811 visited the original settlement near Pittsburgh—and who gave many details which to me appeared to promise many important future advantages. You have since had an opportunity of creating a second settlement [*in Indiana*]. . . . And the particulars of the result of these two experiments would be of real value to me in order to ascertain the practical inconveniences which arise from changes to society from a state of private to public property. . . .

[*Owen asks Rapp to send information about Harmony to his residence in New Lanark, Scotland*]

There is a colony here [*in Scotland*] of about 2,400 persons who I have already placed under new circumstances preparatory to a still more improved arrangement from which incalculable advantages to all classes may be expected. I am now in the midst of preparing a further development of the system. . . . And it will give me pleasure to send you a copy of it. . . . In the meantime I send you copies of such works as I have already published. . . .

Robert Owen

[*no answer from George Rapp to this letter has been found*]

Mr. Melish—author of an 1818 published travel account to the United States.[29]

Source 3

Excerpt from a speech by Robert Owen at Public Hall, New Harmony, Indiana, April 27, 1825.[30]

I have come to this country, to introduce an entire new state of society; to change it from the ignorant, selfish system, to an enlightened social system, which shall gradually unite all interests into one, and remove all cause for conflict between individuals.

The individual system has heretofore universally prevailed; and while it continues, the great mass of mankind must remain, as they comparatively are at present, ignorant, poor, oppressed, and, consequently, vicious, and miserable. Even though it has lasted for numberless ages, virtue and happiness cannot be attained, nor can man, strictly speaking, become a rational being.

Until the individual system shall be entirely abandoned, it will be useless to expect any substantial, permanent improvement in the condition of the human race. The current system ever has been, and must ever remain, directly opposed to universal charity, benevolence and kindness: until the means were discovered, and can be brought into practice, by which universal charity, benevolence and kindness, can be made to pervade the heart and mind of every human being, a state of society in which "peace on earth and good will to man" shall exist, must remain unknown and unenjoyed by mankind.

Source 4

Excerpt from *Domestic Manners of the Americans* by Frances Trollope, 1832.[31]

Frances Trollope (1779–1863) was an English writer and friend of Fanny Wright. Wright recruited Trollope to join the Nashoba community. Trollope traveled to the United States and up the Mississippi River in 1827 with her children, intending to join the community. She left disappointed after spending only ten days in Nashoba. The following excerpt opens on Trollope and her household journeying by wagon with an African American driver in the muddy western Tennessee wilderness from Memphis to Nashoba. Even though she planned to join a community meant to free enslaved black people, her descriptions reveal the racial prejudices of the wider nineteenth-century culture.

The next day we started again, and the clear air, the bright sun, the novel wildness of the dark forest, and our keenly awakened curiosity, made the excursion delightful, and enabled us to bear without shrinking the bumps and bruises we encountered. We soon lost all trace of a road, at least so it appeared to us, for the stumps of the trees, which had been cut away to open a passage, were left standing three feet high. . . . The forest became thicker and more dreary-looking every mile we advanced, but our ever-grinning Negro declared it was a right good road, and that we should be sure to get to Nashoba. . . .

Miss Wright's powerful beliefs enabled her, accustomed to all the comfort and refinement of Europe, to imagine not only that she herself could exist in this wilderness, but that her European friends could enter there, and not feel dismayed at the savage aspect of the scene. Each building consisted of two large rooms furnished in the most simple manner; nor had they as yet collected round them any of those minor comforts which ordinary minds class among the necessaries of life. . . . Her whole heart and soul were occupied by the hope of raising the African to the level of European intellect. . . .

The only white persons we found at Nashoba were my amiable friend, **Mrs. W**, the sister of Miss Wright, and her husband. I think they had between thirty and forty slaves, including children, but when I was there no school had been established. Books and other materials for the great experiment had been collected, and one or two professors engaged, but nothing was yet organized. I found my friend Mrs. W in very bad health, which she confessed she attributed to the climate. This naturally so much alarmed me for my children, that I decided upon leaving the place with as little delay as possible, and did so at the end of ten days.

I do not exactly know what was the immediate cause which induced Miss Wright to abandon a scheme which had taken such possession of her imagination, and on which she had expended so much money; but many months had not elapsed before I learnt, with much pleasure, that she and her sister had also left it. I think it probable that she became aware upon returning to Nashoba, that the climate was too hostile to their health. All I know farther of Nashoba is that Miss Wright found it impossible to free the slaves so she accompanied her slaves to Haiti, and left them there, free, and under the protection of their president.

Mrs. W was Camilla Whitbey, whose husband, Richesson, was the brother of John Whitbey, excerpted below. Both were first Kentucky Shakers, then New Harmony Owenites. Richesson Whitbey subsequently joined the Nashoba community.

Source 5

Excerpts from the account of Mary Dyer, a Shaker apostate.[32]

Mary Marshall Dyer (1780–1867) was one of the best known anti-Shaker writers. She and her husband and five children joined the Enfield, New Hampshire, community in January 1813. Over the next two years, she became dissatisfied with Shaker life. She left in January 1815, even though her husband chose to remain a Shaker. Her children had been legally indentured to the Shakers, and the community refused to allow them to leave the community with their mother. Over the following fifty years, Dyer gave pubic lectures and wrote newspaper articles, pamphlets, and books criticizing the Shakers.

Dyer's work is an example of publications by apostates from communal societies. Apostates are people who abandon a faith and attack the group to which they once belonged. Some complained they had been tricked into joining, others disagreed with the religious practice, or disliked living separate from family members. The goal of apostate publications was to turn the wider community against the organization. In some cases, mobs formed that attacked members or the property of the community. Dyer and another Shaker apostate separated from her children, Eunice Chapman, led such a mob against the Enfield Shakers in 1818.[33]

The first three excerpts below are Mary's words. The final excerpt is a legal deposition from a neighbor, taken as part of Mary's legal suit against the Shakers.

He [*Joseph Dyer*] said, unless I would be a Shaker, he would carry the children to the Shakers and leave me. My sorrow was great—it was the first time I ever knew him discontented with me. I offered to live with him as a slave if he would let me live with my children; but no. Oh! The sorrow at the thought of being separated from my family.

The Shakers . . . treat them ever so cruelly [*children*]. They are not bound to educate the children, nor to give them anything when they become of age, nor to keep them in case they should through misfortune become unprofitable to them—they might cast them upon the town, and they are under no penalty. The Shakers are very severe with children.

Oh, what heart could endure it? I felt the sorrows of an afflicted parent, bereft of her children; my case was desperate; to go any farther from my children was distressing, but to stay [*with the Shakers*] was death.

Testimony of Moody Rich: I, Moody Rich . . . depose and say, that I was present to see Joseph Dyer and Mary Marshall united in marriage in the year 1799—that they lived happily together, until he joined the society of Shakers. . . . I went . . . with his wife to Enfield, to endeavor to prevail upon him to treat her like a wife, and to permit her to see and converse with her children, but was unsuccessful. He utterly refused to live with her, and assigned no reason but his having joined that society. They would not suffer her to converse with her children even in their presence, although urged by her in the most pressing and effecting manner. . . .

I have frequently seen and conversed with [*Joseph*] Dyer, and tried to persuade him to grant his wife [*financial*] support, but he persisted in declaring, "that he considers the marriage contract between them dissolved because of his union with the Shakers. He did not consider himself bound to grant her any support whatever. . . . She is now living upon the charity of her friends and relations. Previous to joining the Shakers, Joseph Dyer possessed handsome property which she had contributed her full share of labor, and industry and economy to acquire.

Source 6

Excerpt from *Beauties of Priestcraft; or, A Short Account of Shakerism* by John Whitbey, a Shaker apostate.[34]

John Whitbey criticized the hierarchical organization of his Shaker community at Pleasant Hill, Kentucky, after learning about the more egalitarian philosophies of Robert Owen. He unsuccessfully tried to reform his community. He and his brother, Richesson, left the Shaker community in 1825 and joined the Owenite New Harmony community. Richesson Whitbey subsequently left New Harmony to join the Nashoba community and married Fanny Wright's sister Camilla.

The 4th of July is already past, and MENTAL INDEPENDENCE is declared; and many feel themselves now engaged in an irrevocable war against the combined powers of superstition, mystery, and mental bondage; though the weapons of their warfare are not made from iron, steel, nor brass. [*Instead the weapons are*] good works, pulling down superstition, false imaginations. . . . The wonderful effects of the New System [*Owenism*], time alone can only unfold. But how lovely would it be, to see nations of people gathered together in small communities of equality, enjoying all the blessings of mental liberty! Where superstition, priestcraft, hypocrisy, anger, emulation and distinction, could never come, nor storms of malice ever blow; but where knowledge, liberty, sincerity, kindness, tranquility and equality forever dwell, and soul-refreshing gales of union and love enrapture the innocent inhabitants.

Source 7

Excerpt from "The Shakers," *Harper's New Monthly Magazine*, July 1857.[35]

Many articles appeared in the nineteenth-century press praising or criticizing utopian communities of the era. The Shakers welcomed tourists and guests, hoping to promote their religion and lifestyle to recruit new members and counter the negative stories from apostates and critics.

The following excerpts are from a magazine article promoting tourism. The author first visited Lebanon Springs, a mineral water spa, before arriving at the Mount Lebanon, New York, Shaker community.

As I walked into the village, serenity and peace seemed to pervade the air! Placidity dwelt upon every face I met. And there were children, too, with cheerful faces peering out from their broad hats and deep bonnets, for they were all dressed like old men and women. I marveled at the sight of children in that isolated world of bachelors and maidens, forgetting that it was a refuge for orphans who are unsheltered in the stormy world without.

I am convinced, from observation and from the testimony of their immediate neighbors, that they live in strict accordance with their beliefs. They are hospitable to strangers, and kind and benevolent toward the community around them. In morals and citizenship, they are above reproach; and they are loved by those who know them best. They have been ridiculed and maligned by those who must have been either ignorant or wicked; for it seems impossible for any candid man, after becoming acquainted with their character, to regard them otherwise than with deepest respect. Surely the sacrifices of the dearest interests of earth [*marriage*] are sufficient guarantees of their sincerity.

Source 8

Excerpt from "Subversion of the Family," *New York Times*, February 20, 1879.[36]

Nineteenth-century utopian communities were often criticized and perceived as a threat to society because of their unique religious doctrines and interpretations of marriage. Early Mormons and the Oneida Perfectionists practiced forms of plural marriage; shockingly different from what was considered normal by their contemporaries. Note that the author also criticized "free-lovers and radical social reformers," a reference to the many different forms of social reform of the era, which included Owenites, Associationists, feminists, and abolitionists.

So far as society at large is concerned, the real mischief is to be found in the false social theory that aims at the subversion of the family and the destruction of those domestic ties upon which the virtue and stability of the people so largely depend. . . . The home is at the foundation of all that is strong in Anglo-Saxon civilization, and gives Christianity much of its power and influence. The sacred relations of husband and wife and a parent and child furnish the basis for a cultivation of the domestic and civic virtues which give strength to the character of a people and promote the progress and well-being of the State. . . . Nothing can take their place. The attempt to substitute a wider social organization for the family has thus far been a ghastly failure. Perfection of body and mind and moral nature . . . are the philosophy of "Father" Noyes, but its practical effect on the men and women subjected to its influence is physical and intellectual deterioration. To relegate the children of a community to the care and nurture of its old women, regardless of parental ties, is to break asunder the bonds that develop the noblest traits of character. . . .

Mormonism, Oneida "Perfectionism," and all the vagaries of free-lovers and radical social reformers, are based on the destruction of family, and threaten society with degeneracy. They degrade women and render them unfit for the highest functions of motherhood, which are not merely to bring children into the world . . . but to also give them the care and nurture that set their growth and development in the right direction. . . . They not only deprive women of this loftiest of tasks, but take it away from them, making their lives barren and desolate, and depriving their offspring of one of the chief advantages intended for them by nature. . . .

Whatever tends to desecrate the sanctity of home life, and weakens domestic ties and obligations, threatens society with degradation. There is enough degradation without these groups forming into societies and adopting an active propaganda. These groups are openly hostile to the improvement of the race, though they profess to be preparing the way for the millennium. Society has a right to protect itself against such insidious undermining.

Whether legislation directly intended for the suppression of a community such as Oneida would be justified is a matter of doubt. It is certain that any attempt to inflame popular feeling against it with a view to bringing about a violent and lawless dispersion of its members would be altogether wrong. But the hollowness of its pretensions as a means of reforming and perfecting human nature can be exposed, and the falseness of its philosophy should be impressed upon the people. Common sense and the better instincts of society should be arrayed against it, and every inducement offered so these groups die out.

Notes

1. Attributed to Max Beerbohm and cited by Lyman Tower Sargent, "The Three Faces of Utopianism Revisited," *Utopian Studies* 5, no. 1 (1994): 1, http://www.jstor.org/stable/20719246.
2. Sargent, "The Three Faces of Utopianism Revisited," 14–15.
3. Arthur Bestor, *Backwoods Utopias* (Philadelphia: University of Pennsylvania Press, 1950), 3–4.
4. Acts 4:32–35 (NIV).
5. Acts 2:44–45 (NIV).
6. Dennis Hardy, *Alternative Communities in Nineteenth Century England* (New York: Longman, 1979), 2–3.
7. Christopher Hill, *The World Turned Upside Down: Radical Ideas during the English Revolution* (New York: Viking Press, 1972), 86–120.
8. Judith A. Graham, "The New Lebanon Shaker Children's Order," *Winterthur Portfolio* 26, no. 4 (Winter 1991): 218, http://www.jstor.org/stable/1181346.

9. Stephen J. Stein, *The Shaker Experience in America* (New Haven, CT: Yale University Press, 1992), 256.

10. D'Ann Campbell, "Women's Life in Utopia: The Shaker Experiment in Sexual Equality Reappraised—1810 to 1860," *New England Quarterly* 51, no. 1 (1978): 23–38, doi:10.2307/364589.

11. Vickie Cimprich, "Free and Freed Shakers and Affiliates of African Descent at Pleasant Hill, Kentucky," *Register of the Kentucky Historical Society*, 111, no. 4 (Autumn 2013): 489–523, http://www.jstor.org/stable/24641051.

12. Kit Firth Cress, "Black Shakers at South Union, Kentucky," *Kentucky Review* 12, no. 1 (Fall 1993): 79–95, https://uknowledge.uky.edu/cgi/viewcontent.cgi?article=1086&context=kentucky-review; "Dictates of Conscience and Feelings of Humanity," *People of Color at South Union, 1807–1860* (Museum exhibition at South Union Shaker Village, South Union, KY, October 2018); Rebekah Brummett, "Beyond Far Off Happenings in Far Off Places," paper presented at Kentucky History Education Conference, Frankfort, Kentucky, July 12, 2018; 1840 United States Federal Census, New Harmony, Posey, Indiana, p. 310 reproduced on Ancestry.com from Sixth Census of the United States, 1840. (NARA microfilm publication M704, 580 rolls), Records of the Bureau of the Census, Record Group 29. National Archives, Washington, DC.

13. Rosemary Radford Reuther, "Utopian and Communal Societies," in *Our Own Voices: Four Centuries of American Women's Religious Writing*, ed. Rosemary Skinner Keller and Rosemary Radford Ruether (San Francisco: Harper San Francisco, 1995), 354.

14. Jean Harvey Baker, "Women in Utopia: The Nineteenth-Century Experience," in *Utopias: The American Experience*, ed. Gairdner B. Moment and Otto F. Kraushaar (Metuchen, NJ: Scarecrow Press, 1980), 56–71; Lawrence Foster, *Women, Family, and Utopia: Communal Experiments of the Shakers, the Oneida Community, and the Mormons* (Syracuse, NY: Syracuse University Press, 1991); Robert S. Fogarty, *Dictionary of American Communal and Utopian History* (Westport, CT: Greenwood Press, 1980), 156.

15. Donald E. Pitzer and Josephine M. Elliott, "New Harmony's First Utopians, 1814–1824," *Indiana Magazine of History* 75, no. 3 (September 1979): 248–49, http://www.jstor.org/stable/27790387.

16. Paul H. Douglas, "Town Planning for the City of God," in *Utopias: The American Experience*, eds. Gairdner B. Moment and Otto F. Kraushaar (Metuchen, NJ: Scarecrow Press, 1980), 103–25; Fogarty, *Dictionary of American Communal and Utopian History*, 142–43.

17. Arthur Bestor, *Backwoods Utopias* (Philadelphia: University of Pennsylvania Press, 1950), 102–10.

18. For a complete account and transcripts of the texts that shocked America, see Celia Morris Eckhardt, *Fanny Wright: Rebel in America* (Cambridge, MA: Harvard University Press, 1984), 108–40.

19. Fanny Wright, "Explanatory Notes on Nashoba, Part 2," *New Harmony Gazette*, February 6, 1828, transcribed in *Jacksonian Miscellanies*, no. 13, April 8, 1997 (accessed June 2018), http://www.jmisc.net/jm970408.htm.

20. Lori D. Ginzberg, "'The Hearts of Your Readers Will Shudder': Fanny Wright, Infidelity, and American Freethought," *American Quarterly* 46, no. 2 (June 1994): 195–226, http://www.jstor.org/stable/2713338; Sheree Sampson, "Reclaiming a Historic Landscape: Frances Wright's Nashoba Plantation in Germantown, Tennessee," *Tennessee Historical Quarterly* 59, no. 4 (Winter 2000): 290–303, http://www.jstor.org/stable/42627588; Helen L. Heineman, "'Starving in That Land of Plenty': New Backgrounds to Frances Trollope's Domestic Manners of the Americans," *American Quarterly* 24, no. 5 (December1972): 643–60, http://www.jstor.org/stable/2711664; Gail Bedermanm, "Revisiting Nashoba: Slavery, Utopia, and Frances Wright in America, 1818–1826," *American Literary History* 17, no. 3 (Autumn 2005): 438–59, http://www.jstor.org/stable/3567902.

21. Complications of pregnancy and childbirth still rank between the sixth and eighth leading causes of death for women between fifteen and thirty-four years of age. Melonie Heron, "Deaths: Leading Causes for 2009," *National Vital Statistics Reports* 61, no. 7 (October 26, 2012): 22 (accessed July 2018), https://www.cdc.gov/nchs/data/nvsr/nvsr61/nvsr61_07.pdf.

22. Carol A. Kolmerten, "Unconscious Sexual Stereotyping in Utopia: A Sample from *The New Harmony Gazette*, 1825–1827," in Gairdner B. Moment and Otto F. Kraushaar, eds., *Utopias: The American Experience*, 72–86; Carol A. Kolmerten, *Women in Utopia: The Ideology of Gender in the American Owenite Communities* (Bloomington: Indiana University Press, 1990), 67, 101.

23. Kolmerten, *Women in Utopia*, 79.

24. Lawrence Foster, "Free Love and Feminism: John Humphrey Noyes and the Oneida Community," *Journal of the Early Republic* 1, no. 2 (Summer 1981): 165–83, http://www.jstor.org/stable/3123007.

25. Church Roll Book of Pleasant Hill (Pleasant Hill, KY: Pleasant Hill Manuscript Collection), 209; Robert Dale Owen, *Threading My Way: Twenty-Seven Years of Autobiography* (New York: G. W. Garleton & Company, 1874), 300–304, https://archive.org/details/twentysevenyear00owengoog.

26. Donald E. Pitzer, "Introduction," in *America's Communal Utopias*, ed. Donald E. Pitzer (Chapel Hill: University of North Carolina Press, 1997), 3–13, eBook Collection, EBSCOhost.

27. Gerrard Winstanley et al., *The True Levellers Standard Advanced* (1649), transcribed by Sandra Jones (Renascence Editions, University of Oregon, 2002), accessed June 2018, https://scholarsbank.uoregon.edu/xmlui/bitstream/handle/1794/863/levellers.pdf?sequence=1&isAllowed=y.

28. Karl J. R. Arndt, comp. and ed., *A Documentary History of the Indiana Decade of the Harmony Society, 1814–1824*, vol. 2 (Indianapolis: Indiana Historical Society, 1978), 89–90.

29. John Melish, *Travels through the United States of America, in the Years 1806 and 1807, and 1809, 1810, and 1811* (Philadelphia and Belfast, 1818), 321–22, https://archive.org/details/travelsthroughun00meli.

30. Robert Owen, "Oration Containing a Declaration of Mental Independence" (speech at Public Hall, New Harmony, Indiana, July 4, 1826), accessed June 2018, http://www.indiana.edu/~kdhist/H105-documents-web/week11/Owen1826.html.

31. Frances Trollope, *Domestic Manners of the Americans* (London: Whittaker, Treacher, & Co., 1832), 42–45, https://archive.org/details/domesticmannerso00troliala/page/n7.

32. Mary Dyer, *A Brief Statement of the Sufferings of Mary Dyer* (Boston: William S. Spear, 1818), 4, 10, 12, 22–23, https://archive.org/details/briefstatementof00dyer/page/n5.

33. Elizabeth A. De Wolfe, *Shaking the Faith: Women, Family, and Mary Marshall Dyer's Anti-Shaker Campaign 1815–1867* (New York: Palgrave Macmillan, 2002), 4–5, 86–87.

34. John Whitbey, *Beauties of Priestcraft: Or, a Short Account of Shakerism*, in *Writings of Shaker Apostates and Anti-shakers, 1782–1850*, vol. 2, ed. Christian Goodwillie Routledge (London: Routledge, 2016), 364. Originally published in *New Harmony Gazette* newspaper in 1826.

35. "The Shakers," *Harper's New Monthly Magazine* (July 1857): 166, 177.

36. "Subversion of the Family," *New York Times* (February 20, 1879): 4, ProQuest Historical Newspapers.

CHAPTER FIVE

Cemeteries and Tombstones

Friends! For your Epitaphs I'm griev'd
Where still so much is said,
One half will never be believ'd
The other never read.

—Alexander Pope, 1736[1]

Essential questions:

- What can cemeteries and tombstones as primary source artifacts reveal about
  - o changing attitudes toward death and commemorating the dead?
  - o social class, status, and roles of men and women? of the wider community?

Cemeteries and tombstones are primary-source artifacts chronicling the stories of individuals and societies. Respectful disposal of human remains and commemoration of the dead have been a part of the human experience since prehistoric times. Some practices have changed little over time. Others have evolved in response to a changing world. The history of cemeteries and tombstones reveals what is old and what is new and why those changes occur. Exploring this story of continuity and change to better understand the present is the greatest reward of thematic social history.

The history of cemeteries and their monuments from the ancient world to the twentieth century is the focus of this chapter. Cemeteries and tombstones are primary source artifacts that, like other death-related objects or texts, reveal social, religious, cultural, artistic, economic, political, or technological trends over time. Funerals, burial or cremation, and permanent memorials have always been costly. How generations have planned for these final expenses is also examined.

A plethora of words have been used in European and American culture to describe places for the dead. In the twenty-first century, the word *cemetery* is commonly used to describe the location of burial sites and memorials to the dead. Cemeteries tend to be places in or near towns and cities, with grass and trees in park-like settings and graves and monuments memorializing the deceased. Our modern concept of a cemetery is historical, grounded in developments since the Industrial Revolution. However, the word *cemetery* is a remnant from ancient cultures. We may use similar words for the dead, but appearances and meanings shift over time.

The Greek prefix *necro-* means death. The ancient Greeks used the word *necropolis* for monuments and graves of the deceased.[2] These "cities of the dead" were located outside the walls of cities, separated from the homes of the living. This separation reflected religious and cultural beliefs about corpses, spirits of the dead, and the afterlife. In the nineteenth century, the word *necropolis* was revived and redefined to describe a new type of planned cemetery *within* the city, such as the Glasgow Necropolis in Scotland.

The word *cemetery* also derives from ancient Greek; literally translated, it means "sleeping place."[3] The Greeks used this word in its literal sense and occasionally as a reference for burial sites. Early Christians in the first four centuries of the Roman Empire adopted the Greek word to describe burial sites, symbolizing Christian beliefs about life after death. To Christians, death is a temporary state, like sleep, to be followed by an afterlife in heaven.

Traditionally, Christianity has also stressed burial over cremation because of the belief one's actual body will be resurrected from the grave at the end of time. Early Christians interred the bodies of their deceased in networks of underground chambers, called catacombs in Latin.[4] Pagan Romans also used catacombs for burial or for cremated remains.

Other words used to reference burial places today have ancient roots and reveal ancient traditions. The word *mausoleum*, describing an imposing building commemorating the burial place of an important person, originated in fourth-century BCE Hellenic history.[5] The word is derived from the name of Mausolus, a Persian king. His monumental shrine, the Mausoleum at Halicarnassus, was designed by Greek architects and considered one of the Seven Wonders of the Ancient World.[6]

A sepulcher, defined as a tomb or burial place, also has distinct religious associations with the cave where Christianity's Jesus was buried.[7] Today, Jerusalem's Church of the Holy Sepulcher commemorates this holy tomb. A potter's field, known as the burial place for the poor or for strangers, also has a Christian association. This phrase derives from a biblical description of the place where Judas, the man who turned Jesus over to the Romans for crucifixion, was buried.[8]

Gravesites, burial practices, and the descriptive words of pagan Germanic, Celtic, and Scandinavian cultures varied. As these groups converted to Christianity, they slowly adopted the Christian practice of interring bodies in special areas designated and consecrated by the Catholic Church. Terms such as *churchyard*, *burying ground*, or *graveyard* designated these Christian sites. *Tomb*, *crypt*, *vault*, *chantry chapel*, *charnel house*, and *ossuary* describe the ultimate destination of human remains and memorials to the deceased in the Middle Ages and Early Modern eras.

The word *cemetery* was revived in the eighteenth century during the Enlightenment and Neoclassic Revival of Greek and Roman art and architecture. Ancient words and symbols reappeared, but reflected new interpretations of religion and death. In the early twentieth century, technology and cultural changes resulted in yet another new name for a burial place—the *memorial park*.

In recent decades, the ancient Latin word *columbarium* has come back in use to describe modern trends.[9] In ancient Rome, columbaria were large community gravesites, sometimes underground, with niches for ashes, and sometimes bodies, of the deceased. Today, as cremation becomes more popular, modern cemeteries are building columbaria to house cinerary urns. Ancient practices and symbols have become modern again.

Cenotaph, a word derived from Greek and Latin, describes an empty tomb commemorating a person whose body was located elsewhere.[10] Today, the word usually refers to a public memorial commemorating those who died in a war.

Cemeteries, old and new, are a very small slice of a much larger theme—death and dying. Preparing for death, performing the rituals immediately before and after death, preparing and disposing of the body of the deceased, and choosing ceremonies and memorials, as well as beliefs about what happens after death and how survivors react to death are all cultural phenomena. These rights and rituals have similarities and distinct differences across time, place, and cultures.

Thanatology, a word coined in the nineteenth century, describes the wide-ranging field of the study of death.[11] Thanatologists study death, its causes, and cultural beliefs surrounding it. This field of study encompasses biology and medicine; philosophy, ethics, and theology; literature, art, and music; history, archaeology, and politics; and psychology, sociology, and anthropology. However, a complete history of human beliefs and practices associated with death is far too broad for the limited scope of this book.

The focus of this chapter is public cemeteries and tombstones. The overview of the history of burial places presents two obvious problems. First, its scope is limited to practices in Europe and the United States. A lack of space, not a lack of importance, prevents an exploration of thousands of years of historical customs from around the globe. Second, the chapter emphasizes widespread and general trends. Unfortunately, many unique cultural practices are not examined. Hopefully, you and your students will continue to explore historical and contemporary global and cultural variations of memorializing the deceased. Customs associated with death tell a universal story of both continuity and change.

SHATTUCK'S SON—FRANK CHESTER. SORREL PATH.

"Thou cam'st—what pleasures new and bright
Thy coming gave:
Thou'rt gone—and every young delight—
Is laid in thy dark grave!
The sigh will rise, in manhood's spite—
The tears will roll;
Grief round me draws her mental night—
And desolates my soul."

MAGOUN MONUMENT. GRIEF. FIR AVENUE.

"A Household's tomb: to Faith how dear!
A part have gone; part linger here;
United all in love and hope,
Our household still!

Together we shall sleep;
Together may we rise;
And sing our morning hymn,
One household still!"

Figure 5.1. **The park-like settings of new nineteenth-century rural cemeteries became tourist destinations, promoted in travel literature of the era. Tourist guidebooks were published for the large cemeteries of major cities, describing monuments of interest and advising the visitor of the most beautiful vistas. This page from an 1854 guidebook for Mount Auburn Cemetery in Boston features monuments for a child and a mother and daughter along with the inscriptions from the stones.**
Nathaniel Dearborn, Dearborn's Guide through Mount Auburn, *1854, 26. (Courtesy of Archive.org)*

Ancient Egypt c. 3100 BCE–641 CE

Ancient Egyptian culture spanned over three thousand years, and rituals related to death, mummification, burial, and memorial architecture evolved over time. However, the custom of interring grave goods along with the body was common throughout ancient Egyptian history. The desert climate helped preserve bodies, grave goods, and papyrus texts. This wealth of material, along with the survival of massive tombs and mortuary complexes of pyramids, mastabas, temples, and other funerary monuments of the wealthiest, may have distorted our modern view of ancient Egyptian culture. It is easy to mistakenly assume ancient Egyptians were more interested in death than life and everyone was mummified, encased in gold, and entombed in a pyramid.

In the earliest centuries, the dead of all social classes were buried in sand pits that naturally dehydrated the body. Over time, mummification, funerals, and burial rituals became more complex, but many details of this evolution of practice are unknown. The mummification of the wealthy was more complicated, and thus more expensive, than the process used for average people. Mummification of Egyptians of all social classes continued into the Roman and Christian eras in the second and third century. The closure of pagan temples by Emperor Theodosius (r. 379–395), the invasion of Egypt by Muslims in the seventh century, and the subsequent acceptance of Islam caused a permanent break with the ancient custom of mummification.[12]

Mummification of the dead may seem strange today, but it is not so different from the modern chemical embalming process used in the funeral industry to preserve bodies. Preserving a corpse with chemicals was not common in ancient, medieval, or early modern Europe. Embalming was only occasionally used to preserve corpses for medical study, not to prepare them for a funeral and burial. Bodies were allowed to naturally decompose in the grave. Modern chemical embalming was introduced during the American Civil War so the bodies of soldiers could be shipped home. This expensive nineteenth-century process became the foundation of the modern commercial funeral industry.[13]

Ancient Greece c. 1600 BCE–c. 600 CE

The stone monuments of wealthy and powerful ancient Greeks made a lasting impression on centuries of Western memorial traditions. Mycenaean bee-hive shaped tombs called tholoi, Greek cremation urns, upright slabs similar to modern tombstones called stelai, and carved statues or two-dimensional reliefs were used as memorials for the cremated ashes or bodies of the dead over the centuries of ancient Greek culture. In the Hellenistic period (323 BCE–31 BCE), giant funerary monuments were constructed by the powerful. It was in this period that the tomb for Mausolus was erected, from which the word *mausoleum* is derived.[14]

The lavish monuments of wealthy sixth-centuries BCE Athenian families were tall stelai, upright slabs of marble or other stone with inscribed epitaphs and realistic or idealized reliefs depicting the deceased. These ancient tombstones inspired the ancient Romans and, a thousand years later, Renaissance artists.

In the eighteenth and nineteenth centuries, wealthy Europeans collected ancient funerary monuments and other antiquities, displayed them in homes and museums, and used them as models for their own tombstones. Eighteenth- and nineteenth-century white marble monuments in England copied the style of Greek stelai. The deceased were depicted in flowing drapery with decorative designs imitating the Greek originals. These copies were not painted but remained in the white and gray tones of natural stone. However, in ancient times, stelai were painted in bright colors.[15]

Much less is known or has survived from the graves of average ancient Greeks. Both burial and cremation were common, but uncertainty surrounds the forms of lasting memorials that were used.

Ancient Rome c. 700 BCE–500 CE

The ancient Romans, like the Greeks, located burial sites outside the city walls. Tombs, catacombs, and cemeteries lined the roads on the outskirts of Roman cities and towns. Some were grand structures, like the enormous mausoleum of Emperor Augustus, constructed in a forty-year period before he actually died. The poorest Romans left no memorial. Their bodies were buried in large pits outside the city along with dead animals and other refuse. Average working people had simple stones or other types of memorials in community burial sites above or underground. Many joined associations that provided a form of life insurance to pay for the cost of a funeral and permanent memorial.

Archaeologists and historians studying ancient customs are challenged by the tiny fraction of surviving funerary remains. The total population of the city of Rome is believed to have been between 10.5 and 14 million. But only about 1.5 percent of those graves have been studied. From graves archeologists have examined, information is gathered from the human remains, memorials, or grave goods. Information about non-elite groups whose lives are generally undocumented, such as freed slaves and children, is especially valuable.[16]

Like the ancient Greeks and modern Americans, the Romans practiced both burial and cremation. Cremation was predominant until the early second century when burial became increasingly popular. Older scholarship assumed the influence of Christianity caused the shift from cremation to burial, but most modern scholars argue that changes in customs cannot be explained so easily. Ancient burial customs appear to be more closely tied with family traditions than religious doctrine.[17]

Cremated remains of average people were memorialized on grave altars and placed inside chests of stone, lead, terracotta, or wood, or in urns, vases, or pots. The remains were housed above ground in cemeteries or in buildings with niches, such as community mausoleums or columbaria. Flowers, food, or drinks were offered to the dead; lamps or candles were lit on certain days; and family occasions were celebrated at the grave. Many of these facilities also had dedicated spaces for funeral-related ceremonies and annual memorial banquets.[18]

By the second century, a chronic shortage of burial space led to an increasing number of interments in shared sarcophagi or niches, previously used for a single deceased person. Extensive underground catacomb networks were constructed in the suburbs outside of the city to meet the demand for the growing population. These have been estimated to extend for over six hundred miles and contain space for six million dead.[19]

The passages of catacombs were lined with loculi, rectangular niches just large enough for a body and stacked six or seven high, similar to bunk beds. After a body was placed in the niche, the opening was sealed with tiles or slabs of stone or terra-cotta. Symbols and inscriptions were placed on the niche cover or medallions or other items were set in the mortar beside the panel to memorialize the deceased.[20]

By the early third century, most bodies were placed directly in the niches along the walls of catacomb corridors. For those who could afford the expense, the body was placed in a sarcophagus, a carved stone box similar to a coffin that also served as a monument. By the fourth century, the ancient Greeks were also using stone sarcophagi. Privileged families were entombed in sarcophagi in private, decorated rooms within the catacombs.[21]

As the Roman Empire declined, old monuments of all types were pillaged and reused to build homes, churches, and new gravesite memorials. Pagan Roman sarcophagi were reused for Christian saints in the early Middle Ages, reflections of a period of economic decline when transportation systems, trade networks, and skilled craft industries of the Romans were destroyed. The reuse of old monuments in new contexts is not unusual. Ancient Egyptian dynasties reused, reinscribed, and repurposed the antique monuments of previous dynasties. Reuse of the monuments and symbols of previous cultures served to associate admired qualities of the old regimes with the goals of the new civilization.[22]

The Middle Ages c. 500–c. 1500

While burial became more prominent in the late Roman Empire, the funeral and commemorative traditions of non-Roman groups such as the Celts and Germanic tribes varied widely. Some groups cremated the dead, such as the Anglo-Saxons between the fifth to the seventh century. The Norse practiced both cremation and burial. Other groups buried the dead, individually or in groups, in mounds, cairns (stacks of stone), cists (a coffin or curial chamber made of stone or a hollowed tree), or barrows (long mounds of earth). The inclusion of grave goods was common.

As Christianity spread throughout Europe from the third to the twelfth century, burial slowly became standard practice. Recent scholarship has demonstrated that burial practices of families and social groups did not abruptly shift upon conversion to Christianity, but evolved over time. Local family and community funeral and commemoration traditions remained prominent for centuries after Christianity was adopted.

For example, the people of England had mostly converted to Christianity by the early seventh century but evidence indicates the Church had little influence over local burial practices until the eighth and ninth centuries.[23] Early medieval crosses, sarcophagi, or other surviving memorials often have both Christian and pagan symbols. The first documented mention of burial in a churchyard comes from the mid-eighth century.

As the influence of the Catholic Church grew, people were generally buried in or beside their parish church. Not surprisingly, power, money, and status mattered in medieval burial and commemoration. Two medieval traditions of burial and commemoration seem strange to many modern Americans—burial within a church and removal of the bones to a charnel house or ossuary for storage.

Over the centuries of the Middle Ages, the purpose of a church as a site for worship was transformed. Churches also served as indoor graveyards with memorials to the wealthy, powerful, or famous. The most desirable locations for burials were nearest to the relics of the saints, located in the main altar of every medieval church. For example, Westminster Abbey in London contains the bodies, ashes, or cenotaphs of over three thousand people dating from its construction in the thirteenth century to modern times.

In the earlier Middle Ages, the remains of clergy; royalty; and, over time, the nobility were likely to be located inside the church in the floor, along the wall, or crypt of the church. Corpses were placed in stone sarcophagi or under stone or metal slabs covering a grave located in the floor. These memorials were often carved with epitaphs, effigies of the deceased, and symbols of the family.

By the end of the Middle Ages, up to half of the dead were buried in the church. Over time, lesser nobility and even wealthy merchants demanded to be buried within the church. Chantry chapels were dedicated spaces within a larger church or built adjacent to the church to house the dead whose families could afford the expense. Technically, a chantry was a donation to pay for the religious service of Mass to be performed for the soul of the deceased. These services for the dead often took place in chantry chapels.

Chantry chapels often became private spaces because their construction or decoration was paid for by wealthy families who hired the most prestigious artists of their era to decorate these chapels.[24] Since many European churches have been in use for centuries, graves inside the church represent a hierarchy of rank and status as well as changing artistic and architectural styles. The tension between the functions of the church for religious worship and the pressures to use the interior space for burial and memorials is very evident.

The sixteenth- and seventeenth-century Renaissance Medici Chapels, adjacent to the fifteenth-century Church of San Lorenzo in Florence, Italy, are an example. These chapels were constructed to house the tombs and holy services for members of the Medici family. They also serve as extravagant memorials to wealth and power and examples of the revival of ancient sculpture and mortuary forms by artists and architects such as Michelangelo.

Over the centuries, the Catholic Church attempted to limit these indoor burials to only the holiest people or members of royal families. But burial within a church was also a business ensuring the economic stability of churches. Indoor burial space and endowments for religious ceremonies for the dead came at a price; a price well worth it for those seeking religious and social prestige.

Burial within the church decreased significantly with the Reformation, but church crypt burials continued for those who could afford the space. In sixteenth-century Reformation England, Parliament prohibited payments for services for

Figure 5.2. In the Middle Ages, corpses were shrouded in fabric and placed directly into the grave. The wealthiest were interred inside the church or in its underground vaults. This image from a fifteenth-century manuscript depicts burial in a consecrated churchyard with the exposed bones of those previously buried. These were symbolic, reminding viewers they would also face death. Cross-shaped grave markers with triangular tops are depicted in the background.

"Office of the Dead," in Book of Hours, *Yates Thompson 3, f. 201v, c. 1440–1450, https://bit.ly/2BQS6lB. (Courtesy of the British Library)*

the dead and the crown confiscated the endowments left in chantry funds. These laws greatly reduced the vast wealth of ninety churches, over one hundred religious hospitals for pilgrims or the sick, and over two thousand guild and private chantry endowments.[25]

The medieval graves of those who could not afford burial inside the church were located in the churchyard in an area declared holy by a priest. Burial in churchyards was limited to baptized Christians. Unbaptized children, heretics, lepers, those expelled from the Church by excommunication, and Jews were not allowed to be buried in the consecrated ground near the church. Even simple ceremonies and burial spaces for average people required fees to be paid to the church. Most medieval graves of average people had no permanent marker.

Bodies of the deceased were placed directly in the ground. Over the centuries, as churchyards were filled, burial space was reused again and again. After bodies decomposed, the bones were exhumed and placed in vaults under the church or special buildings near or adjacent to the church. By the twelfth and thirteenth centuries, charnel houses or ossuaries, vaults for storing human bones, were common. This practice continued in parts of Catholic Europe until the nineteenth century.

The Saint Louis Cemeteries, opened in New Orleans, Louisiana, in the late eighteenth and early nineteenth centuries, featured above-ground burial vaults with spaces intended for multiple uses. As the vaults filled, the skeletal remains were moved to an ossuary at the bottom of the larger family vault or to a communal space.[26]

Holy Innocents' Cemetery and its charnel house in Paris, a burial ground used since the twelfth century, contained the remains of over one million people. The need for burial space was so high that corpses were not allowed to remain in the soil for more than a couple years. In 1780, the pressure of its overworked soil caused the collapse of basements in adjacent apartment buildings. The cemetery was closed, and Paris began a program of cemetery reform.

The secular ossuary of the Paris Catacombs was established and contains the remains of millions relocated from crowded Paris cemeteries. First, the bones of at least six million people were transferred from the city's cemeteries to the Paris Catacombs, former mines turned into an underground ossuary. Second, Paris opened a new style of civic cemetery, inspiring a movement in cemetery design called the rural or garden cemetery. This new concept in the burial and commemoration of the dead spread across Europe and to the United States in the early nineteenth century.[27]

Reusing cemetery space and moving human remains is shocking to many modern Americans. Many customs of gravesite veneration are relatively new, developing in the nineteenth century. Today, various state-level laws make the disturbance or relocation of cemeteries, graves, grave markers, and human remains an illegal act.

American Burial Customs

Native American burial customs varied over time and place and were impacted by different environments, social structures, and spiritual beliefs. Above-ground burials in trees, scaffolds, canoes, or boxes on stilts were common among groups on the plains or in the Pacific Northwest. Other groups such as those along the Mississippi River used permanent earth mounds for corpses or cremated remains. Some tribes buried remains in earthenware urns. As Native Americans came into contact with Christian missionaries and European settlers, many of their burial and memorial customs evolved.[28]

Americans often imagine European colonists arriving in the New World and making a distinct break from the late medieval cultural traditions of Europe. However, these impressions are usually incorrect. While new cemetery and commemoration traditions developed over time, old ones continued to be practiced or reinterpreted for generations.

The earliest burials of European explorers and colonists in the New World took place in the closest convenient location, not in dedicated burial grounds. These early graves were either unmarked or marked with makeshift markers. As communities formed, permanent family and church graveyards were established.

In seventeenth-century New England Puritan Congregationalist colonies, burying grounds located near church meetinghouses were established. Since these communities allowed only one religious denomination, one burying ground served the entire community. Other colonies with an established faith supported by the colonial government and taxes, such as Virginia's Anglican establishment, created consecrated churchyards for burial of the faithful. As in Europe, those outside the faith were interred separately.

In the tradition of medieval churchyards, colonial burying grounds were not carefully tended with ornamental plantings like modern cemeteries. Graves were haphazardly placed and in some cases the space was leased as pasture for animals or other community events. Markers were constructed of wood or local stone, crafted locally, with names and dates and memento mori epitaphs or symbols reminding those passing that death was inevitable (see figure 5.1). In Virginia, where stone suitable for carving was not available, monuments were imported from England by those who could afford the expense.

An excavation of burial sites of the Jamestown colony revealed only twenty-five marked graves in the church and its burying ground. However, it is likely over three hundred burials took place in those early years. In the European tradition, two marked and numerous unmarked burials were excavated inside the church. Several of these contained the remains of more than one person. As in Europe, the two marked graves were of men of high status—a knight and a minister.

The establishment of family cemeteries in America broke with European traditions. In Europe, only elite families had family chapels, crypts, or mausoleums located on their property, but even this custom was not the norm. In the colonies, family graveyards were most common in the middle colonies and on the frontiers of white settlement. This new tradition was created by the challenges of long-distance transportation and sparse settlement patterns. Moving a corpse long distances from a remote plantation or frontier fort or cabin to a consecrated churchyard was impossible. The government of colonial Virginia recognized this problem and issued a law allowing family cemeteries in the 1620s.[29]

As various churches were established in new colonial communities, an accompanying graveyard was opened, but burial was generally restricted to members of that denomination. The family graveyard provided a solution for those who did not want, or were not allowed, burial in the consecrated ground of another Christian denomination.[30]

By the late 1700s and early 1800s, many of the graveyards in the oldest American cities were overcrowded. The cemeteries and vaults of large, urban churches were packed after over a century of use. New York's Anglican Trinity Church was consecrated in 1697. One hundred years later, contemporaries estimated over one hundred thousand were entombed in the vaults or buried in the cemetery. People were also concerned about the effect of overused cemeteries on the health of the living. Even though scientific theories of the spread of disease were not fully understood, many believed graveyards could exude disease-causing gas. As in Europe, demand to relocate existing graveyards and open new ones outside cities grew.[31]

In 1796, the town of New Haven, Connecticut, responded to these concerns by establishing a new burial place. The Old Burying Ground, located in the center of town and in use for 157 years, was crowded and chaotic. A new ten-acre graveyard located away from the congested parts of the town was leveled, enclosed, and divided into geometric lots available for purchase.

The location, landscape design, and monuments of New Haven Burying Ground represented a new era of civic pride, changing religious belief, artistic design, and cemetery governance and economics in America. The cemetery was not owned by a single family, church, or city government as in the past. Instead, it was established as a corporation of private lot holders, a model for future cemetery developers. Individuals or families purchasing a lot were allowed burial, and the chartered corporation was to cover the costs of future maintenance.[32]

In the New Haven Burying Ground and other new American cemeteries, old memento mori, grim symbols of death, fell out of favor, and new symbols from the Neoclassical Revival were preferred, such as urns and weeping willows. These shifts symbolized new views about death and dying.

Similar concerns about overcrowding and sanitation also inspired new styles of cemeteries in England and France in the late eighteenth century. In 1804, the first cemetery in the European garden or rural cemetery style was Père Lachaise, located on the outskirts of Paris. Père Lachaise was designed with winding paths, beautiful views, and dramatic monuments in ancient and modern styles. This movement in cemetery design referenced an idealized rural past while serving the growing urban population of the future.[33] The old symbols of death were being replaced by new symbols, discussed in the following chapter.

Rural or Garden Cemeteries: New Styles for a New Era

The nineteenth-century rural cemeteries were not remote places in the countryside. Instead, the descriptor *rural* or *garden cemetery* referenced locations on the outskirts of major cities that were landscaped, parklike settings. The landscape design was influenced by Romantic visions of a lost rural landscape and the gardening styles of the era. Burial was removed from the city but kept close enough so one could easily travel by carriage or urban trains to visit. Mourners and tourists were encouraged to wander among the tombs, consider the history of those buried there, enjoy the views, and appreciate the architecture of the monuments.

Figure 5.3. Funeral and burial traditions change over time, but many communities continue to follow traditional or unique customs. In this 1940 photograph from Kentucky, centuries old traditions were still followed. Four men carry the deceased in a homemade coffin to the family cemetery. By the 1940s, many Americans had turned preparing the body and funeral over to commercial funeral parlors, with burial in new memorial park cemeteries.
Marion Post Wolcott, photographer, "Mountain people carrying a homemade coffin near Jackson, Kentucky in Breathitt County," 1940. (Courtesy of Library of Congress)

Americans quickly adopted the new trend. Mount Auburn, founded on the outskirts of Boston in 1831, was the first American rural cemetery. Many other cities followed the trend. Examples include Laurel Hill in Philadelphia, founded in 1836; New York's Greenwood Cemetery, founded in 1838; Louisville's Cave Hill, founded in 1848; Hollywood Cemetery in Richmond, Virginia, founded in 1849; and Chicago's Graceland, founded in 1860. Smaller cities and growing towns followed the trend to showcase their own civic pride and economic success.

These new cemeteries broke with many graveyard traditions of previous centuries. First, the permanent family plot was central in the design. These monuments and their symbols reflected the importance of status, family, and religion and represented the nineteenth-century industrial economy, growing affluent middle and upper classes, and changing religious beliefs about the afterlife. Second, the overall design of the cemeteries reflected new trends in landscaping and became tourist destinations and badges of civic pride.

Rural cemeteries were business ventures, unconnected to a single faith or family. Like the New Haven Burying Ground, rural cemeteries were incorporated; lot-holders became shareholders. Generally, anyone with the money could purchase the space to be buried. This new style of management, separated from church and state, reflected the emerging business practices of a wider industrial economy. Rural cemeteries quickly became the desirable place to be buried and markers of social status for a community.

Family plots were the focus of sales in rural cemeteries. In the family plot, a large central monument dominated, with markers for individual family members surrounding it. Therefore, cemeteries reflected the wider nineteenth-century culture, in which home and family were central to the success of the nation. In life, mothers were to create a pleasant domestic environment and be models of kindness, virtue, religion, and charity. The realm of fathers lay outside the home, in the rational world of government and industry. Boys and girls were to learn these different, gendered roles so the success of the nation could continue into the future.

In death, the economic success of the father was communicated through large, imposing, and expensive monuments. The domestic talent and virtue of the mother were represented in sentimental and religious symbolism. The deaths of children were memorialized through symbols representing their innocence and angelic existence in the afterlife.

The overall design of rural cemeteries reflected several merging trends. Americans were nostalgic for a rural heritage perceived to be disappearing as cities grew. At the same time, they wanted to convey pride in the accomplishments of their cities and their most important inhabitants. Monuments to famous residents were prominent, providing a patriotic history lesson for the visitors. The remains of important founders were often relocated from an older burial ground to the new cemetery and marked with an impressive contemporary monument. For example, an imposing 1884 monument marks the relocated remains of Red Jacket, a Native American ally of the colonists during the Revolutionary War, at the entrance of the Forest Lawn Cemetery in Buffalo, New York.[34]

Landscaping and domestic gardening were especially popular pursuits in the late eighteenth and nineteenth centuries. This popularity influenced the creation of park-like designs, the landscaping of individual family plots, and the natural symbols on tombstones. Cemetery founders invested in massive earthmoving projects, altering the land to create picturesque ponds, terraces, and even hills and valleys. The roads within the cemetery were carefully planned curving avenues and paths with beautiful vistas. Plot owners were responsible for the plantings in individual plots. Family members, or professional gardeners hired by the family, planted flowers, shrubs, and trees and added ornamental fencing and benches.

Periodical literature, published travel accounts, and tourist guidebooks encouraged cemetery tourism. Visitors were directed to the graves of important people, unusual markers, and the loveliest views. Famous people visited rural cemeteries and published accounts of their visits, thus encouraging more visitors. An Englishman and friend of Nathaniel Hawthorne noted, "Cemeteries here are all the 'rage': people lounge in them, and used them . . . for walking, making love, weeping, sentimentalizing, and every thing in short."[35]

Tourists searched for examples of sublime, picturesque, and pastoral scenery, three aesthetic concepts popularized in eighteenth-century romantic literature. Pastoral scenes were characterized by a landscape tamed by humans—perfectly manicured gardens and idealized farm settings. *Picturesque* was a descriptor for spiritually uplifting beauty created by God and nature without the intervention of humans, featuring wildlife, majestic mountains, scenic rivers. The word *sublime* described nature at its most dangerous, with violent storms, raging rivers, and dramatic canyons and cliffs, reminding the viewer of God's power over the lives and deaths of humans.

This symbolic language of landscape was, in essence, a gentler version of the medieval memento mori. Both reminded viewers of the need to seek salvation and of God's power in life and death. Rural cemetery landscaping and scenery reinforced the emotional cultural conceptions of death and the afterlife popular in the nineteenth century.

Today, these nineteenth-century rural cemeteries are usually located inside urban areas because cities expanded around them. While burial continues in many of these historical cemeteries today, much of the original landscaping has been altered to accommodate power lawnmowers and new beliefs about death and burial. However, visits by twenty-first-century tourists continue the tradition of the cemetery as public park. Modern visitors still search for the graves of important people and admire the monuments. But instead of searching for spiritual meaning in symbols and scenery, modern visitors are more likely to search for ghosts.

From Cemeteries to Memorial Parks

The appearance of new cemeteries changed in the closing decades of the nineteenth century and early twentieth century, a reflection of changing technology, business practices, and experiences with and views of death. Technological innovation, the industrial process, and improved transportation resulted in mass-produced and standardized tombstone designs. Straight rows of evenly spaced monuments could be mowed quickly with new power equipment, allowing for fewer groundskeepers. The complicated and ornate landscaping of the rural cemetery fell out of style.

The process of death and funerals changed. Prior to the late nineteenth century, funeral preparations were performed by family members. Most people died at home. Before the Civil War, embalming was practically unknown; family members washed and dressed the deceased. For most average households, coffins and tombstones were ordered from local carpenters or stone carvers or made at home. Middle- and upper-class households might purchase items associated with death such as mourning clothing, stationary, or monuments, but for most, burial was a simple religious and family affair.

Between 1850 and 1920, the modern, commercial funeral home industry developed. New services and products were introduced and marketed to mourning families. Chemical embalming was introduced during the Civil War to ship soldiers' corpses long distances by train. For a fee, professional undertakers embalmed bodies for burial; provided coffins, mourning stationary, and other items required by mourning etiquette; arranged funeral and graveside services; placed obituary notices; and provided hearses to transport the body to the cemetery. Over time, funeral gatherings and services were moved from homes and churches to funeral parlors or funeral homes, another service with a fee attached.[36]

In the early twentieth century, the memorial park style of cemetery management spread across the nation from its origins in Southern California. Beginning in 1913, Hubert Eaton, a California businessman, combined modern marketing and advertising methods to sell life insurance, cemetery plots as real estate investments, and everything needed for funeral services to families and individuals *before* they were actually needed at death.

His Forest Lawn Memorial Park in Glendale, California, rejected somber views of death and the old-fashioned clutter of family monuments in nineteenth-century cemeteries. Memorial park cemeteries had simple, modernist designs. The grounds were wide expanses of green grass. Evergreen trees lined the avenues, but were carefully placed so views across the lawns were uninterrupted. Individual bronze monuments flush to the ground marked the graves of the deceased.

The only visible monuments in Forest Lawn were inspiring white marble copies of famous patriotic and religious sculptures. For example, copies of Michelangelo's *David* and statues of patriots like George Washington were featured on the lawn. The Great Mausoleum was constructed for those who preferred crypt burial. It featured a stained-glass window of Da Vinci's *The Last Supper*.[37]

Memorial parks represented America's changing views of death and dying. Grave markers focused on the importance of individuals, not the primacy of the family. The symbolism of the historical, patriotic, and religious statuary was widely known and appreciated, chosen to appeal to a wide swath of Americans. Memorial parks abandoned symbolism explicitly referencing death or dying. Centuries of cemetery traditions were reinterpreted and final resting places were expected to be serene, peaceful, pleasant, positive, and sacred, but in a universal, secular manner.[38]

While social class distinctions seemed to disappear in the memorial park design, looks were deceiving. Pricing of lots in the memorial park followed typical patterns, with the highest priced lots closest to the featured statuary. Private vaults and walled outdoor grave sites were provided for the rich and famous at extra cost. Many Hollywood celebrities are buried at Forest Lawn Memorial Park. For example, pop star Michael Jackson rests in one of the highest-priced and most private locations in the Great Mausoleum.

Throughout American history and far into the first half of the twentieth century, people of color were usually excluded from burial in the churchyards of all-white churches or prevented from purchasing plots at many private cemeteries. Some civic cemeteries allowed burial in segregated sections. The early twentieth century memorial park cemeteries were no exception; their promoters catered to a white middle-class clientele. Arlington National Cemetery, established in 1864 during the closing years of the Civil War, originally allowed the burial of African American soldiers but in a section separate from whites. Segregation by race and rank in Arlington did not end until 1948, after World War II.[39]

In 1955, 90 percent of all public cemeteries were estimated to have racially restrictive rules and regulations. As late as 1969, the widow of an African American Vietnam veteran was denied the right to purchase a plot in an all-white private Alabama cemetery. In court, the cemetery's race-based and discriminatory burial practices were declared illegal.[40]

Burial in memorial parks or more traditional cemeteries and the services of the funeral home industry were the norm for most Americans throughout the twentieth century. Traditions developed in the late nineteenth and early twentieth centuries still dominate funeral customs in many regions of the nation. Funeral homes continue to oversee the rituals of death: removing of the body of the deceased from the hospital or nursing home; embalming, preparing and placing the body in a casket; planning viewings of the body and visitations by survivors in a funeral home setting; announcing the death through obituaries; organizing the funeral service; transporting the body to the cemetery; and even creating memorial albums for the survivors.

Figure 5.4. The wealth and status of a family was communicated through the large family plots featured in nineteenth-century rural cemeteries. Families purchased ornate landscaping with flowers, shrubs, trees, and ornamental fencing, along with a large central monument and smaller ones for individual family members. These 1854 advertisements in a guidebook for Boston's Mount Auburn cemetery represent the growing commercialism of the funeral industry.
Nathaniel Dearborn, Dearborn's Guide through Mount Auburn, 1854, *56–57. (Courtesy of Archive.org)*

Modern Cemetery Trends

Cemetery, memorial, and funeral trends continue to evolve. In 2017, the American funeral home industry was worth $16 billion, employing over one hundred twenty thousand people in over nineteen thousand funeral homes. But declines in traditional religious practice and changing attitudes toward death and dying are likely to cause a decline in the industry in the next decades. However, funeral-related businesses will continue to seek new ways to profit while consumers demand more individualized and less expensive services.[41]

In recent decades, more and more Americans are choosing nontraditional and less expensive methods to memorialize the deceased and deal with bodily remains. Cremation has become a more popular and less expensive option than traditional burial. About half of all Americans were cremated at death in 2018, up from less than 4 percent in 1960. Rates of cremation in the United States are expected to rise to 79 percent by 2035.[42] While many choose to place remains in a special container and house them in a modern columbarium, this practice is not required. Cremated remains can be scattered or placed wherever survivors choose.

"Green" or natural burials in "memorial woodlands" are another modern trend representing new interest in preserving natural resources and the environment. The deceased are buried in biodegradable caskets without embalming. Instead of tombstones, bodies can be buried with GPS devices, so friends and family members can locate the exact location in subsequent years. Memorials and cemeteries for pets have become more common, signifying the growing emotional attachment of Americans to their pets.

Industrialization changed cemeteries and funeral customs in the late nineteenth and early twentieth centuries; the digital technology revolution is driving change today. Funeral and memorial services are renamed "life celebrations" and feature multimedia presentations and live online streaming. Printed obituaries in newspapers are being replaced by online tributes. Coffins, urns, and grave markers can be purchased direct by the consumer online. Computer technology allows tombstones to be even more personalized with engraved photographs and unique images and symbols. Digital technology makes grave markers interactive with electronic codes linked to websites and social media memorials and life stories.[43]

Wealth, Status, Sex, and Gender in Cemeteries

Cemeteries and burial customs offer a microcosm of a community's views on class, status, and gender. Historically, men were far more likely to be prominent in burial places than women. Permanent memorials and the preservation of human remains require wealth. The majority of the dead from the past are invisible.

Less archaeological and historical information can be discovered on the practices of average people the farther one reaches back in time. Most bodies or grave markers have disappeared over time. Archeologists conclude that formal burial practices have a history of over one hundred thousand years, with actual evidence of special treatment of the dead going back as far as two million years. However, most grave evidence has been completely erased by time or remains undiscovered. What has been discovered may not be what the majority of a culture practiced, but may instead be unique or unusual.[44]

Additional biological factors make certain groups of the dead invisible to archaeologists. The bones of children and women are smaller than those of men and therefore disintegrate quicker. Other historical practices cause children to disappear from the archaeological record—shallow burial, infanticide, and burial of children in different locations from the adults. In some cultures, bodies were not buried but left to the elements. These remains disintegrated or were quickly dispersed. Evidence from cultures using cremation disappears unless lasting monuments are constructed.[45]

Some climates preserve the human remains and artifacts of gravesites better than others. For example, ancient Egypt is often characterized as a culture obsessed with death, funerals, and lasting memorials to the dead. But the arid desert of Egypt allowed many more artifacts to survive over the millennia. Other prehistoric or ancient cultures may have also ostentatiously memorialized the dead but the evidence has not survived.

Cultural assumptions about sex and gender roles are prominent in graveyards and memorials. Until the twentieth century, monuments commemorating males were larger and more common. In family cemetery plots, the name of the father occupied the most prominent position; wives and children were noted in smaller letters or on smaller monuments in satellite positions. Until recent history, the civic monuments commemorating individuals were almost exclusively for males.

A study of tombstone epitaphs from 1770 to 1920 in a New Hampshire cemetery documented different gender expectations for males and females. Overall, the epitaphs communicated messages indicating men found meaning in public commerce, while women were expected to be in private, domestic roles, usually caring for children. Men were commonly described as pious, of exemplary conduct, or useful. On the other hand, women were described as beautiful daughters, affectionate and cherished companions, and tender mothers.

In this study, 84 percent of the adult female headstones identified women as the wife of a man and 12 percent as the daughter of a man. Even unmarried women seventy years of age or older were listed as "daughter of." In contrast, men were never identified as the "husband of" a woman. Adult males were never listed as a son; only boys. Pronouns on women's stones were limited to Mrs., Miss, mother, or widow. On the other hand, men were just not Mr., they were also Reverend, Deacon, Dr., Elder, Esq., Hon., or members of professional organizations or the military.[46]

The burial sites of the wealthy tend to last the longest and attract the most attention. Stone monuments and the precious objects in wealthy graves are often better protected. Written documents are more likely to exist and survive, documenting the lives and deaths of the upper classes. King Tutankhamun, an undistinguished ruler in his own time, is well known in the twenty-first century because his tomb was constructed of stone and full of treasure. Little evidence remains of the uncounted poor and average people who created his tomb. The eighteenth-century quote that "nothing can be said to be certain, except death and taxes"[47] may be true for everyone, but both tax bills and gravesites are rarely equal.

Socioeconomic status matters in graveyards. Some sections have always been far more desirable than others. In the Middle Ages, members of the clergy and the nobility were interred inside the church or in the crypt while average people lay in unmarked graves outside. From the nineteenth century until today, the most desirable and expensive sites are the most visible ones near the entrance, along the main avenues, or in locations with scenic views by ponds or on hills. Throughout time, the gravesites and tombstones of average people, if they exist at all, are smaller, simpler, and more likely to be overlooked than the monuments to the rich and powerful.

A study of tombstones from the 1880s to 1987 in the Chicago area categorized monuments by cost, based on the socioeconomic status of the family of the deceased. The most expensive and therefore upper-class monuments tended to be large mausoleums housing nuclear or extended families and dynastic plots with a large family marker surrounded by smaller tombstones of individual family members. The moderate or middle-class range included smaller mausoleums and family plots with smaller monuments. Small individual stones with simple lettering indicated the lower class. The number in each category corresponded with the demographics of the community.[48]

However, automatically associating a grave marker or grave goods with wealth, social status, specific religious practice, or other cultural practices can be problematic. Scholars note some cultural communities choose to spend more or less than would be expected because of religious beliefs and traditions. For example, some historical communities such as the Quakers and Shakers chose extremely simple markers or no individual markers at all as a reflection of their faith, not their economic success.[49] The grave goods in ancient and medieval burial sites may signify occupation, status, wealth, religion, or patterns of economic activity. Absence of written records makes it difficult to verify many archaeological conclusions.

For thousands of years, average people with limited financial resources have planned for the costs associated with death. Throughout history, people knew the costs of funerals and burial could overwhelm the average household.

Funeral Planning Then and Now

Even in the ancient world, burials and monuments were costly. In the city of Rome during the late Republic and early years of the Empire, the price of land and burial plots grew with the population. Average people, including the free, slaves, and ex-slaves, joined cooperative burial clubs called collegia. For modest membership dues, members received some sort of inscribed stone and a burial site. Generally, the Roman government was hostile to voluntary associations because of fear they would create political dissension. But burial clubs were allowed and became a widespread feature of Roman society throughout the empire.

Some partial lists of the mostly male club members and commemorations of members have survived. Several of the common burial chambers have been uncovered by archaeologists.

Some Roman burial clubs centered on the temple of the sponsoring deity. Others were more secular associations of people who purchased space in a collective burial chamber. One excavated columbarium held the slaves and ex-slaves of Livia, the wife of Emperor Augustus, with over three thousand burial urns in a chamber of about six hundred fifty square feet and about twenty-two feet high. Others have been discovered with six hundred to seven hundred urns, as well as smaller ones. Each individual space was marked with inscriptions including the name of the deceased and the relationship of the commemorator. Relatives of the dead had access to the burial spaces for commemorative occasions.

Roman burial clubs also served as social organizations with regular feasts and business meetings. Members gathered on holidays associated with the dead and the feasts took place in banqueting rooms built above or adjoining the collective tombs.[50]

Medieval guilds offered their members various forms of burial insurance. The families of guild members were given money for funeral expenses and a grave. Guildsmen were expected to keep a vigil at the sickbed of fellow members, attend his burial, and carry his coffin. From the mid-sixteenth century until the end of the eighteenth century, these early forms of insurance increased.[51]

In seventeenth- and eighteenth-century Europe and America, burial clubs, fraternal organizations such as the Masons, community members, and churches provided informal and organized support for funeral expenses, especially for widows and orphans. The development and growth of the modern life insurance industry began in the nineteenth century.[52]

In America, support for funeral and burial costs often came from the church or community. Most churches provided burial plots free to members. After the Civil War, many African American churches provided not only church cemetery plots, but also offered membership in burial societies for a small monthly fee to pay funeral expenses. The charitable organization of African American women, Daughters of Zion, founded a cemetery in 1873 in Charlottesville, Virginia. Black people of all social classes were interred in this cemetery from the 1870s until the end of the charitable association in 1933.[53]

Mutual benefit associations paralleled older fraternal orders such as the Masons and Odd Fellows by providing both financial security and group identity. These organizations offered practical social and economic benefits to members through the practice of mutual aid. Mutual benefit associations were especially appealing to immigrants and African Americans who were often excluded from the fraternal orders. Traditionally members received modest sums donated by the local lodge at the death of a member.

The life insurance industry began in the early nineteenth century, offering policies to cover the costs of death. What had been "burial" insurance for centuries was renamed "life" insurance to refocus attention from the death of a person to the life of the survivors. Like today, life insurance did not guarantee the policyholder a longer or better life. Instead, these policies provided money to cover various expenses when the policyholder died. The early policies were aimed primarily to cover burial expenses. Modern twenty-first-century life insurance may also pay debts of the deceased or provide money to the named survivors.

Advertising for nineteenth-century life insurance focused on the prominent themes of contemporary culture—the costs of a suitable funeral and burial, the importance of family and responsibility of the father to provide, the growth of the science of statistics underpinning the insurance industry, and the economic uncertainly of working American families. In 1868, the Ancient Order of United Workmen became the first fraternity to offer insurance policies providing a death benefit to members. This insurance provided predetermined sums derived from assessments levied on the entire state or national membership rather than donations from local lodge members.

The life insurance industry grew as Americans entered the wage labor market in urban factories, far from traditional forms of community support. Policies for factory workers were designed to be paid for in weekly installments ranging from five to seventy cents a week. For this investment, the family of the policyholder might receive $120 in 1895, or $150 in 1920. But if payments lapsed, so did the benefit.[54]

The existence of one such organization, Woodmen of America founded in 1883, has left a lasting mark on late nineteenth- and early twentieth-century cemeteries—the tree stone tombstone. Symbolism for the new organization was derived from the image of the pioneer woodsmen; even though its founder and most of its members had nothing to do with the lumber industry. Tree stones were not unique to this organization; this and other tombstone symbols will be discussed in more depth in the following chapter.

In 1890, the organization began a program to provide tombstones for its members, originally limited to white males between the ages of twenty-one and fifty.[55] Even though tree stones are often associated with this organization, they were not the only style available. The earliest monuments were shafts topped by a draped urn as well as a seven-and-a-half-foot tree trunk with the Woodmen of the World emblem. Woodmen tree trunk monuments varied over time and location. The original design was replaced by shorter models in the early twentieth century. Some were in the form of cut and stacked logs.

Stone carvers' manuals typically included the instructions for carving the Woodmen of the World seal and major monument companies carried one or two designs for Woodmen monuments (see figure 5.5).

Later in the program, local organizations could choose a monument from a local dealer and be reimbursed. The $100 benefit could be used to purchase a modest monument or subsidize the purchase of a larger monument. The organization required the inscription "Erected by Woodmen of the World," and later, "Here rests a Woodman of the World" appear on the monument to advertise this unique life insurance benefit.

Figure 5.5. Tree stones were a popular tombstone style from the 1850s through the 1920s. This style was recommended and paid for by the Woodmen of America's burial insurance program. These three options featuring the Woodmen of the World emblem appeared in a cemetery monument catalog from around 1900. However, many tree stones were chosen to memorialize individuals or families not associated with this organization.
Quality Monuments, Catalog of Columbus Marble Works, Columbus, Mississippi, 1900, 34–35. (Courtesy of Archive.org)

The program was very successful, but was discontinued in 1932. By 1905, the Pacific Jurisdiction Woodmen of the World had erected 2,385 stone and zinc monuments throughout the Northwest. But since the amount of the benefit never rose beyond $100, the size and complexity of monuments declined over time.[56]

Like people over the centuries, average modern Americans also plan for funeral and burial or cremation expenses for years before their expected demise. Today, funerals are often the third-largest expense in one's lifetime, behind houses and cars.[57] The average American funeral with burial costs is nearly $9,000. Cemetery plots for burial average around $1,000, and like traditional real estate, prices increase in crowded urban areas and desirable locations. Typical granite monuments start at around $1,200.[58]

Traditionally, the wealthy have spent the most on burial and funerals. But this long-term trend has shifted in recent years. Since 1996, low-income families have been consistently ranked as the highest spenders on funerals and burial relative to their total expenditures. On the other hand, funeral spending by the wealthiest was less than the national average. In 2014, the top 1 percent spent less on funerals than everyone else; while the poor spent a 26 percent greater share than the national average.[59]

In the Classroom

The primary sources for this chapter are your local cemeteries. To prepare for a field trip to a local cemetery, make arrangements in advance and review the rules of the cemetery with your students before departure. Rules may vary from cemetery to cemetery, but one of special note is students should never lean or climb on the monuments for both their own safety and to preserve often fragile stones.

Consult with the cemetery manager, cemetery preservation groups, and local historical societies to learn if tours are available. These organizations may also have additional primary sources such as burial, cemetery deed, and plot registers. They may also recommend articles or books about the development and history of your local cemeteries.

Quality publications outlining classroom activities and ideas for using tombstones and cemeteries in the classroom are available in print and online. Many encourage students to seek out monuments of important people and focus upon their accomplishments and importance in the community. While this can be significant, it fails to recognize the wider focus of social history—to identify patterns in the lives of average people over time. The following suggestions and those described in the next chapter focus on tombstones and cemeteries as primary source evidence for social, religious, cultural, artistic, economic, political, or technological continuity and change.

A scavenger hunt for common symbols or styles of monuments is an engaging introductory activity. Students can research the meaning and history of chosen symbols or monuments before or after the cemetery visit. Many guides to cemetery iconography are available online and in print, but quality varies. Symbols rarely have one meaning, so beware of sources suggesting a single meaning for a popular symbol. This is discussed in more depth in the next chapter. *Stories in Stone, A Field Guide to Cemetery Symbolism and Iconography* by Douglas Keister is a quality and affordable guide available in print.

In the cemetery, pairs of students search for common symbols from a provided list. Examples can be documented with photographs for later analysis. The list will vary depending on the community and the era of the cemetery, but might include common religious symbols; Greek, Roman, or Egyptian symbols; flowers, plants, birds, animals; images related to the profession of the deceased; or symbols of organizations such as the Masons or Woodmen of the World. Students can also be asked to locate various styles of monuments such as Classical, Gothic, Egyptian Revival, or tree stones.

Students can practice "doing history" by collecting data in the cemetery and using qualitative analysis to make conclusions. This activity is described in the next chapter. Many cemetery restoration and documentation groups and projects exist across the country. Encourage participation in these efforts to find, document, photograph, map, and protect family, church, and civic cemeteries.

Notes

1. Alexander Pope, 1736, quoted in Karl S. Guthke, "Do-It-Yourself Immortality: Writing One's Own Epitaph," in *Markers* XX (2003): 125, https://archive.org/details/markers20asso/page/n1.
2. *Oxford English Dictionary Online*, s.v. "necropolis, n.," http://www.oed.com/.
3. Ibid., s.v. "cemetery, n."
4. Ibid., s.v. "catacomb, n."
5. Ibid., s.v. "mausoleum, n."
6. Ibid., s.v. "mausoleum, n."
7. Ibid., s.v. "sepulchre, n."
8. Matthew 27:5–10 (NIV).
9. *Oxford English Dictionary Online*, s.v. "columbarium, n."
10. Ibid., s.v. "cenotaph, n."
11. Ibid., s.v. "thanatology, n."
12. Robert S. Bianchi, "Egyptian Mummies: Myth and Reality," *Archaeology* 35, no. 2 (1982): 18–25, http://www.jstor.org/stable/41727852.
13. Drew Gilpin Faust, *This Republic of Suffering: Death and the American Civil War* (New York: Alfred A. Knopf, 2009), 92; Erich Brenner, "Human Body Preservation: Old and New Techniques," *Journal of Anatomy* 224, no. 3: 316–44, https://www.ncbi.nlm.nih.gov/pmc/articles/PMC3931544/.
14. James Stevens Curl, *Death and Architecture* (Gloucestershire, England: Sutton Publishing, 2002), 21–34.
15. Graham Oliver, "Images of Death: Inscribed Funerary Monuments from Fourth-Century Athens to Neo-Classical England," *Bulletin of the Institute of Classical Studies* 75 (2000): 125–41, http://www.jstor.org/stable/43767719.
16. Christine Schenk, "Commemorating the Dead: Roman Funerary Customs and Practices," in *Crispina and Her Sisters: Women and Authority in Early Christianity* (Minneapolis: Augsburg Fortress, 2017), 161–62, http://www.jstor.org/stable/j.ctt1tm7gz6.10.
17. Schenk, "Commemorating the Dead," 164–66.
18. Curl, *Death and Architecture*, 41.
19. Schenk, "Commemorating the Dead," 164–66.
20. Curl, *Death and Architecture*, 67.

21. Schenk, "Commemorating the Dead," 164–66.

22. Paul Binski, *Medieval Death: Ritual and Representation* (Ithaca, NY: Cornell University Press, 1996), 80; Barbara Gilli, "The Past in the Present: The Reuse of Ancient Material in the 12th Dynasty," *Aegyptus* 89 (2009): 89–110, http://www.jstor.org/stable/23375031.

23. James Frederick Gerrard, "Synthesis, Chronology, and 'Late Roman' Cemeteries in Britain," *American Journal of Archaeology* 119, no. 4 (2015): 565–72, doi:10.3764/aja.119.4.0565; Adrian Maldonado, "What Does Early Christianity Look Like? Mortuary Archaeology and Conversion in Late Iron Age Scotland," *Scottish Archaeological Journal* 33, nos. 1–2 (2011): 39–54, http://www.jstor.org/stable/43923909; Marios Costambeys, "Burial Topography and the Power of the Church in Fifth- and Sixth-Century Rome," *Papers of the British School at Rome* 69 (2001): 169–89, http://www.jstor.org/stable/40311009.

24. Binski, *Medieval Death, Ritual and Representation*, 32, 56, 72, 116.

25. Ibid., 99.

26. Paul Koudounaris, *The Empire of Death: A Cultural History of Ossuaries and Charnel Houses* (London: Thames & Hudson, 2011), 224.

27. David Charles Sloane, *The Last Great Necessity: Cemeteries in American History* (Baltimore: Johns Hopkins University Press, 1991), 28.

28. Elizabeth Walton Potter and Beth M. Bolton, "Burial Customs and Cemeteries in American History," in *Guidelines for Evaluating and Registering Cemeteries and Burial Places*, National Register Bulletin (Washington, DC: US Department of the Interior, National Park Service, 1992), https://www.nps.gov/nr/publications/bulletins/nrb41/nrb41_5.htm.

29. Elizabeth A. Crowell and Norman Vardney Mackie, "Funerary Monuments and Burial Patterns of Colonial Tidewater Virginia, 1607–1776," *Markers* VII (1990): 103–38, https://archive.org/details/markers07asso.

30. John R. Stilgoe, *Common Landscape of America, 1580 to 1845* (New Haven, CT: Yale University Press, 1982), 227–31.

31. Sloane, *The Last Great Necessity*, 34–40.

32. Ibid., 31–32.

33. Blanche M. G. Linden, *Silent City on a Hill, Picturesque Landscapes of Memory and Boston's Mount Auburn Cemetery* (Boston: University of Massachusetts Press, 2007).

34. "The Graves of Red Jacket," *Western New York Heritage*, accessed June 2018, https://www.wnyheritage.org/content/the_graves_of_red_jacket/index.html.

35. Henry Arthur Bright, *Happy Country This America: The Travel Diary of Henry Arthur Bright*, ed. Anne Henry Ehrenpreis (Columbus: Ohio State University Press, 1978), 118.

36. James F. Farrell, *Inventing the American Way of Death, 1830–1920* (Philadelphia: Temple University Press), 146–52.

37. Sloane, *The Last Great Necessity*, 159–72.

38. Ibid., 159–90.

39. Harry Truman, Executive Order 9981, Harry S. Truman Presidential Library & Museum, https://www.trumanlibrary.org/9981.htm.

40. Kitty Rogers, "Integrating the City of the Dead: The Integration of Cemeteries and the Evolution of Property Law, 1900–1969," *Alabama Law Review* 56, no. 4 (Summer 2005): 1153–66 (accessed July 2018), https://www.law.ua.edu/pubs/lrarticles/Volume%2056/Issue%204/Rogers.pdf.

41. Virginia R. Beard and William C. Burger, "Change and Innovation in the Funeral Industry: A Typology of Motivations," *OMEGA—Journal of Death and Dying* 75, no. 1 (October 2015): 47–68, https://doi.org/10.1177/0030222815612605.

42. "Funerals of the Future," *Economist* (April 16, 2018): 51–53.

43. Ibid.

44. Jennie Bradbury and Chris Scarre, "Introduction: Engaging with the Dead," in *Engaging with the Dead: Exploring Changing Human Beliefs about Death, Mortality and the Human Body*, ed. Jennie Bradbury and Chris Scarre (Philadelphia: Oxbow Books, 2017), 1, http://www.jstor.org/stable/j.ctt1vgw6s0.3.

45. Ibid., 2.

46. Lynn Rainville, "Hanover Deathscapes: Mortuary Variability in New Hampshire, 1770–1920," *Ethnohistory* 46, no. 3 (Summer 1999): 570–71, http://www.jstor.org/stable/483201.

47. Fred Shapiro, "Quotes Uncovered: Death and Taxes," February 17, 2011 (accessed July 2018), http://freakonomics.com/2011/02/17/quotes-uncovered-death-and-taxes/.

48. Paula J. Fenza, "Communities of the Dead: Tombstones as a Reflection of Social Organization," *Markers* VI (1989): 136–57, https://archive.org/details/markers06asso.

49. Ibid.

50. Keith Hopkins, *Death and Renewal* (Sociological Studies in Roman History), vol. 2 (Cambridge: Cambridge University Press, 1983), 211–16; Richard P. Saller and Brent D. Shaw, "Tombstones and Roman Family Relations in the Principate: Civilians, Soldiers and Slaves," *Journal of Roman Studies* 74 (1984): 124–56, http://www.jstor.org/stable/299012.

51. Marco H. D. Van Leeuwen, "Guilds and Middle-Class Welfare, 1550–1800: Provisions for Burial, Sickness, Old Age, and Widowhood," *Economic History Review* 65, no. 1 (February 2012): 61–90, https://www.jstor.org/stable/41475545.

52. Farrell, *Inventing the American Way of Death*, 66–73.

53. Lynn Rainville, *Hidden History: African American Cemeteries in Central Virginia* (Charlottesville: University Press of Virginia, 2016), 73–74.

54. Farrell, *Inventing the American Way of Death*, 66–73.

55. Annette Stott, "The Woodmen of the World Monument Program," *Markers* XX (2003): 1–29, https://archive.org/details/markers20asso.

56. Ibid., 1–29.

57. Beard and Burger, "Change and Innovation in the Funeral Industry," 62.

58. "Funerals of the Future," 51–53; Statistics, National Funeral Directors Association, accessed July 2018, http://www.nfda.org/news/statistics.

59. Elizabeth Currid-Halkett, *The Sum of Small Things: A Theory of the Aspirational Class* (Princeton, NJ: Princeton University Press, 2017), 33.

CHAPTER SIX

Remembering the Dead

Symbols and Scrapbooks

A scrapbook "is not a grave in which you have buried all these good and beautiful thoughts, but a living treasure always open to your hand."

—E. W. Gurley, *Scrap-Books and How to Make Them*, 1880[1]

Essential questions:

- How do you want to be remembered?
- How do we save memories?

Through time, humans have imagined and sought better lives. The previous chapters explore the peaks and valleys of this timeless search for impossible cures, visionary societies, and utopian dreams. People also hope to be remembered after death. Tombstones, epitaphs, obituaries, and scrapbooks commemorate lives of the dead. All are unique primary sources expressing the human desire to remember and be remembered.

Tombstone Symbols: Remembering in Stone

Tombstones and cemeteries are symbols, symbols of the deceased and symbols of their culture. Symbols represent abstract ideas larger than themselves in images or words. Symbols tell stories about how cultures think about life and death. The ancient Greeks had a similar word for symbol meaning a token or ticket.[2] Symbols are tickets into cultures of the past.

Funerary symbols have remarkably long lives. Trees, obelisks, roses, and urns have been used in art and architecture for thousands of years. But each of these symbols may appear similar over time, interpretations are subjective and flexible, varying between individuals, cultures, and historical eras. One can't assume an ancient Greek urn or Egyptian sphinx has the same meaning in twenty-first-century America as it did in previous historical eras.

Iconography, the interpretation of meanings and uses of images, is an important element in the study of cemeteries and tombstones. In cemeteries, iconographers list and categorize decorative carvings and images and seek to learn why those images were chosen, their meanings, and historical traditions. This search for meaning can be especially difficult because the meaning of cemetery symbols changes over time, a reflection of shifting attitudes toward death, religion, family, and social class. Popular trends and individual tastes also influence tombstone design.

To complicate matters, tombstone epitaphs and symbols can represent two opposing ideas at the same time. For example, the same symbol can represent both hope and despair. A weeping angel might represent a family's despair at the finality of death and the loss of a loved one, as well as hope the loved one resides in heaven.

Figure 6.1. ***Memento mori*, Latin for "Remember you must die," describes a Christian emphasis on preparing for death. Memento mori symbols reminded the viewer to always be prepared for death. At death, sinners went to hell but the faithful went to heaven, so these symbols served as a grim warning. Memento mori symbols were popular in the Middle Ages in art and funeral monuments but fell out of style in the late eighteenth century. Several memento mori symbols appear on this tombstone marking the grave of a Boston woman who died in 1745. The skeleton is snuffing out a candle, symbolizing the end of life. An angel holds an hour glass, a symbol of life passing quickly. Death's heads, skulls with bones or wings, were also featured on early colonial tombstones.**
Tombstone of Rebecca Sanders, died 1745, King's Chapel Burying Ground, Boston, Massachusetts. (Courtesy of the author)

Botanical symbols such as roses, lilies, vines, or tree stumps are especially open to ambiguous interpretations. The life cycle of a plant from seed to death can symbolize the fleeting nature of life or the promise of rebirth. These symbols can represent personality qualities of the deceased or feelings or desires of those still living. One symbol can have secular, religious, and historical meanings.[3]

Tree stones, discussed as symbols for Woodmen of America in the previous chapter, have accumulated dozens of symbolic meanings over time. A tree might be a reference to the Tree of Life in the Garden of Eden, described in Genesis, a text of Jewish and Christian faiths. Or it could be derived from many other historical and current religions. Trees of life can symbolize eternal life or fertility. Tree stones might be a secular reference to a family tree and thus the importance of family. A tree stump might symbolize a life cut short; or it might simply be a popular motif of the era.

Tree tombstones were not unique to those insured by Woodmen's burial insurance. Tree stones began to be popular in the 1850s in American cemeteries, years before Woodmen of America's insurance program began. Their popularity waned in the 1920s and 1930s (see figure 5.5).

Before tree stones were associated with the Woodmen of America, they were a popular midwestern regional trend. For example, the log motif was a distinctive trademark of an Indiana family of stone carvers, the Durlaufs, in the late nineteenth and early twentieth centuries. In Indiana, 2,414 tree markers have been identified ranging from eight inches to fifteen feet high in 245 different cemeteries.[4]

Tree stones also reflect European and American rustic design styles popular in the nineteenth century. English design books began featuring rustic designs of twigs, branches, bark, leaves, and vines for indoor and outdoor furniture and decorative household objects beginning in the late eighteenth century. The style was frequently used in the newly fashionable rural cemeteries. The Arts and Crafts movement of design (1880s–1920s) continued to promote the motif.[5]

Preferences for this back-to-nature imagery contrasted with the increasing urbanization of the era. It was part of a wider nostalgia for a simple, rural life in a century of economic and technological change.[6]

Flower motifs were especially popular on nineteenth-century tombstones. The Victorian era has been characterized as a time when flowers were used to communicate specific and often secret meanings. Books that paired various flowers with sentimental emotions were especially popular in nineteenth-century France, England, and America. However, many different meanings were attributed to the same plants and flowers in these books.

Historian Beverly Seaton demonstrated that people of the era did not view the "language of flowers" as authoritative. Most of these publications were simply interesting gifts and read as a popular pastime. These books were among many consumer products capitalizing on the popularity of gardening, giving flowers as gifts, and using flowers as decorative home or wardrobe accessories.[7]

Depictions of flowers on tombstones and epitaphs with floral references were popular and promoted as symbolic for commercial gain. Variations of "Budded on earth to bloom in heaven" appeared on American tombstones as early as 1834, and records indicate stone carvers received explicit orders for this particular phrase. This epitaph could be interpreted as a message of consolation or as a tribute to the personality of the deceased. The Sears *Tombstones and Monuments* (1902) included this in a two-page list of epitaph choices, noting "used frequently on work we have made in the past." It was a bargain because its twenty-eight letters only cost seventy cents to inscribe.[8]

While the history and meanings of natural and floral symbols are difficult to pinpoint, tracing the historical origins of other themes is more straightforward. Depictions of corpses and skeletons became popular in art and funeral monuments in the late Middle Ages. Many scholars point to the monumental impact of the Black Death as the origin of these trends. Collectively known as memento mori, a Latin phrase for "Remember you must die," these symbols remind the living that death is universal. People from all stations of life were reminded they must prepare for death. The dance of death or danse macabre stressed similar themes and was also a popular theme in art (see figure 6.1).

In the fifteenth and sixteenth centuries, a *transi*, memento mori, or cadaver tomb became a style of funerary monument for the wealthy. A transi is the depiction in art of a decomposing cadaver. The two- or three-dimensional monuments, or paintings depicted a two-level, open coffin. On top was a *gisant*, or effigy, of the deceased and below was a skeleton or shrouded or decomposing corpse. The depictions warned viewers that even the wealthy die and face their maker.[9]

Skulls with crossed bones, skulls with wings called death's heads, skeletons, scythes, and coffins were featured on the earliest American colonial tombstones (see figure 6.1). However, by the mid-eighteenth century, these symbols of grim views of life, death, and salvation were changing, resulting in a shift in graveyard symbolism. Over time, skulls with bones or wings were less common on tombstones and more inviting cherubs, human faces with wings, took their place. By the end of the eighteenth century, urns and willow trees had become new fashionable motifs. Three movements inspired these changes—the Great Awakening of the 1730s and 1740s, Romanticism, and the revival of classic art and architecture.

The Great Awakening impacted American attitudes toward life and death. Previously, Protestant Calvinist beliefs in predestination reminded believers that the prospects for a happy afterlife were slim. This doctrine held that only a few "elect" Christians could enter heaven; all others were damned to hell. These unforgiving religious beliefs gave way to a more optimistic view of salvation in the eighteenth century, in which every individual, through faith and a worthy life, could go to heaven after death. The cherub was a symbol reflecting this more optimistic attitude toward life after death.

Urns, weeping willows, and ancient Greek and Roman design elements reflected the mid-eighteenth-century Neoclassicism movement and late eighteenth-century Romanticism. Neoclassicism in the visual arts, architecture, and literature was inspired by the rediscovery of the ancient Roman cities of Herculaneum and Pompeii, in 1738 and 1748 respectively. At the same time, Greco-Roman ideals were revived and merged with the emerging ideals of the Enlightenment. Visits to the cradles of civilization in Athens and Rome were a requirement of the Grand Tour of Europeans and, later, Americans. As a result, monuments reminiscent of Greek temples, columns, figures dressed in togas, acanthus leaves, funerary urns, and other classical elements became increasingly popular.

The weeping willow tree, imported to America in the 1730s, became associated with mourning and melancholic themes of the Romantic movement. This symbol reached the peak of its popularity when it was reported in the 1820s that Napoleon asked to be buried under a weeping willow tree on St. Helena, the island of his final exile. Images of a mourner beside a classical urn on a pedestal under a weeping willow tree became incredibly popular on tombstones, in art, prints, jewelry, and even as embroidery designs to commemorate the deceased into the late nineteenth century.[10]

Gothic Revival was the second most popular design style in nineteenth-century American towns, cities, and cemeteries. Gothic Revival originated from a revived eighteenth century-European interest and reinterpretation of medieval history. Gothic Revival funeral monuments incorporated pointed arches, ornate lettering, crosses, and other decorative elements reminiscent of medieval cathedrals.

By the late nineteenth century, Egyptian Revival symbols and architectural styles became the hot new trend for cemetery gateways, monuments, and public memorials. Obelisk tombstones; pyramid mausoleums; flat-roofed mastabas; and wide, curved lotus-topped columns proliferated. Sphinxes; winged orb or sun-disks, with or without cobra heads; and ouroboros (snakes eating their tail) were common motifs. Many of these originally pagan symbols were given new associations with Christianity through references to the biblical accounts of Hebrew enslavement in Egypt. Egyptian Revival symbols and architecture was also popular for prisons, firehouses, railroad depots, bridges, and even churches and synagogues.[11]

Nineteenth-century Egyptomania was inspired by historical events of the era. Everything Egyptian became incredibly popular in Europe after the French (1798–1801) and British occupation (1882–1922) of Egypt. The Rosetta Stone, a stele with Greek and ancient hieroglyphic inscriptions discovered by the French invaders, provided the key for Francois Champollion's translation of hieroglyphics in 1822. These events, along with the popularity of travel to Egypt promoted by published tourist guides and accounts of Egyptian tours, fueled the trend.

The ancient Egyptian customs and monuments also inspired the ancient Romans. The Emperor Augustus commemorated his defeat of Cleopatra and Mark Anthony and the addition of Egypt to the Roman Empire by moving an Egyptian obelisk to the Circus Maximus in the city of Rome. It had been commissioned by Ramses II over one thousand years before Augustus and was one of seven Egyptian obelisks relocated to Rome.

The ancient Romans also adopted Egyptian styles for funeral monuments. The monument for the first-century BCE senator Gaius Cestius was a white marble-faced pyramid over eighty feet high. The surviving inscription noted the

Figure 6.2. Egyptian Revival styles were popular in nineteenth- and early twentieth-century cemeteries. The Sphinx erected in Boston's Mt. Auburn Cemetery (1872) commemorated the end of the Civil War. The body of a lion symbolized the enslaved, while the woman's face with an American bald eagle on her headdress symbolized white Americans. Together, this was meant to represent how white and black Americans would build a new future. The Latin inscription on the pedestal translates to "American Union Preserved; African Slavery Destroyed; by the Uprising of a Great People; by the Blood of Fallen Heroes." In Richmond, Virginia's Hollywood Cemetery, a ninety-foot-high granite pyramid completed in 1869 was chosen as a memorial to the eighteen thousand Confederate soldiers buried in the cemetery.

Photographs, Milmore's Sphinx, Mt. Auburn Cemetery, Cambridge, MA, and Monument to Confederate Dead, Hollywood Cemetery, Richmond, VA, both between 1890 and 1901, Detroit Publishing Co. (Courtesy of Library of Congress)

pyramid took 330 days to build. This ancient Roman monument, styled on an even more ancient Egyptian form, still stands today adjacent to a cemetery opened in the eighteenth century for non-Catholics.

Ancient symbols are reused and reinterpreted over time and the meanings of those symbols are malleable. The Sphinx Monument, designed and donated by Jacob Bigelow and installed in Mt. Auburn Cemetery in Boston as a public monument in 1872, commemorated Union soldiers in the Civil War. Bigelow's sphinx reinterpreted and blended Egyptian and American symbols.

Bigelow's sphinx monument was widely misunderstood and misinterpreted during his lifetime and after his death, despite his efforts to explain the symbolism. Bigelow's benevolent female sphinx was meant to symbolize a new nation. However, it was misinterpreted as the treacherous female sphinx of Greek myth who destroyed those who could not answer her riddles.[12] Ironically, the Egyptian Revival style was also used for a ninety-foot granite pyramid erected in Richmond, Virginia's Hollywood Cemetery in 1869 to commemorate the eighteen thousand Confederate soldiers buried nearby (see figure 6.2).

Cemetery symbols, like utopian ideals and traditional cures, have histories extending for centuries. Some elements of the tradition retain age-old associations, others are redefined and reinterpreted by new generations for new purposes. Flowers, trees, and pyramids are still popular images in graphic art. But few would associate these with death or the afterlife. Today, memento mori symbols such as skeletons, skulls, and decaying corpses have more to do with the commercialized holiday of Halloween or zombies. Few would perceive these as religious warnings that life is short and one must prepare for death. Humans have recycled symbols for millennia, but their meanings are unique to a time and place.

The Culture of Mourning in the Nineteenth Century

Mourning for the dead was an especially prominent theme in the nineteenth century, especially from the 1830s to the 1880s. Historians have outlined a variety of reasons: changing eighteenth-century religious attitudes toward death; the influence of Romanticism; Queen Victoria's extended mourning for Prince Albert, who died in 1861; high mortality rates, especially during the Civil War years; a growing middle-class seeking to distinguish itself through elaborate rules of etiquette; and the growth of a funeral industry promoting consumer spending. All of these factors influenced how people viewed death as well as how they mourned, buried, and memorialized the dead. This culture of mourning produced ephemera that was saved, clipped, and pasted into scrapbooks of the era.

The concept of the Good Death was an integral part of death and mourning in European and American culture. Since the fifteenth century, *Ars moriendi*, or Art of Dying, books instructed Catholic and Protestant Christians how to feel about and prepare for death. Jeremy Taylor's English version, *The Rule and Exercise of Holy Dying* (1651), was widely reprinted, adapted, and admired far into the nineteenth century. This and other texts instructed one how to gladly accept death, resist the temptations of despair and worldly attachment to life, pray, and model one's death after Jesus.[13]

By the nineteenth century, the Good Death was expected to take place in one's home with family members assembled around the deathbed. It was important for family and friends to witness a death so all could be assured the dying person's soul was pure and ready to go to heaven. Those assembled heard the final words of the dying person and repeated them to friends and relatives who could not be present. Final words demonstrated the purity of one's soul, summarized one's life, and communicated important, religious lessons to the living.[14]

Conceptions of the Good Death and proper mourning were described, promoted, and reinforced in every form of media of the era. Etiquette books provided advice on behavior and appropriate clothing for the bereaved. Tourist guides promoted visits to cemeteries. Newspapers and magazines printed elaborate obituaries, poetry, and stories related to death and mourning. Songs, hymns, sermons, and religious tracts dwelt on the themes of the Good Death, Christian bereavement, and heavenly rewards. Popular prints and other visual media presented idealized images of death and mourning.

Popular novels of the day, labeled consolation literature by subsequent scholars, provided models for behavior for both the dying and the mourning survivors. Characters such as Charles Dickens's Little Nell in *The Old Curiosity Shop* (1841) or Harriet Beecher Stowe's Eva in *Uncle Tom's Cabin* (1852) served as models for exemplary deaths. Popular poems and stories communicated, over and over, contemporary cultural expectations for the Good Death and the process of mourning of surviving family and friends, continually reinforcing its importance.

The Gates Ajar (1868) by Elizabeth Stuart Phelps Ward, a best-selling novel in this genre, recounted the emotional and religious struggles of Mary Cabot after the death of her brother, a soldier in the Civil War. The title was a reference to the gates of heaven. *The Gates Ajar* and its 1883 and 1887 sequels inspired popular songs. Images of the gates of heaven were widely used symbols at funerals, on tombstones, and in cemetery design. Ward's novels described emotional visits to cemeteries, the imagined activities of loved ones in heaven, and visions of a future when loved ones would be reunited in this utopian afterlife (see figure 6.3).[15]

Mourning poetry, tributes to the deceased, and poems expressing grief for named and unnamed dead were common in nineteenth-century newspapers. Clippings pasted in scrapbooks of both men and women of the era reflect this trend. In 1841, a Massachusetts man transcribed 186 pages of mourning poetry in an album he entitled "For the Infant Dead" as a gift for his wife a year after the death of their child.[16]

Themes of death and mourning were especially prominent during and after the American Civil War. Songs, poetry, and other literature of the era proliferated as thousands died on the battlefield or in military camps. Families at home hoped someone was present to care for loved ones as they died and record their final words.[17]

Descriptions of a dying soldier's Good Death were very popular in newspapers, often reprinted, clipped, and saved in scrapbooks of the era. One Civil War poem, Mary Woolsey Howland's "Mortally Wounded" (1863), was published dozens of times over a number of years in broadsides, newspapers, magazines, and stories. As it was republished, the name of its original author was lost or omitted. The author, context, and story behind this poem were changed to resonate with different audiences. Henry Ingersoll Bowditch, a northern abolitionist, included three copies of the poem in his scrapbooks mourning and memorializing his son killed in the Civil War.[18]

Another popular poem, "Somebody's Darling" by Marie La Coste, appeared in poetry anthologies and scrapbooks of both Northerners and Southerners. The poem about the death of a soldier mentioned no specific battle, war, or cause of death. The "somebody" mourning the soldier could have been a father, mother, sister, wife, or girlfriend. "The Blue and The Gray," composed by Northerner Francis Miles Finch (1827–1907) after the war, was widely recirculated on both sides and saved by both black and white scrapbookers.[19]

Even after the Civil War, poems such as Bret Harte's "A Second Review of the Grand Army," Kate Putnam's "Driving Home the Cows" (both published in 1865), and Walt Whitman's "Ashes of Soldiers" (1872) imagined the return of the dead soldiers.[20]

Civil War–era scrapbooks and diaries provide insights into many characteristics of the era. Julia Wheelock, an Iowa teacher who became a Civil War nurse, compiled scrapbooks of newspaper and magazine poetry and story clippings about her experiences.[21] Other scrapbooks of newspaper clippings document the partisanship and bias of Southern or Northern newspapers, covering battles and local, regional, or national politics.[22]

Scrapbooks created by African Americans after the Civil War contained stories from black and white newspapers about deaths from lynchings and other racial violence. For example, Charles Hunter (c. 1851–1931) clipped stories from North Carolina newspapers to compare how whites and blacks were treated when accused of crimes. His documentation demonstrated whites received light sentences while blacks were lynched.[23]

By the mid-nineteenth century, mourning was increasingly expressed through the purchase of consumer goods. The growing funeral industry reinterpreted old customs and invented new ones to sell products and services. Specially printed death announcements, funeral notices, invitations, memorial cards, and visiting cards were promoted. After photography was introduced, photographs were taken and distributed of the deceased in the casket, alone and surrounded by the family and funeral attendees. Special scrapbooks and albums were available for purchase to save and display these items.

Mourning fashion was prescribed for both men and women: black clothing and jewelry made from polished or unpolished jet or the hair of the deceased.[24] Hairwork was popular beginning in the 1770s and throughout the 1800s. Wearing or displaying the hair of a loved one served as a literal reminder of the loved one and one's feelings for that person. Hair jewelry also sent an outward message to observers, communicating the emotions and dedication of the wearer to preserving the memory of the deceased.

Novels described tear-wrenching scenes of characters on their deathbeds cutting their hair to give as mementos to friends and family. The dying wish of Eva, in *Uncle Tom's Cabin*, was to give her golden curls to both her family members and the family's slaves.[25] Treasured locks of hair of the deceased were often saved in scrapbooks and fashioned into lasting mementos.

Creating items from the hair of living or deceased friends and family was a popular form of nineteenth-century "fancy work," decorative needlework or crafts for wear or home décor. Hair was fashioned into elaborate wreaths, pictures, or miniature cemetery scenes with urns, weeping willows, and tombs to be displayed under glass. The hair of loved ones

Figure 6.3. Popular nineteenth-century novels and other literature communicated cultural expectations for a Good Death and the process and etiquette for mourning. *The Gates Ajar* (1868) by Elizabeth Stuart Phelps Ward was a best-selling novel about the mourning of Mary Cabot after the death of her brother, a soldier in the Civil War. The title was a reference to the gates of heaven and the joy loved ones could expect when re-united in heaven after death. The novel inspired songs, and images of open gates became a popular funeral and cemetery motif.

Sheet Music, "How the Gates Came Ajar" by Eastburn, 1872. (Courtesy Archive.org and Newberry Sheet Music Digital Collection)

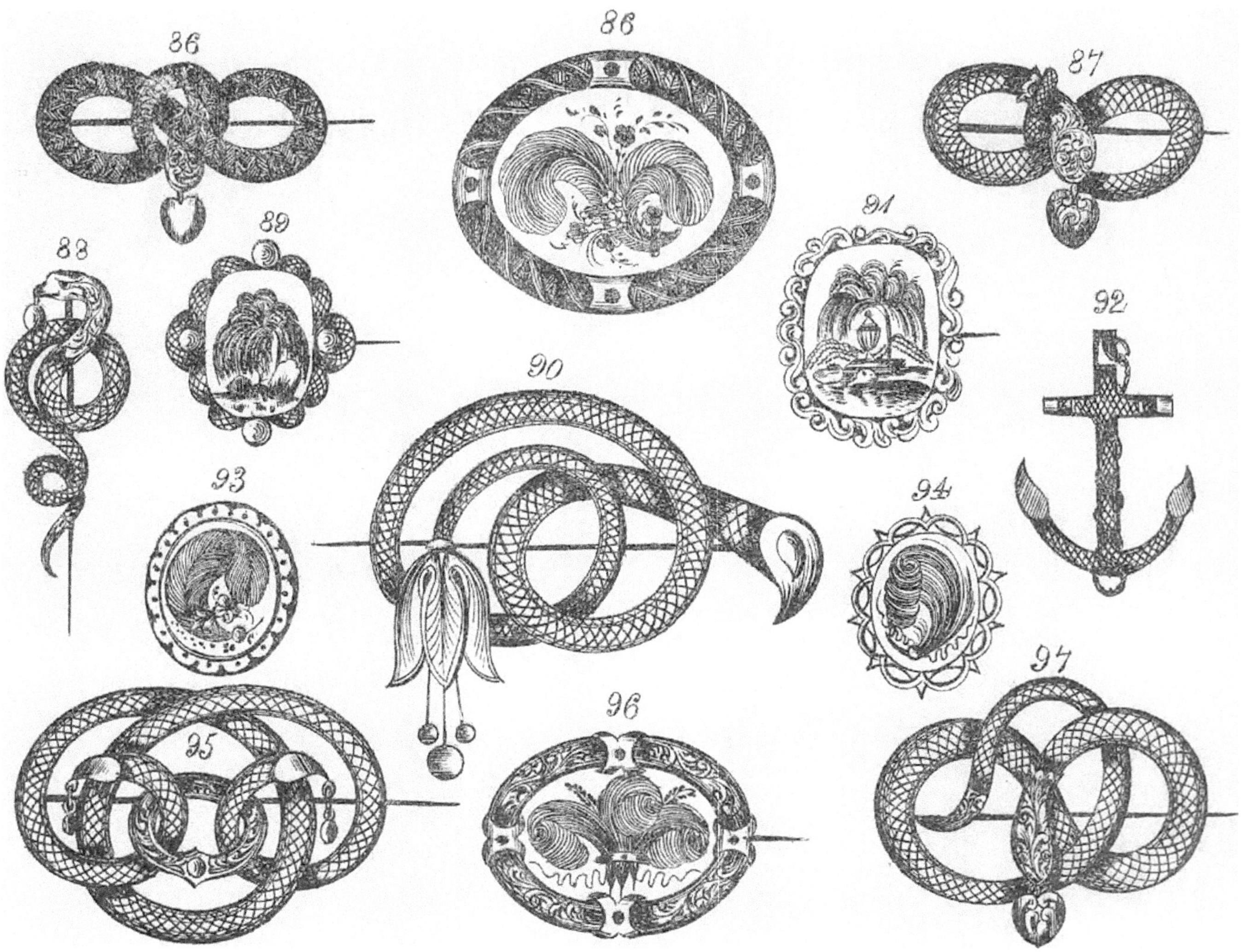

Figure 6.4. Hairwork, creating jewelry, wreaths, pictures, or other decorative objects, was popular throughout the nineteenth century. These items were fashioned from the hair of loved ones, living or deceased. Popular magazines include patterns for items to make at home and professional hairworkers created items with hair provided by the customer. Above is a page of brooch designs from an 1864 pattern book of hair jewelry. For numbers 89 and 91, the hair was dissolved to make a special paint. Note that these are mourning brooches with the popular cemetery symbols, a weeping willow and urn. The feathery designs in 86, 94, 96, and 93 were made from swirls of hair. For the remainder of the designs, the hair was woven using a special loom to make the rope-like portions of the brooch.
From The Jewellers' Book of Patterns in Hair Work, *1864. (Courtesy of Archive.org)*

could be made into a special paint and used to create portraits or larger pictures that might also include photographs or poetry. Miniature portraits were painted on small ivory discs and mounted in jewelry settings (see figure 6.4).

Popular women's magazines such as *Godey's Lady's Book* featured patterns to make jewelry or other decorative items from hair. One could choose styles and jewelry settings from catalogs and pay a professional hair worker to create the item. One advertiser offered to create "mementoes of the dead"—wreaths or bouquets made from the relics of deceased friends such as hair, pieces of clothing, shrouds, coffins, old shoes, stockings, or other personal articles. Hairwork fell out of style in the early twentieth century as attitudes toward death and mourning changed.[26]

Scrapbooks: Remembering with Scissors and Paper

Scrapbooks, today and in the past, are personal stories created from repurposed media and ephemera of the era. Scrapbooking began as a hobby and pastime in the same decades of the nineteenth century that mourning conventions became prominent. Both originated in the 1830s. Both trends grew as industrialization, new technology, and advertising created consumer goods and the desire to buy them. Advertising trade cards and other print ephemera as well as clippings from growing numbers of newspapers and magazines were saved in scrapbooks. Nineteenth-century scrapbooks are personal reflections that often cast light on the wider culture of death and mourning.

Before printed books and newspapers were widely available, literate people kept commonplace books. A commonplace book was a collection of meaningful excerpts, collected for future reference and often organized under individual thematic headings. The purposes were as varied as the creators but, in general, commonplace books organized information from reading for future reference and use.

Medieval scholars created *florilegia* or "books of flowers" with excerpts from the Bible and the works of important theologians to be remembered for devotions or in sermons. Renaissance scholars collected important passages from ancient Greek and Latin literature to be used as models or quoted in their own work.[27]

For centuries, students were instructed to keep commonplace books so they could remember important passages and advice from other sources. A young George Washington compiled a list of 110 rules of etiquette from various sources in a commonplace book he named "Rules of Civility and Decent Behavior in Company and Conversation." Many historical and literary figures compiled commonplace books of excerpts or quotes for future use in their writing or speeches.

As the book publishing industry grew, the commonplace books of famous men were printed and sold. John Locke even published an instruction book for creating commonplace books—*A Method of Making Commonplace Books* (1706).[28] Over time, printed reference books of important quotations and literary extracts replaced handwritten commonplace books. *John Bartlett's Familiar Quotations*, first printed in 1885 and currently in its eighteenth edition, is a sort of commonplace book, providing indexed quotations for the reference of writers and speechmakers.

Nineteenth-century scrapbooks were reinventions of the commonplace book. In the new era of affordable newspapers and magazines, memorable passages no longer needed to be handwritten. By the 1820s, inexpensive newspapers were more common. Men, women, and children of all social classes and ethnicities used scissors to cut out information related to their interests, instead of copying it by hand. At first, clippings were pasted on recycled paper or books no longer needed, such as record or ledger books. "Cutting and pasting" in the modern era originates from this practice.

Scrapbooking was widely promoted. Teachers were encouraged to create reference scrapbooks of teaching ideas and information relevant to their curriculum. Children were believed to benefit from scrapbooking, as it was thought to improve organizational, artistic, and literacy skills.[29] In 1864, an African American church newspaper advised black children to follow the model of Frederick Douglass, saving useful information in scrapbooks for future reference. The same story was reprinted as advice for white children in at least two newspapers for white audiences.[30]

Scrapbooking as a hobby was viewed as frugal and worthwhile, but it could also be charitable. Middle-class publications encouraged children to make scrapbooks for poor, invalid children. Church groups made scrapbooks of religious clippings for shut-ins. Fiction of the era portrayed poor but grateful children receiving uplifting scrapbooks as gifts that resulted in life-changing improvements.[31]

Creating scrapbooks was not just educational or entertaining, it was also a professional pursuit. Scrapbooks could organize factual information and serve as a record of accomplishments. Statesmen such as Abraham Lincoln, Frederick Douglass, and Charles Sumner, writers such as Horatio Alger, Lydia Maria Child, and Jack London kept scrapbooks. Organizations focused on women's suffrage and the abolition of slavery created scrapbooks of clippings and other ephemera documenting their activities. Professionals from physicians to actors to ministers kept scrapbooks documenting their careers.[32]

The nineteenth-century scrapbook was a pastime; a consumer good; and a reflection of the growth of media, industrialization, mass marketing, capitalism, and the middle class. Not only was scrapbooking highly recommended in middle-class magazines, newspapers, and advice books of the era, scrapbook and scrapbook accessories were also mass marketed. By the late 1820s and 1830s, one could purchase blank books especially for scrapbooking. In 1873, Mark Twain, a scrapbooker himself, patented and sold scrapbooks with self-adhesive glue strips included.[33]

Clippings from newspapers and magazines are prominent in nineteenth-century scrapbooks. In previous centuries, printed materials had been far too expensive to cut up or throw away. New printing and paper manufacturing technologies made publication cheaper. Publishers of periodicals learned they could earn higher profits through advertising sales, and they therefore lowered the price of subscriptions. Circulation grew, and more new publications appeared. As prices dropped, readers saved the most important information and discarded the rest (see figure 6.5).

Newspapers contained far more than just the news to be read, clipped, or saved. They also published diverse facts, tips, and short bits of scientific, historic, or agricultural miscellany. This fragmented information was especially popular with scrapbook collectors. Some newspapers even used the headline "for the scrapbook" for these sections of the newspaper. Especially popular items, such as mourning poems, were clipped and pasted over and over into scrapbooks by people all over the nation.[34]

Newspapers obtained assorted information, poems, columns, and other material for publication from subscription services, or "exchanges" with other regional or national publications. Membership in an exchange allowed for free reprinting as long as credit was given to the original source. Information cut and pasted from other publications might cite the original source and author; other times the work was altered, renamed, reattributed, or printed with no source named at all.[35] Popular content recirculated in various publications for years or even decades, similar to the circulation of viral internet information today.

In the late 1870s, clipping bureaus provided a new media service that impacted both scrapbooking and the funeral industry. Clipping bureaus were businesses that scanned and clipped items from current newspapers on topics of interest to clients. Employees, usually women, scanned dozens of newspapers searching for keywords or topics. Relevant articles were literally cut out, sorted, labeled with the date of publication and clipping bureau's logo, and periodically delivered to clients. Clients could gauge the interest, or lack of it, in their chosen topics through regional and national newspaper coverage.[36]

Authors requested reviews of their work. Politicians followed coverage of their actions or collected information relevant to legislative initiatives. Lawyers, doctors, or other professionals asked for information on topics relevant to their careers. Socialites used clipping bureaus to track their rising or falling popularity in the press. Clipping bureaus offered the additional service of compiling clippings into scrapbooks for clients.[37]

Clipping bureaus were also valuable to commercial industries seeking to target potential customers. Funeral industry businesses requested packets of death notices and obituaries. Mourning families were identified as potential customers for cemetery plots, tombstones, and other relevant services. Obituaries also gave crooks the information needed to swindle survivors, collect falsified debts, and even burglarize homes during memorial services. Clipping bureaus' services were similar to modern-day internet search engines, media monitoring services, and related technology used to track and monitor the internet use of individuals for both legitimate and criminal financial gain

Obituaries, also called memorial advertisements, death notices, or death announcements, typically included the date of death, surviving and deceased family members, and biographical details. Daily newspapers were more likely to include details of funeral arrangements. Death notices in weekly newspapers, often published after the funeral, notified the community of a death. Fees were usually charged to print an obituary, therefore the deaths of many went unreported in the press.

Before the nineteenth-century culture of mourning, these notices were brief. However, in the 1800s obituaries became longer, reflecting the culture's fascination with mourning and death. Some described a "good death"—the moments or hours before death, religious activities and preparations made prior to death, and pleas for readers to prepare themselves spiritually for death. Flowery accounts of friends and family present at the moment of death along with texts of their prayers, hymns, or poetry were included. Some included descriptions of future reunions in heaven.[38]

Mark Twain satirized collecting obituaries and the cultures' obsession with death in *The Adventures of Huckleberry Finn*. In the novel, Huck learns about young, deceased Emmeline Grangerford and her obsession with death. He sees pictures she drew of mourning women and tombstones and her scrapbook full of clippings about accidents, the suffering of the sick or injured, and obituaries. He even gets to hear an example of Emmeline's mourning poetry, "Ode to Stephen Dowling Bots" about a boy who drowned in a well. Huck learns the following from the Grangerford family: "Every time a man died, or a woman died, or a child died, she [*Emmeline*] would be on hand with her 'tribute' before he was cold. She called them tributes. The neighbors said it was the doctor first, then Emmeline, then the undertaker—the undertaker never got in ahead of Emmeline but once."[39]

By the 1870s obituaries began to focus less on religious faith and heavenly homes and more on the secular life achievements of the deceased.[40] By the turn of the twentieth century, scrapbooks and mourning trends parted ways, again influenced by changing technology and shifting attitudes about death and dying. Death, funerals, and burials were ceasing to become private family experiences. Death moved to hospitals; funerals took place in commercial, public spaces provided by funeral homes or parlors; and memorial park burial became more individual and secular. Scrapbooks featured less about death and mourning and more about life captured with a new technology, the camera.

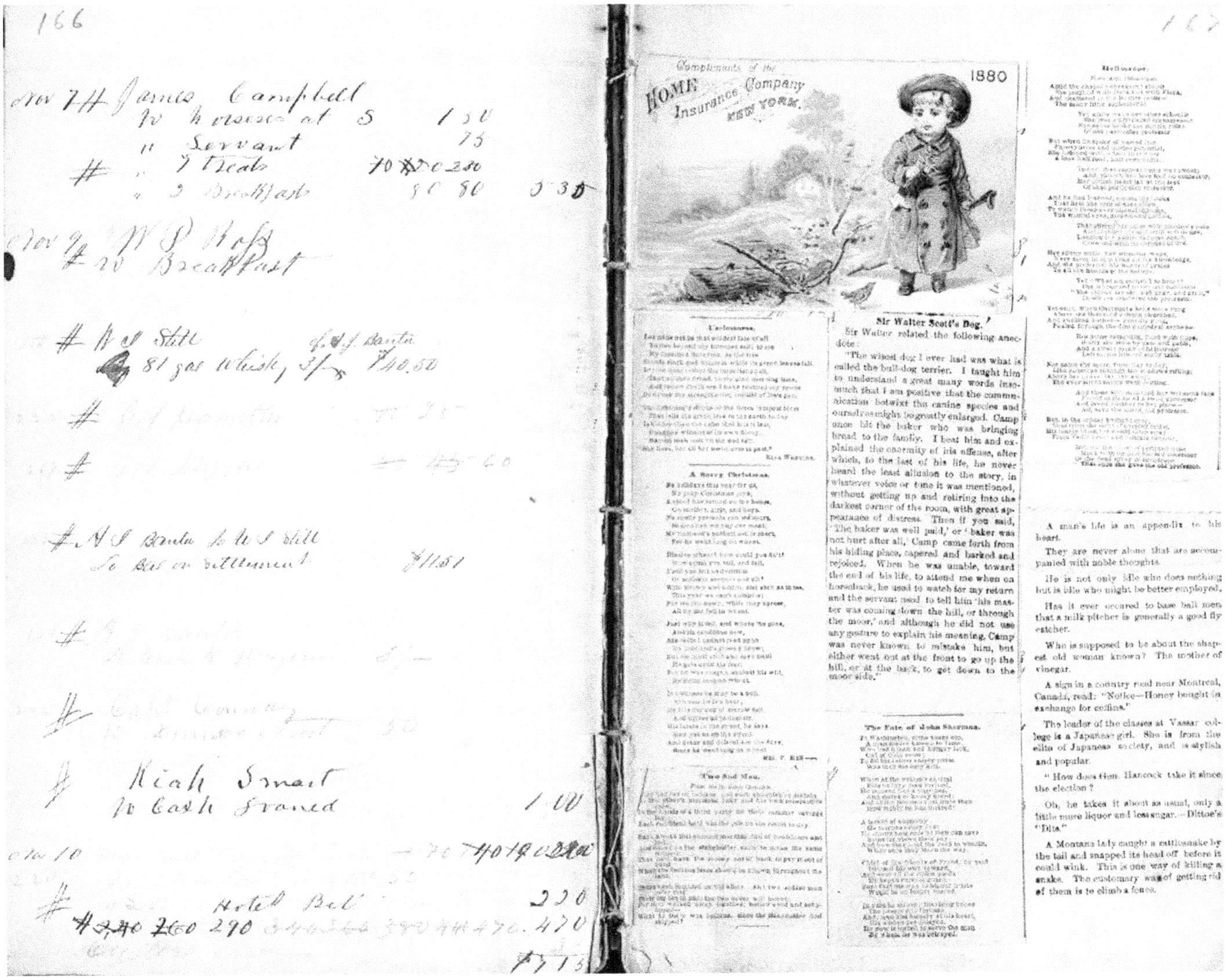

Figure 6.5. Men, women, and children of all social classes and ethnicities created scrapbooks. Clippings of texts and other ephemera were pasted on recycled paper or books or in commercially available blank scrapbooks. This example, dating from between 1857 and the 1880s, was created using an old ledger from a livery stable, a business where horses were boarded or rented. On the left, the original ledger pages are visible. The scrapbook contains newspaper clippings and a few images such as the trade card for an insurance company at the top. The creator is unknown.
Livery Stable Ledger/Scrapbook, 1879–1881. (Courtesy of Eastern Kentucky University Special Collections and Archives, Richmond, KY)

In the Classroom

One tombstone, epitaph, or obituary represents the life and death of one person and efforts by that individual's family and friends to remember. A scrapbook signifies what is important and saved by one individual. Each of these items are important primary sources for reconstructing the life of a single person or family.

However, historians study patterns and trends of a wider culture. Historians examine sets of primary sources to identify recurring trends or patterns representing attitudes or issues of an era. Tombstones, obituaries, or scrapbooks can become primary source sets for student analysis. The ability to identify patterns, trends, and relationships in the media of an era is a key skill for critical analysis

In the previous chapter, the conclusions of two studies using groups of tombstones and epitaphs were discussed. In the first, conclusions were made about the gender roles of men and women between the late eighteenth and early twentieth centuries based on an analysis of tombstone epitaphs. In the second, the styles of tombstones were analyzed for conclusions about economic status in cemeteries and in the wider community.[41]

Students can perform similar research using data from obituaries or tombstones. Historical obituaries are easily accessible in newspaper databases such as the Library of Congress's Chronicling America, Historic American Newspapers collection located at https://chroniclingamerica.loc.gov/. Choose local newspapers for insights into the patterns and trends in your community.

Historical and contemporary epitaphs are as close as your local cemetery. Epitaphs are short statements or phrases written in memory of the deceased and carved on tombstones or memorials. They serve as a brief record of a person's life and serve as reminders of the deceased. Epitaphs range from unique statements written for one individual by a friend or family member to phrases selected from a list or catalog of popular choices. Some people write their own epitaphs which are included with their will or pre-arranged plans for funeral and burial.

Analyzing groups of primary sources introduces the methods of qualitative analysis, a technique used by social scientists for sets of non-numerical data. This process is typically conducted as follows:

1. Preview the topic and the potential data to be collected. Students will need to know what information is typically included in newspaper obituaries. Or if tombstones are to be analyzed, familiarize students with styles, symbols, epitaphs, and other information recorded on tombstones.
2. Formulate research questions. Brainstorm possible research questions to be answered using systematic data collection. For example, if analyzing epitaphs, asks student to brainstorm what they might learn by analyzing epitaphs on tombstones in a fifty-year time period. Provide some prompts such as: Are epitaphs original statements? Do the themes of epitaphs change over time? If so, how do they change? Do epitaphs differ according to the sex or age of the deceased? What data could be collected to answer these questions? After students explore various research questions, narrow to one or two key questions.
3. Create a framework for collecting data from which conclusions can be made to answer the chosen research questions. Ask students to collaborate and create a data collection form for gathering the information needed to answer their research questions.
4. Collect data. Students visit a local cemetery and systematically record relevant information. Or students analyze the contents of sets of obituaries from designated time periods or geographic regions, noting what information is included or omitted.
5. Data analysis. After data have been collected, ask students to quickly review the data and identify patterns, trends, or relationships. Revisit their research questions. Then, formulate a plan for analysis that will address the research questions. Modern historians often enter collected information in computer programs designed especially for data analysis. A basic spreadsheet program can serve the same purpose for this activity, allowing students to enter and sort in various ways. For example, if epitaphs are sorted by date, similarities may appear in the epitaphs from the same time period. Epitaphs sorted by the sex of the deceased may reveal a prominent pattern in the theme of the inscriptions. Encourage students to use simple statistics and create charts or graphs that illustrate their findings.
6. In the final step, students attempt to answer their research questions using the evidence from their data analysis. Researchers often discover data are inconclusive or the data collected fail to answer the proposed questions. Or prominent trends or patterns appear to answer questions not previously considered. Students are likely to discover more questions to answer. Discuss these new questions and brainstorm what additional information might be required to answer them and how or where it could be obtained.

Essential Question: How Do You Want to Be Remembered?

Obituaries and epitaphs are usually written about the deceased by surviving family and friends. Discussing the differences between how we portray ourselves and how we are portrayed by others can introduce an important concept in primary source analysis—the identities of authors, their motives, and purposes matter. Historical epitaphs are accessible online and in published collections from the ancient world to the present. Seventy-five percent of all surviving ancient Latin inscriptions come from epitaphs.[42] (See https://teachingwiththemes.com/ for sources for historical epitaphs.)

Select a set of historical or modern epitaphs for analysis. Ask students to consider the author, the author's relationship to the deceased, and the purpose and motive for writing or selecting the information included. Consider what was not included. Explore how writing or reporting about the deceased differs from writing about the living.

Another possibility is to ask students to write their own obituaries or epitaphs. Then consider how these might be different if written by a friend or relative. Obviously, this activity may not be appropriate for all students.

Essential Question: How Do We Save Memories?

Many historical methods of honoring the dead seem strange to modern sensibilities. For example, when students learn saving the hair of deceased loved ones for scrapbooks, ornamental jewelry, or art was common in the eighteenth and nineteenth centuries, they usually pronounce the practice weird and creepy. However, this antique practice is little different from modern trends in which extracted DNA or the ashes of the deceased loved ones are captured in lockets, keepsake jewelry, or works of art.

However, scrapbooks are a method of saving memories familiar to modern students. Scrapbooks are personal stories created from re-purposed media and ephemera, digital or paper. Nineteenth-century scrapbooks were created to capture and remember information, people, events, and thoughts.

Many scrapbooks from the era, like the one of fictional Emmeline Grangerford, were memorials to the deceased. They were filled with clipped mourning poems and obituaries from newspapers and magazines as well as ephemera such as funeral notices, funeral speeches, and specially printed mourning visiting cards and stationary. These scrapbooks are not so different from modern memorial websites. The purpose was the same, only the media have changed.

When exploring themes related to death, teachers must be careful to select topics and ask questions appropriate for the age and maturity of their students. However, asking students to explore the general motivation for creating scrapbooks in the past and present places the focus on saving memories.

Museums and archives often contain historical scrapbooks. Many historical scrapbooks have been digitally reproduced online (see https://teachingwiththemes.com/ for suggestions). Ask students to explore historical scrapbooks and make comparisons with modern forms of scrapbooking and saving memories. Explore the functions of various social media sites such as Pinterest, Facebook, and blogs in saving and reusing information. Speculate if modern online scrapbooks will survive over time. Discuss the problems future historians may face when accessing old digital records.

The following questions can be used to focus discussion and analysis:

- How can historians determine the date and creator of a historical scrapbook if the information is not explicitly provided on the cover or title page?
- What stories does a scrapbook tell about an individual? What types of events are included and not included? How does a scrapbooker "edit" her or his story? How does one choose what to include in a scrapbook? What to ignore?
- Who creates scrapbooks now? In the past? What are the similarities and differences in scrapbooks and scrapbook-makers now and then? Is digital and paper scrapbooking a free or low-cost hobby? Why or why not?
- What can historians learn and conclude about an individual, a society, or a group of people from several scrapbooks from the same time period? What themes are prominent? What themes are absent?
- What types of media are reused or repurposed in a digital and paper scrapbook? Technology has changed scrapbooking; how have the themes and contents of scrapbooks changed? Stayed the same?
- Commonplace books and scrapbooks are aids for organizing information. How has organizing information changed over time? How are modern methods of managing information the same or different than in the past? What has changed? What has stayed the same?

Notes

1. E. W. Gurley, *Scrap-Books and How to Make Them* (New York: Authors' Publishing Company, 1880), 56.
2. *Oxford English Dictionary Online*, s.v. "symbol, n.1," http://www.oed.com/.
3. Carl Lindahl, "Transition Symbolism on Tombstones," *Western Folklore* 45, no. 3 (July 1986): 168–69, 173–75, http://www.jstor.org/stable/1499433.
4. Susanne S. Ridlen, "Tree-Stump Tombstones: The Influence of Traditional Cultural Values on Funerary Art in Indiana in the 1890s" (PhD dissertation, Indiana University, 1992), 13, 146, 353; Simon J. Bronner, "The Durlauf Family: Three Generations of Stonecarvers in Southern Indiana," *Pioneer America* 13, no. 1 (March 1981): 17–26, http://www.jstor.org/stable/29763614.
5. Ridlen, "Tree-Stump Tombstones," 52–70.
6. Warren E. Roberts, "Traditional Tools as Symbols: Some Examples from Indiana Tombstones," *Pioneer America* 12, no. 1 (February 1980): 54–63, http://www.jstor.org/stable/29763600; Bronner, "The Durlauf Family," 17–26; Ridlen, "Tree-Stump Tombstones," 52–70.
7. Beverly Seaton, *The Language of Flowers: A History* (Charlottesville: University Press of Virginia, 1995), 16–35.

8. June Hadden-Hobbs, "Say It with Flowers in the Victorian Cemetery," *Markers* XIX (June 2002): 240–71, https://archive.org/stream/markers19asso#page/240/mode/2up.

9. Paul Binski, *Medieval Death: Ritual and Representation* (Ithaca, NY: Cornell University Press, 1996), 142–47.

10. Blanche M. G. Linden, "The Willow Tree and Urn Motif: Changing Ideas about Death and Nature," *Markers* I (1979–1980): 149–55, https://archive.org/details/markers01asso; Edwin Dethlefsen and James Deetz, "Death's Heads, Cherubs, and Willow Trees: Experimental Archaeology in Colonial Cemeteries," *American Antiquity* 31, no. 4 (April 1966): 502–10, http://www.jstor.org/stable/2694382.

11. Joy M. Giguere, *Characteristically American: Memorial Architecture, National Identity, and the Egyptian Revival* (Knoxville: University of Tennessee Press, 2014), 9, 69–71, eBook Collection, EBSCOhost.

12. Ibid., 140–62.

13. Drew Gilpin Faust, *This Republic of Suffering: Death and the American Civil War* (New York: Alfred A. Knopf, 2009), 9; Jeremy Taylor, *The Rule and Exercises of Holy Dying*, 1850 ed., https://archive.org/stream/ruleandexercise18taylgoog#page/n12.

14. Faust, *This Republic of Suffering*, 3–31.

15. Ann Douglas, "Heaven Our Home: Consolation Literature in the Northern United States, 1830–1880," *American Quarterly* 26, no. 5 (December 1974): 510, http://www.jstor.org/stable/2711887.

16. Ellen Gruber Garvey, *Writing with Scissors: American Scrapbooks from the Civil War to the Harlem Renaissance* (Oxford: Oxford University Press, 2013), 115–16.

17. Faust, *This Republic of Suffering*, 3–31.

18. Garvey, *Writing with Scissors*, 41–47.

19. Ibid., 123–24.

20. Ibid., 127, 130.

21. Daneen Wardrop, *Civil War Nurse Narratives, 1863–1870* (Iowa City: University of Iowa Press, 2015), 177–204, http://www.jstor.org/stable/j.ctt20p596k.11.

22. Garvey, *Writing with Scissors*, 104–10.

23. Ibid., 151.

24. Ann Schofield, "The Fashion of Mourning," in *Representations of Death in Nineteenth-Century US Writing and Culture*, ed. Lucy Elizabeth Frank (Abingdon, UK: Routledge, 2017), 157–71, Collection, EBSCOhost.

25. Harriet Beecher Stowe, *Uncle Tom's Cabin*, chapter 26, https://www.gutenberg.org/files/203/203-h/203-h.htm.

26. Helen Sheumaker, *Love Entwined: The Curious History of Hairwork in America* (Philadelphia: University of Pennsylvania Press, 2007), 57.

27. Earle Havens, *Commonplace Books: A History of Manuscripts and Printed Books from Antiquity to the Twentieth Century* (New Haven, CT: Yale University Press, 2001), 8–9.

28. John Locke, *A Method of Making Commonplace Books*, 1706, https://archive.org/details/gu_newmethodmaki00lock.

29. Susan Tucker, Katherine Ott, and Patricia P. Buckler, eds., *Scrapbook in American Life* (Philadelphia: Temple University Press 2006), 9–11.

30. Garvey, *Writing with Scissors*, 134–35.

31. Ibid., 51–52.

32. Ibid., 4.

33. Tucker, Ott, and Buckler, eds. *Scrapbook in American Life*, 10.

34. Garvey, *Writing with Scissors*, 6.

35. Ibid., 29–36.

36. Ibid., 236, 243–45.

37. "Scissors Snip Press Notices for all Sorts," *New York Times* (November 16, 1924): X17, ProQuest Historical Newspapers.

38. Eleanor Agnew, "The Romantic Rhetoric of Nineteenth Century Obituaries: 'She Gave a Few Faint Gasps and Died,'" paper presented at Conference on College Composition and Communication, Washington, DC (March 23–25, 1995); James F. Farrell, *Inventing the American Way of Death, 1830–1920* (Philadelphia: Temple University Press), 187–90.

39. Mark Twain, *Adventures of Huckleberry Finn* (New York: Charles L. Webster and Company, 1885), chapter 17, https://www.gutenberg.org/files/76/76-h/76-h.htm.

40. Farrell, *Inventing the American Way of Death*, 187–90.

41. Lynn Rainville, "Hanover Deathscapes: Mortuary Variability in New Hampshire, 1770–1920," *Ethnohistory* 46, no. 3 (Summer 1999): 570–71, http://www.jstor.org/stable/483201; Paula J. Fenza, "Communities of the Dead: Tombstones as a Reflection of Social Organization," *Markers* VI (1989): 136–57, https://archive.org/details/markers06asso.

42. Richard P. Saller and Brent D. Shaw, "Tombstones and Roman Family Relations in the Principate: Civilians, Soldiers and Slaves," *Journal of Roman Studies* 74 (1984): 124–56, http://www.jstor.org/stable/299012.

Works Cited

Adams, Samuel Hopkins. *The Great American Fraud.* New York: Collier and Son, 1912. https://www.gutenberg.org/files/44325/44325-h/44325-h.htm.

Agnew, Eleanor. "The Romantic Rhetoric of Nineteenth Century Obituaries: 'She Gave a Few Faint Gasps and Died.'" Paper presented at Conference on College Composition and Communication, Washington, DC, March 23–25, 1995.

"Aislinge Meic Con Glinne." Corpus of Electronic Texts. Edition: T308002. Electronic edition compiled by Beatrix Färber. Accessed June 2018. https://celt.ucc.ie//published/T308002/index.html.

Anderson, Ann. *Snake Oil, Hustlers and Hambones: The American Medicine Show.* Jefferson, NC: McFarland, 2002.

Appel, Toby A. "The Thomsonian Movement, the Regular Profession, and the State in Antebellum Connecticut: A Case Study of the Repeal of Early Medical Licensing Laws." *Journal of the History of Medicine and Allied Sciences* 65, no. 2 (April 2010): 153–86. http://www.jstor.org/stable/24632012.

Arndt, Karl J. R., comp. and ed. *A Documentary History of the Indiana Decade of the Harmony Society, 1814–1824.* Vol. 2. Indianapolis: Indiana Historical Society, 1978.

Association Medical Journal. "Four Strongholds of Quackery in the Fourth Estate." *Association Medical Journal* 1, no. 24 (June 17, 1853): 518–20. http://www.jstor.org/stable/25494700.

Athenaeus. *The Deipnosophists of Athenaeus of Naucratis*, trans. Charles Burton Gulick. London: William Heinemann, 1929. Excerpted in "Learning Dreamers and Dissenters," British Library. Accessed June 2018. http://www.bl.uk/learning/histcitizen/21cc/utopia/perfection1/athenaeus1/perfect.html.

Bacon, Francis. *The Advancement of Learning.* 1605, 2nd book, XI. http://www.philosophy-index.com/bacon/advancement-learning/ii-x.php.

Baker, Jean Harvey. "Women in Utopia: The 19th Century Experience." In *Utopias: The American Experience*, edited by Gairdner B. Moment and Otto F. Kraushaar, 56–71. Metuchen, NJ: Scarecrow Press, 1980.

Beard, Virginia R., and William C. Burger. "Change and Innovation in the Funeral Industry: A Typology of Motivations." *OMEGA: Journal of Death and Dying* 75, no. 1 (October 2015): 47–68. https://doi.org/10.1177/0030222815612605.

Beauchamp, Gorman. "The Dream of Cockaigne: Some Motives for the Utopias of Escape." *Centennial Review* 25, no. 4 (Fall 1981): 345–62. http://www.jstor.org/stable/23739084.

Bedermanm, Gail. "Revisiting Nashoba: Slavery, Utopia, and Frances Wright in America, 1818–1826." *American Literary History* 17, no. 3 (Autumn 2005): 438–59. http://www.jstor.org/stable/3567902.

Bell, Whitfield J., Jr. "Medical Practice in Colonial America." *Bulletin of the History of Medicine* 31, no. 5 (September–October 1957): 442–53. http://www.jstor.org/stable/44449174.

Bestor, Arthur. *Backwoods Utopias.* Philadelphia: University of Pennsylvania Press, 1950.

Bianchi, Robert S. "Egyptian Mummies: Myth and Reality." *Archaeology* 35, no. 2 (1982): 18–25. http://www.jstor.org/stable/41727852.

Bingham, A. Walker. *The Snake-Oil Syndrome: Patent Medicine Advertising.* Hanover, MA: Christopher Publishing House, 1994.

Binski, Paul. *Medieval Death, Ritual and Representation.* Ithaca, NY: Cornell University Press, 1996.

Blegen, Theodore C., trans. *Norwegian Emigrant Songs and Ballads.* Vol. 14. London: H. Milford, 1936. In Norwegian-American Historical Association Online. Accessed July 2018. http://www.stolaf.edu/naha/pubs/nas/volume14/vol14_5.htm.

Bok, Edward. "Dr. Pierce's Favorite Prescription: A Retraction." *Ladies' Home Journal* 21, July 1904,18. https://babel.hathitrust.org/cgi/pt?id=mdp.39015020919042;view=1up;seq=465.

———. "The 'Patent-Medicine' Curse." *Ladies' Home Journal* 21, May 1904, 18. https://babel.hathitrust.org/cgi/pt?id=mdp.39015020919042;view=1up;seq=343.

Botkin, Benjamin A. "Mythical Places of the Florida Negro." In *A Treasury of Southern Folklore*. New York: Crown Publishers, 1949.

Boudry, Maarten, Stefaan Blancke, and Massimo Pigliucci. "What Makes Weird Beliefs Thrive? The Epidemiology of Pseudoscience." *Philosophical Psychology* 28, no. 8 (2015): 1177–98. http://dx.doi.org/10.1080/09515089.2014.971946.

Brady, Erika. "Folk Medicine." In *The New Encyclopedia of Southern Culture*, edited by Charles Reagan Wilson and James G. Thomas, vol. 2, 76–80. Chapel Hill: University of North Carolina Press, 2012.

———, ed. *Healing Logics: Culture and Medicine in Modern Health Belief Systems*. Logan: Utah State University Press, 2001. doi:10.2307/j.ctt46nwrq.

Brenner, Erich. "Human Body Preservation: Old and New Techniques." *Journal of Anatomy* 224, no. 3 (March 2014): 316–44. US National Library of Medicine National Institutes of Health. https://www.ncbi.nlm.nih.gov/pmc/articles/PMC3931544/.

Bright, Henry Arthur. *Happy Country This America: The Travel Diary of Henry Arthur Bright*, edited by Anne Henry Ehrenpreis. Columbus: Ohio State University Press, 1978.

Bronner, Simon J. "The Durlauf Family: Three Generations of Stonecarvers in Southern Indiana." *Pioneer America* 13, no. 1 (March 1981): 17–26. http://www.jstor.org/stable/29763614.

Brummett, Rebekah. "Beyond Far Off Happenings in Far Off Places." Paper presented at Kentucky History Education Conference, Frankfort, Kentucky, July 12, 2018.

Buchan, William. *Domestic Medicine*. London: Joseph Crukshank, Robert Bell, and James Muir, 1784. https://archive.org/details/domesticmedicin00buchgoog/page/n4.

Burke, Peter. *Popular Culture in Early Modern Europe*. New York: New York University Press, 1978.

Bynum, William. *History of Medicine: A Very Short Introduction*. Oxford: Oxford University Press, 2008.

Byrd, William, and Edmund Ruffin. *The Westover Manuscripts: Containing the History of the Dividing Line Betwixt Virginia and North Carolina; A Journey to the Land of Eden, A.D. 1733; and A Progress to the Mines*. Petersburg, VA: Edmund and Julian C. Ruffin, 1841. Accessed April 2018. https://docsouth.unc.edu/nc/byrd/byrd.html.

Campbell, D'Ann. "Women's Life in Utopia: The Shaker Experiment in Sexual Equality Reappraised—1810 to 1860." *New England Quarterly* 51, no. 1 (1978): 23–38. doi:10.2307/364589.

Caplan, Arthur L. "The Concepts of Health, Illness, and Disease." In *Companion Encyclopedia of the History of Medicine*, edited by William Bynum and Roy Porter, vol. 1, 233–48. New York: Routledge, 1997.

Capp, Al. *The Short Life and Happy Times of the Shmoo*. Woodstock, NY: Overlook Press.

Car, J., B. Lang, A. Colledge, C. Ung, and A. Majeed. "Interventions for Enhancing Consumers' Online Health Literacy." *Cochrane Database of Systematic Reviews* 15, no. 6 (June 2015). doi: 10.1002/14651858.CD007092.pub2. US National Library of Medicine National Institutes of Health. https://www.ncbi.nlm.nih.gov/pubmed/21678364.

Carter, Richard. *Valuable Vegetable Medical Prescriptions, for the Cure of all Nervous and Putrid Disorders*. Frankfort, KY: Gerard & Berry, 1815. https://collections.nlm.nih.gov/catalog/nlm:nlmuid–2545048R-bk.

Caulfield, Timothy. *The Cure for Everything*. Boston, MA: Beacon Press, 2012.

Center for Place-Based Learning and Community Engagement. "What Is Place-Based Education?" Accessed December 2018. https://promiseofplace.org/what-is-pbe/what-is-place-based-education.

Child, Lydia Maria. *The Family Nurse; or, Companion of the Frugal Housewife*. Boston: C. J. Hendee, 1837. https://catalog.hathitrust.org/Record/006125465.

Chu, J. T., M. P. Wang, C. Shen, K. Viswanath, T. H. Lam, and S. S. C. Chan. "How, When and Why People Seek Health Information Online: Qualitative Study in Hong Kong." *Interactive Journal of Medical Research* 6, no. 2 (2017). doi:10.2196/ijmr.7000. https://www.i-jmr.org/2017/2/e24/.

Church Roll Book of Pleasant Hill. Pleasant Hill, Kentucky: Pleasant Hill Manuscript Collection.

Cimprich, Vickie. "Free and Freed Shakers and Affiliates of African Descent at Pleasant Hill, Kentucky." *Register of the Kentucky Historical Society* 111, no. 4 (Autumn 2013): 489–523. http://www.jstor.org/stable/24641051.

Claeys, Gregory. *Searching for Utopia: The History of an Idea*. New York: Thames & Hudson.

Claridge, R. T. *Hydropathy; or, The Cold Water Cure*. London: J. Madden and Company, 1842. https://archive.org/details/39002086176733.med.yale.edu/page/n7.

Cohn, Norman. *The Pursuit of the Millennium*. New York: Oxford University Press, 1970.

Costambeys, Marios. "Burial Topography and the Power of the Church in Fifth- and Sixth-Century Rome." *Papers of the British School at Rome* 69 (2001): 169–89. http://www.jstor.org/stable/40311009.

Cowen, David. *Medicine and Health in New Jersey: A History*. Princeton, NJ: D. Van Nostrand, 1964.

Cress, Kit Firth. "Black Shakers at South Union, Kentucky." *Kentucky Review* 12, no. 1 (Fall 1993): 79–95. https://uknowledge.uky.edu/cgi/viewcontent.cgi?article=1086&context=kentucky-review.

Cronosolon. "First Table of Laws." Internet Sacred Text Archive. Accessed June 2018. http://www.sacred-texts.com/cla/luc/wl4/wl423.htm.

Crowell, Elizabeth A., and Norman Vardney Mackie. "Funerary Monuments and Burial Patterns of Colonial Tidewater Virginia, 1607–1776." *Markers* VII (1990): 103–38. https://archive.org/details/markers07asso.

Curl, James Stevens. *Death and Architecture*. Gloucestershire, UK: Sutton Publishing, 2002.

Currid-Halkett, Elizabeth. *The Sum of Small Things: A Theory of the Aspirational Class*. Princeton, NJ: Princeton University Press, 2017.

de la Piña, Carolyn Thomas. *The Body Electric: How Strange Machines Built the Modern American*. New York: New York University Press, 2003.

Del Giudice, Luisa. "Mountains of Cheese and Rivers of Wine: Paesi di Cuccagna and Other Gastronomic Utopias. In *Imagined States, Nationalism, Utopia, and Longing in Oral Cultures*, edited by Luisa Del Giudice and Gerald Porter, 11–63. Logan: Utah State University Press, 2001. http://www.jstor.org/stable/j.ctt46nxsn.4.

Dethlefsen, Edwin, and James Deetz. "Death's Heads, Cherubs, and Willow Trees: Experimental Archaeology in Colonial Cemeteries." *American Antiquity* 31, no. 4 (April 1966): 502–10. http://www.jstor.org/stable/2694382.

De Wolfe, Elizabeth A. *Shaking the Faith, Women, Family, and Mary Marshall Dyer's Anti-Shaker Campaign 1815–1867*. New York: Palgrave, Macmillan, 2002.

D'Itri, Patricia A., and Frank M. D'Itri. *Mercury Contamination: A Human Tragedy*. New York: John Wiley & Sons, 1977.

Donegan, Jane B. *Hydropathic Highway to Health, Women and Water-Cure in Antebellum America*. New York: Greenwood Press, 1986.

Donohue, Julie. "A History of Drug Advertising: The Evolving Roles of Consumers and Consumer Protection." *Milbank Quarterly* 84, no. 4 (2006): 659–99. http://www.jstor.org/stable/25098137.

Douglas, Ann. "Heaven Our Home: Consolation Literature in the Northern United States, 1830–1880." *American Quarterly* 26, no. 5 (December 1974): 496–515. http://www.jstor.org/stable/2711887.

Douglas, Paul H. "Town Planning for the City of God." In *Utopias: The American Experience*, edited by Gairdner B. Moment and Otto F. Kraushaar, 103–25. Metuchen, NJ: Scarecrow Press, 1980.

Dronsfield, Alan, and Pete Ellis. "Phosphorus—Food for Thought." *Education in Chemistry* (blog). Royal Society of Chemistry, November 1, 2009. Accessed December 2018. https://eic.rsc.org/feature/phosphorus-food-for-thought/2020208.article.

Dyer, Mary. *A Brief Statement of the Sufferings of Mary Dyer*. Boston: William S. Spear, 1818. https://archive.org/details/briefstatementof00dyer/page/n5.

Eckhardt, Celia Morris. *Fanny Wright: Rebel in America*. Cambridge, MA: Harvard University Press, 1984.

The Economist. "Funerals of the Future." April 16, 2018.

Estes, J. Worth. "The Shakers and their Proprietary Medicines." *Bulletin of the History of Medicine* 65, no. 2 (Summer 1991): 162–84.

Farrell, James F. *Inventing the American Way of Death, 1830–1920*. Philadelphia: Temple University Press.

Faust, Drew Gilpin. *This Republic of Suffering: Death and the American Civil War*. New York: Alfred A. Knopf.

Fenza, Paula J. "Communities of the Dead: Tombstones as a Reflection of Social Organization." *Markers* VI (1989): 136–57. https://archive.org/details/markers06asso.

Firth, C. H., ed. "A Proper New Ballad Called The Summons to New England." In *An American Garland, Being a Collection of Ballads Relating to America*, 27–30. Oxford: B. H. Blackwell, 1915. https://archive.org/details/anamericangarlan00firtiala/page/n5.

Fitting, Peter. "A Short History of Utopian Studies." *Science Fiction Studies* 36, no. 1 (March 2009): 121–31. http://www.jstor.org/stable/25475211.

Flannery, Michael A. "The Early Botanical Medical Movement as a Reflection of Life, Liberty, and Literacy in Jacksonian America." *Journal of the Medical Library Association* 90, no. 4 (2002): 442–54. US National Library of Medicine National Institutes of Health. https://www.ncbi.nlm.nih.gov/pmc/articles/PMC128961/.

Fogarty, Robert S. *Dictionary of American Communal and Utopian History*. Westport, CT: Greenwood Press, 1980.

Foster, Lawrence. "Free Love and Feminism: John Humphrey Noyes and the Oneida Community." *Journal of the Early Republic* 1, no. 2 (Summer 1981): 165–83. http://www.jstor.org/stable/3123007.

———. *Women, Family, and Utopia: Communal Experiments of the Shakers, the Oneida Community, and the Mormons*. Syracuse, NY: Syracuse University Press, 1991.

Fox, Susannah, and Maeve Duggan. "Health Online 2013." Pew Research Center, Internet & Technology, January 15, 2013. Accessed March 2018. http://www.pewinternet.org/2013/01/15/health-online–2013/.

Franklin, Benjamin. "Information to Those Who Would Remove to America." In *The Works of the Late Dr. Benjamin Franklin: Consisting of His Life Written by Himself, Together with Essays, Humorous, Moral, & Literary, Chiefly in the Manner of the Spectator*. New York: John Tiebout, 1799. Accessed April 2018. https://play.google.com/store/books/details?id=l10zAQAAMAAJ&rdid=book-l10zAQAAMAAJ&rdot=1.

Fuller, Robert C. "Alternative Medicine." In *Encyclopedia of Social History*, edited by Mary Kupiec Cayton, Elliott J. Gorn, and Peter W. Williams, vol. 3, 2379. New York: Charles Scribner's Sons, 1993.

Garvey, Ellen Gruber. *Writing with Scissors: American Scrapbooks from the Civil War to the Harlem Renaissance*. Oxford: Oxford University Press, 2013.

Gelfand, Toby. "The History of the Medical Profession." In *Companion Encyclopedia of the History of Medicine*, edited by William Bynum and Roy Porter, vol. 2, 233–48. New York: Routledge, 1997.

Gentilcore, David. "'Charlatans, Mountebanks and Other Similar People': The Regulation and Role of Itinerant Practitioners in Early Modern Italy." *Social History* 20, no. 3 (October 1995): 297–314. http://www.jstor.org/stable/4286294.

Gerrard, James Frederick. "Synthesis, Chronology, and 'Late Roman' Cemeteries in Britain." *American Journal of Archaeology* 119, no. 4 (2015): 565–72. doi:10.3764/aja.119.4.0565.

Giguere, Joy M. *Characteristically American: Memorial Architecture, National Identity, and the Egyptian Revival*. Knoxville: University of Tennessee Press, 2014. eBook Collection, EBSCOhost.

Gilli, Barbara. "The Past in the Present: The Reuse of Ancient Material in the 12th Dynasty." *Aegyptus* 89 (2009): 89–110. http://www.jstor.org/stable/23375031.

Ginzberg, Lori D. "'The Hearts of Your Readers Will Shudder': Fanny Wright, Infidelity, and American Freethought." *American Quarterly* 46, no. 2 (June 1994): 195–226. http://www.jstor.org/stable/2713338.

Graham, Judith A. "The New Lebanon Shaker Children's Order." *Winterthur Portfolio* 26, no. 4 (Winter 1991): 215–29. http://www.jstor.org/stable/1181346.

Green, Henry. Interview, Federal Writers' Project: Slave Narrative Project. Vol. 2, Arkansas, Part 3, Gadson-Isom. 1936, 99–100. Library of Congress. https://www.loc.gov/resource/mesn.023/?sp=99.

Griffenhagen, George B., and James Harvey Young. "Old English Patent Medicines in America." *Pharmacy in History* 34, no. 4 (1992): 199–229. https://www.jstor.org/stable/41111487.

Guerra, Francisco. "Medical Almanacs of the American Colonial Period." *Journal of the History of Medicine and Allied Sciences* 16, no. 3 (July 1961): 234–55. http://www.jstor.org/stable/24620679.

Gurley, E. W. *Scrap-Books and How to Make Them*. New York: Authors' Publishing Company, 1880.

Guthke, Karl S. "Do-It-Yourself Immortality: Writing One's Own Epitaph." *Markers* XX (1980): 111–53. https://archive.org/details/markers20asso/page/n1.

Hadden-Hobbs, June. "Say It with Flowers in the Victorian Cemetery." *Markers* XIX (June 2002): 240–71. https://archive.org/stream/markers19asso#page/240/mode/2up.

Hardy, Dennis. *Alternative Communities in Nineteenth Century England*. New York: Longman, 1979.

Harper's New Monthly Magazine. "The Shakers." July 1857, 164–77.

Havens, Earle. *Commonplace Books, A History of Manuscripts and Printed Books from Antiquity to the Twentieth Century*. New Haven, CT: Yale University/University Press of New England, 2001.

Hedrick, Joan D. *Harriet Beecher Stowe, A Life*. New York: Oxford University Press, 1994.

Heineman, Helen L. "'Starving in That Land of Plenty': New Backgrounds to Frances Trollope's Domestic Manners of the Americans." *American Quarterly* 24, no. 5 (December 1972): 643–60. http://www.jstor.org/stable/2711664.

Helfand, William H. *Quack, Quack, Quack: The Sellers of Nostrums in Prints, Posters, Ephemera and Books*. New York: Grolier Club, 2002.

Helman, Cecil G. "'Feed a Cold, Starve a Fever': Folk Models of Infection in an English Suburban Community, and Their Relation to Medical Treatment." *Culture, Medicine and Psychiatry* 2 (1978): 107–37.

Heron, Melonie. "Deaths: Leading Causes for 2009." *National Vital Statistics Reports* 61, no. 7 (October 26, 2012): 22. Accessed July 2018. https://www.cdc.gov/nchs/data/nvsr/nvsr61/nvsr61_07.pdf.

Hesiod, *Works and Days*. Translated by Richmond Lattimore. Ann Arbor: University of Michigan Press, 1959.

Hicks, John D. "The Political Career of Ignatius Donnelly." *Mississippi Valley Historical Review* 8, nos. 1–2 (June–September 1921): 80–132. http://www.jstor.org/stable/1889278.

Hill, Christopher. *The World Turned Upside Down: Radical Ideas during the English Revolution*. New York: Viking Press, 1972.

Hopkins, Keith. *Death and Renewal* (Sociological Studies in Roman History). Vol. 2. Cambridge: Cambridge University Press, 1983.

Horace. "Epode 16." *The Odes and Epodes of Horace*. Translated by Joseph P. Clancy. Chicago: University of Chicago Press, 1960.

Humphrey, George. "Dr. Long, The Oracle of Harley Street, 1830." *The Printshop Window: Caricature and Graphic Satire in the Long Eighteenth-Century* (blog). July 14, 2015. Accessed December 2018, https://theprintshopwindow.wordpress.com/2015/07/14/dr-long-the-oracle-of-harley-street–1830/.

"An Invitation to Lubberland." Printed for J. Deacon, at the Angel in Gilt-spur-street, c. 1685. English Broadside Ballad Archive, EBBA 30687. British Library, Roxburghe. https://ebba.english.ucsb.edu/ballad/30687/xml.

Juhnke, Eric S. *Quacks and Crusaders: The Fabulous Careers of John Brinkley, Norman Baker, and Harry Hoxsey*. Lawrence: University Press of Kansas, 2002.

Kesselman, Amy. "The 'Freedom Suit': Feminism and Dress Reform in the United States, 1848–1875." *Gender and Society* 5, no. 4 (December 1991): 495–510. http://www.jstor.org/stable/190097.

King, Dan. *Quackery Unmasked*. Boston: D. Clapp, 1858. https://archive.org/details/57310420R.nlm.nih.gov.

King, Martin Luther, Jr. "I've Been to the Mountaintop." Speech given in Memphis, Tennessee, April 3, 1968. Accessed June 2018. https://www.americanrhetoric.com/speeches/mlkivebeentothemountaintop.htm.

Kolmerten, Carol A. "Unconscious Sexual Stereotyping in Utopia: A Sample from *The New Harmony Gazette*, 1825–1827." In *Utopias: The American Experience*, edited by Gairdner B. Moment and Otto F. Kraushaar, 72–86. Metuchen, NJ: Scarecrow Press, 1980.

———. *Women in Utopia: The Ideology of Gender in the American Owenite Communities*. Bloomington: Indiana University Press, 1990.

Koudounaris, Paul. *The Empire of Death: A Cultural History of Ossuaries and Charnel Houses*. London: Thames & Hudson, 2011.

"The Land of Cokaygne. Accessed June 2018. https://web.archive.org/web/20050207153710/http://www.thegoldendream.com/landofcokaygne.htm.

"The Land of Cockaygne." Harley Manuscript 913, ff. 3r–6v, British Library. Accessed June 2018. http://www.soton.ac.uk/wpwt/trans/cockaygn/coctrans.htm.

Lau, Joe Y. F. *An Introduction to Critical Thinking and Creativity: Think More, Think Better*. Hoboken, NJ: John Wiley & Sons, 2011.

Legan, Marshall Scott. "Hydropathy in America: A Nineteenth Century Panacea." *Bulletin of the History of Medicine* 45, no. 3 (May–June 1971): 267–80. http://www.jstor.org/stable/44451210.

Lindahl, Carl. "Transition Symbolism on Tombstones." *Western Folklore* 45, no. 3 (July 1986): 165–85. http://www.jstor.org/stable/1499433.

Linden, Blanche M. G. *Silent City on a Hill, Picturesque Landscapes of Memory and Boston's Mount Auburn Cemetery*. Boston: University of Massachusetts Press, 2007.

———. "The Willow Tree and Urn Motif: Changing Ideas about Death and Nature." *Markers* I (1979/1980): 149–55. https://archive.org/details/markers01asso.

Lochrie, Karma. *Nowhere in the Middle Ages*. Philadelphia: University of Pennsylvania Press, 2016.

Locke, John. *A Method of Making Commonplace Books*. 1706. https://archive.org/details/gu_newmethodmaki00lock.

Lucian. "A True Story." Translated by A. M. Harmon. Vol. 1. Cambridge, MA: Harvard University Press, 1913.

Madden, Etta M., and Martha L. Finch. "Introduction." In *Eating in Eden: Food and American Utopias*, edited by Etta M. Madden and Martha L. Finch. Lincoln: University of Nebraska Press, 2006.

Maldonado, Adrian. "What Does Early Christianity Look Like? Mortuary Archaeology and Conversion in Late Iron Age Scotland." *Scottish Archaeological Journal* 33, nos. 1–2 (2011): 39–54. http://www.jstor.org/stable/43923909.

Manuel, Frank E., and Fritzie P. Manuel. *Utopian Thought in the Western World*. Cambridge, MA: Belknap Press of Harvard University Press, 1979.

Mason, Augustus. *The Quackery of the Age: A Satire on the Times*. Boston: White, Lewis & Potter, Printers, 1845. https://collections.nlm.nih.gov/bookviewer?PID=nlm:nlmuid-101198816-bk#page/1/mode/2up.

McClintock, Harry. "Big Rock Candy Mountain." Accessed June 2018. https://genius.com/Harry-mcclintock-big-rock-candy-mountain-lyrics.

McGrew, Sarah, Teresa Ortega, Joel Breakstone, and Sam Wineburg. "The Challenge That's Bigger Than Fake News: Civic Reasoning in a Social Media Environment." *American Educator* 41, no. 3 (Fall 2017): 4–9.

McMurtrie, Douglas C. "Early Kentucky Medical Imprints with a Bibliography to 1830." *Register of Kentucky State Historical Society* 31, no. 96 (July 1933): 256–70.

McNamara, Brooks. "The Indian Medicine Show." *Educational Theatre Journal* 23, no. 4 (December 1971): 431–44. http://www.jstor.org/stable/3205750.

McTighe, Jay, and Grant Wiggins. *Essential Questions: Opening Doors to Student Understanding*. Alexandria, VA: Association for Supervision & Curriculum Development, 2013.

Metlitzki, Dorothee. *The Matter of Araby in Medieval England*. New Haven, CT: Yale University Press, 1977.

More, Thomas. "Six Lines on The Island of Utopia, written by Anemolius, Poet Laureate, and Nephew to Hytholody by his Sister." In *Utopia*. Edited by George M. Logan. Translated by Robert M. Adams, 3rd edition. Cambridge: Cambridge University Press, 2016.

———. *Utopia*. Book I. Open Utopia edition. Accessed July 2018. http://theopenutopia.org/full-text/book-i-of-utopia/.

Moreland, J., T. L. French, and G. P. Cumming. "The Prevalence of Online Health Information Seeking among Patients in Scotland: A Cross-Sectional Exploratory Study." *JMIR Research Protocols* 4, no. 3 (July 2015). doi:10.2196/resprot.4010.

Morton, A. L. *The English Utopia*. London: Lawrence & Wishart, 1922.

Moss, Kay. *Southern Folk Medicine, 1750–1820*. Columbia: University of South Carolina Press, 1999. eBook Collection, EBSCOhost.

Mumford, Lewis. *The Story of Utopias*. New York: Boni and Liveright, 1962. https://archive.org/details/storyutopias00mumfgoog/page/n32.

Murphy, Lamar Riley. *Enter the Physician: The Transformation of Domestic Medicine 1760–1860*. Tuscaloosa: University of Alabama Press, 1991.

National Funeral Directors Association. "Statistics." Accessed July 2018. http://www.nfda.org/news/statistics.

National Geographic Society. National Geography Standard 2. https://www.nationalgeographic.org/standards/national-geography-standards/2/.

National Institutes of Health, Office of Dietary Supplements. "Dietary Supplements." Updated June 24, 2011. Accessed March 2018. https://ods.od.nih.gov/factsheets/DietarySupplements-HealthProfessional/.

New York Times. "Death Stirs Action on Radium 'Cures.'" April 2, 1932. ProQuest Historical Newspapers.

———. "Eben M. Byers Dies of Radium Poisoning." April 1, 1932. ProQuest Historical Newspapers.

———. "Scissors Snip Press Notices for all Sorts." November 16, 1924. ProQuest Historical Newspapers.

———. "Subversion of the Family." February 20, 1879. ProQuest Historical Newspapers.

Nutton, Vivian. "Humoralism." In *Companion Encyclopedia of the History of Medicine*, edited by William Bynum and Roy Porter, vol. 1, 281–91. New York: Routledge, 1997.

O'Connor. Bonnie B., and David J. Hufford. "Understanding Folk Medicine." In *Healing Logics: Culture and Medicine in Modern Health Belief Systems*, edited by Erika Brady, 13–36. Logan: Utah State University Press, 2001. doi:10.2307/j.ctt46nwrq.

Odum, Howard Washington, and Guy Benton Johnson. *Negro Workaday Songs*. Chapel Hill: University of North Carolina Press, 1926. https://archive.org/details/negroworkadayson00odum/page/n7.

Offit, Paul A. *Do You Believe in Magic? The Sense and Nonsense of Alternative Medicine*. New York: HarperCollins, 2013.

Oliver, Graham. "Images of Death: Inscribed Funerary Monuments from Fourth-Century Athens to Neo-Classical England." *Bulletin of the Institute of Classical Studies* 75 (2000): 125–41. http://www.jstor.org/stable/43767719.

Owen, Robert. "Oration Containing a Declaration of Mental Independence." Speech at Public Hall, New Harmony, Indiana, July 4, 1826. Accessed June 2018. http://www.indiana.edu/~kdhist/H105-documents-web/week11/Owen1826.html.

Owen, Robert Dale. *Threading My Way: Twenty-Seven Years of Autobiography*. New York: G. W. Garleton & Company, 1874. https://archive.org/details/twentysevenyear00owengoog.

Paulas, John. "How to Read Athenaeus' 'Deipnosophists.'" *American Journal of Philology* 133, no. 3 (Fall 2012): 403–39. http://www.jstor.org/stable/23269874.

Pew Research Center, Internet & Technology. "The Internet and Health." February 12, 2013. Accessed December 2018. http://www.pewinternet.org/2013/02/12/the-internet-and-health/.

Pitzer, Donald E. *America's Communal Utopias*. Chapel Hill: University of North Carolina Press, 1997. eBook Collection, EBSCOhost.

Pitzer, Donald E., and Josephine M. Elliott. "New Harmony's First Utopians, 1814–1824," *Indiana Magazine of History* 75, no. 3 (September 1979): 225–300. http://www.jstor.org/stable/27790387.

Plato. *Critias*. Translated by Benjamin Jowett. New York: C. Scribner's Sons, 1871. http://classics.mit.edu/Plato/critias.html.

Pleij, Herman. *Dreaming of Cockaigne: Medieval Fantasies of the Perfect Life*. New York: Columbia University Press.

Potter, Elizabeth Walton, and Beth M. Bolton. "Burial Customs and Cemeteries in American History." In *Guidelines for Evaluating and Registering Cemeteries and Burial Places*. National Register Bulletin. Washington, DC: United States Department of the Interior, National Park Service, 1992. https://www.nps.gov/nr/publications/bulletins/nrb41/nrb41_5.htm.

"Press Clippings and the Nostrum Enterprise." In *Nostrums and Quackery: Articles on the Nostrum Evil and Quackery*. Reprinted from *Journal of the American Medical Association*. Chicago: American Medical Association, 1911. https://archive.org/stream/nostrumsquackery00amerrich#page/498/mode/2up.

Rainville, Lynn. "Hanover Deathscapes: Mortuary Variability in New Hampshire, 1770–1920." *Ethnohistory* 46, no. 3 (Summer 1999): 570–71. http://www.jstor.org/stable/483201.

———. *Hidden History: African American Cemeteries in Central Virginia*. Charlottesville: University Press of Virginia, 2016.

Rammel, Hal. *Nowhere in America: The Big Rock Candy Mountain and Other Comic Utopias*. Urbana: University of Illinois Press, 1990.

Reese, David Meredith. *Humbugs of New-York: Being a Remonstrance against Popular Delusion*. New York: John S. Taylor, 1838. https://archive.org/details/humbugsofnewyork01rees/page/n5.

Reitz, John C. "A History of Cutoff Rules as a Form of Caveat Emptor." *American Journal of Comparative Law* 36, no. 3 (Summer 1988): 437–72. https://www.jstor.org/stable/840343.

Resor, Cynthia, and S. Kay Gandy. "Dreaming of a Better Life: Utopia as a Focus for Thematic, Interdisciplinary Instruction." *Clearing House: A Journal of Educational Strategies, Issues and Ideas* 87, no. 1 (204): 1–8. doi: 10.1080/00098655.2013.813432.

Reuther, Rosemary Radford. "Utopian and Communal Societies." In *Our Own Voices: Four Centuries of American Women's Religious Writing*, edited by Rosemary Skinner Keller and Rosemary Radford Ruether, 341–82. San Francisco: HarperCollins, 1995.

Ricks, Christopher. *Tennyson*. Berkeley: University of California Press, 1989.

Ridlen, Susanne S. "Tree-Stump Tombstones: The Influence of Traditional Cultural Values on Funerary Art in Indiana in the 1890s." PhD dissertation, Indiana University, 1992.

Rippere, Vicky. "The Survival of Traditional Medicine in Lay Medical Views: An Empirical Approach to the History of Medicine." *Medical History* 25, no. 4 (1981): 411–14. US National Library of Medicine National Institutes of Health. https://www.ncbi.nlm.nih.gov/pmc/articles/PMC1139071/.

Roberts, Warren E. "Traditional Tools as Symbols: Some Examples from Indiana Tombstones." *Pioneer America* 12, no. 1 (February 1980): 54–63. http://www.jstor.org/stable/29763600.

Rogers, Kitty. "Integrating the City of the Dead: The Integration of Cemeteries and the Evolution of Property Law, 1900–1969." *Alabama Law Review* 56, no. 4 (Summer 2005): 1153–66. Accessed July 2018. https://www.law.ua.edu/pubs/lrarticles/Volume%2056/Issue%204/Rogers.pdf.

Rothstein, William G. "The Medical Profession." In *Encyclopedia of American Social History*, edited by Mary Kupiec Cayton, Elliott J. Gorn, and Peter W. Williams, vol. 3, 2363–78. New York: Charles Scribner's Sons, 1993.

Saller, Richard P., and Brent D. Shaw. "Tombstones and Roman Family Relations in the Principate: Civilians, Soldiers and Slaves." *Journal of Roman Studies* 74 (1984): 124–56. http://www.jstor.org/stable/299012.

Sampson, Sheree. "Reclaiming a Historic Landscape: Frances Wright's Nashoba Plantation in Germantown, Tennessee." *Tennessee Historical Quarterly* 59, no. 4 (Winter 2000): 290–303. http://www.jstor.org/stable/42627588.

Sargent, Lyman Tower. "The Three Faces of Utopianism Revisited." *Utopian Studies* 5, no. 1 (1994): 1–37. http://www.jstor.org/stable/20719246.

———. *Utopianism: A Very Short Introduction*. Oxford: Oxford University Press, 2010.

Seaton, Beverly. *The Language of Flowers: A History*. Charlottesville: University Press of Virginia, 1995.

Schenk, Christine. *Crispina and Her Sisters: Women and Authority in Early Christianity*. Minneapolis: Augsburg Fortress, 2017. http://www.jstor.org/stable/j.ctt1tm7gz6.10.

Schofield, Ann. "The Fashion of Mourning." In *Representations of Death in Nineteenth-Century US Writing and Culture*, edited by Lucy Elizabeth Frank, 157–71. Abingdon, UK: Routledge, 2017. eCollection, EBSCOhost.

Scriven, George B. "Doctors, Drugs, and Apothecaries of Seventeenth Century Maryland." *Bulletin of the History of Medicine* 37, no. 6 (November/December 1963): 516–22. http://www.jstor.org/stable/44446987.

Shapiro, Fred. "Quotes Uncovered: Death and Taxes." February 17, 2011. Accessed July 2018. http://freakonomics.com/2011/02/17/quotes-uncovered-death-and-taxes/.

Sheumaker, Helen. *Love Entwined: The Curious History of Hairwork in America*. Philadelphia: University of Pennsylvania Press, 2007.

Simms, William Gilmore. "Hydropathy: or the Cold Water Cure." *Magnolia* (October 1842): 257–60. http://simms.library.sc.edu/view_item.php?item=152559.

Sloane, David Charles. *The Last Great Necessity, Cemeteries in American History*. Baltimore: Johns Hopkins University Press, 1991.

Stein, Stephen J. *The Shaker Experience in America*. New Haven, CT: Yale University Press, 1992.

Stilgoe, John R. *Common Landscape of America, 1580 to 1845*. New Haven, CT: Yale University Press, 1982.

Stott, Annette. "The Woodmen of the World Monument Program." *Markers* XX (2003): 1–29. https://archive.org/details/markers20asso.

Stowe, Harriet Beecher. *Uncle Tom's Cabin*. 1852. https://www.gutenberg.org/files/203/203-h/203-h.htm.

Sullivan, Mark. "Did Mr. Bok Tell the Truth?" *Ladies' Home Journal* 23 (January 1906): 18. https://babel.hathitrust.org/cgi/pt?id=mdp.39015011447888;view=1up;seq=109.

———. "The Inside Story of a Sham, by Which Thousands of People Are Daily Hoodwinked, and to Which the Most Prominent Men and Women in America Have Loaned Their Names." *Ladies' Home Journal* 23 (January 1906): 14. https://babel.hathitrust.org/cgi/pt?id=mdp.39015011447888;view=1up;seq=105.

Taylor, Jeremy. *The Rule and Exercises of Holy Dying*. 1850. https://archive.org/stream/ruleandexercise18taylgoog#page/n12.

Temin, Peter. "The Origin of Compulsory Drug Prescriptions." *Journal of Law & Economics* 22, no. 1 (April 1979): 91–105. http://www.jstor.org/stable/725214.

Tennent, John. *Every Man His Own Doctor; or, The Poor Planter's Physician*. National Humanities Center Resource Toolbox. Accessed July 2018. http://nationalhumanitiescenter.org/pds/becomingamer/ideas/text7/homemedicalguides.pdf.

Thomson, Samuel. *Guide to Health, or Botanic Family Physician*. Brockville, ON: W. Willes, printed by Wm. Buell Jr. & Company, 1831. https://archive.org/details/cihm_01684/page/n5.

Trollope, Frances. *Domestic Manners of the Americans*. London: Whittaker, Treacher, & Co., 1832. https://archive.org/details/domesticmannerso00troliala/page/n7.

Truman, Harry. Executive Order 9981. Harry S. Truman Presidential Library & Museum. Accessed July 2018. https://www.trumanlibrary.org/9981.htm.

Tucker, Susan, Katherine Ott, and Patricia P. Buckler, eds. *Scrapbook in American Life*. Philadelphia: Temple University Press, 2006.

Twain, Mark. *Adventures of Huckleberry Finn*. New York: Charles L. Webster and Company, 1885. https://www.gutenberg.org/files/76/76-h/76-h.htm.

United States Department of Agriculture, Bureau of Chemistry. *Service and Regulatory Announcements*. Supplement 29. Issued October 17, 1917. Notice 4944, 592. Accessed July 2018. http://goo.gl/a2AXI.

United States Federal Census. New Harmony, Posey, Indiana, p. 310. Reproduced on Ancestry.com from Sixth Census of the United States, 1840 (NARA microfilm publication M704, 580 rolls), Records of the Bureau of the Census, Record Group 29. National Archives, Washington, DC.

United States Food and Drug Administration. "CPG Sec. 120.500 Health Fraud: Factors in Considering Regulatory Action." Accessed July 2018. https://www.fda.gov/ICECI/ComplianceManuals/CompliancePolicyGuidanceManual/ucm073838.htm.

Valuck, Robert J., Suzanne Poirier, and Robert G. Mrtek. "Patent Medicine Muckraking: Influences on American Pharmacy, Social Reform, and Foreign Authors." *Pharmacy in History* 34, no. 4 (1992): 183–92. http://www.jstor.org/stable/41111483.

Van Leeuwen, Marco H. D. "Guilds and Middle-Class Welfare, 1550–1800: Provisions for Burial, Sickness, Old Age, and Widowhood." *Economic History Review* 65, no. 1 (February 2012): 61–90. https://www.jstor.org/stable/41475545.

Veeresham, Ciddi. "Natural Products Derived from Plants as a Source of Drugs." *Journal of Advanced Pharmaceutical Technology & Research* 3, no. 4 (October–December 2012): 200–201. US National Library of Medicine National Institutes of Health. https://www.ncbi.nlm.nih.gov/pmc/articles/PMC3560124/.

Ventola, C. Lee. "Direct-to-Consumer Pharmaceutical Advertising: Therapeutic or Toxic?" *Pharmacy and Therapeutics* 36, no. 10 (2011): 669–84. US National Library of Medicine National Institutes of Health. https://www.ncbi.nlm.nih.gov/pmc/articles/PMC3278148/.

Vieira, Fátima. "The Concept of Utopia." In *Cambridge Companion to Utopian Literature*, edited by Gregory Claeys, 3–27. Cambridge: Cambridge University Press, 2010. doi:10.1017/CCOL9780521886659.001.

Wardrop, Daneen. *Civil War Nurse Narratives, 1863–1870*. Iowa City: University of Iowa Press, 2015. http://www.jstor.org/stable/j.ctt20p596k.11.

Western New York Heritage. "The Graves of Red Jacket." Accessed June 2018. https://www.wnyheritage.org/content/the_graves_of_red_jacket/index.html.

Whitbey, John. *Beauties of Priestcraft: Or, a Short Account of Shakerism*. Originally published in *New Harmony Gazette* newspaper in 1826. In *Writings of Shaker Apostates and Anti-shakers, 1782–1850*, edited by Christian Goodwillie, vol. 2, 315–64. London: Routledge, 2016.

Wilkie A., and R. Mata. "Cognitive Bias." In *Encyclopedia of Human Behavior*, edited by V. S. Ramachandran, 2nd edition, vol. 1, 531–35. Cambridge, MA: Academic Press, 2012.

Wineburg, Sam, Sarah McGrew, Joel Breakstone, and Teresa Ortega. "Evaluating Information: The Cornerstone of Civic Online Reasoning." 2016. Stanford Digital Repository. http://purl.stanford.edu/fv751yt5934.

Winstanley, Gerrard, et al. *The True Levellers Standard Advanced* (1649). Transcribed by Sandra Jones. Renascence Editions, University of Oregon, 2002. Accessed June 2018. https://scholarsbank.uoregon.edu/xmlui/bitstream/handle/1794/863/levellers.pdf?sequence=1&isAllowed=y.

Wolinsky, Howard. "Disease Mongering and Drug Marketing." *EMBO Reports* 6, no. 7 (2005): 612–14. doi 10.1038/sj.embor.7400476. US National Library of Medicine National Institutes of Health. https://www.ncbi.nlm.nih.gov/pmc/articles/PMC1369125/.

Wright, Fanny. "Explanatory Notes on Nashoba, Part 2." In *New Harmony Gazette*, February 6, 1828. Transcribed in *Jacksonian Miscellanies*, no. 13, April 8, 1997. Accessed June 2018. http://www.jmisc.net/jm970408.htm.

Wrobel, Arthur. *Pseudo-Science and Society in 19th-Century America*. Lexington: University Press of Kentucky, 2015. eBook Collection, EBSCOhost.

Young, James Harvey. *The Medical Messiahs: A Social History of Health Quackery in Twentieth Century America*. Princeton, NJ: Princeton University Press, 1967.

———. "Patent Medicines: An Early Example of Competitive Marketing." *Journal of Economic History* 20, no. 4 (December 1960): 648–56. http://www.jstor.org/stable/2114405.

———. "Patent Medicines: The Early Post-Frontier Phase." *Journal of the Illinois State Historical Society* 46, no. 3 (Autumn 1953): 254–64. http://www.jstor.org/stable/40189311.

———. *The Toadstool Millionaires: A Social History of Patent Medicines in America*. Princeton, NJ: Princeton University Press, Princeton Legacy Library, 1961, 2015.

Index

Note: Page references for figures are italicized.

About the Author

Cynthia Williams Resor taught high school social studies and sixth grade before deciding to pursue her dream of obtaining a PhD in history. She is a professor at Eastern Kentucky University and has taught undergraduate and graduate teacher education courses, social studies for teachers, medieval history, US history survey courses, humanities, and study-abroad classes. She has published journal articles and two books and conducts professional development sessions related to history and social studies education.

Cynthia loves history, especially the history of daily life and ordinary people, and she is always trying to spread her enthusiasm about history inside and outside the classroom. She worked as a costumed interpreter, a "fake" Shaker, at the Shaker Village at Pleasant Hill in central Kentucky. She surprises her students by appearing in historical costumes. She is obsessed with genealogy and local history and makes her students visit local historical sites. Cynthia forces her family and friends to visit old cemeteries and take vacations with her to historical sites, especially utopian communities. She lives in an old house and collects hair jewelry, old advice books, cookbooks, and other random ephemera from the past. Her dream job is a tour guide with a time-traveling machine.

Journalism and media literacy are of special interest to Cynthia. She studied journalism and mass communications in college, before the internet was invented and when dinosaurs roamed the earth. She had a short career as a newspaper reporter before becoming a teacher. While she has adapted to the new electronic age, she still enjoys reading "antique" media on real paper.

www.ingramcontent.com/pod-product-compliance
Ingram Content Group UK Ltd.
Pitfield, Milton Keynes, MK11 3LW, UK
UKHW051933150926
475560UK00005B/366

9 781475 832044